Praise For

Pushing Through Invisible Barriers

"*Pushing Through Invisible Barriers* is an apt description not only of Tena Friesen's personal life story but also her relentless pioneer pursuit of life-long learning and giving meaningful expression and value to that learning.

This is a must read for those interested in the life of a Mennonite pioneer, whether this be in Osler, La Crete, or Tumbler Ridge, whether it is in the setting of family, church, school or community, or whether it is engaging the ageless cycles of life and death, birth and rebirth, and breaking with or affirming tradition.

All the chapters provide unique perspectives that consistently reflect Tena's strong personal faith. "God has been my faithful Companion and Guide in my walk through life."

We scarce have time to pause in our reading to try out the tasty Mennonite recipes interspersed throughout the book.

This first time author has produced a first time winner."

John Janzen, B.A., B.Ed., M.Ed,
Low German Coordinator, MCC Canada

"Tena Friesen's *Pushing Through Invisible Barriers* is a repository of historical fact blended with a personal, first-hand account of a people and an era. Every bit as charming and accessible as Laura Ingalls Wilder's *Little House on the Prairie*, it is a gem of a book. A must read for those who value their Canadian heritage and who seek to understand where they have come from and on whose shoulders they stand."

Rebecca J. Hefty, author and staff writer/editor,
Mission Builders International of Youth With a Mission (YWAM)

i

"To have lived a full life, experiencing difficult times and good times is wonderful, but taking the time and energy to record such a life is a gift to family, community and country. A life beginning at the end of the depression years, through the war years followed by pioneering conditions to a satisfying completion in retirement is truly remarkable. This book is a sincere, honest account of a life where challenges were courageously accepted. At the same time, the author had a goal of reaching the moon for her family and community and landed on a number of stars more beautiful than the moon could ever have been. Her faith and trust in God as understood at various stages in her life resulted in actions with sensitivity, compassion, love and gratitude. A life lived in hope has been translated into a loving family, friends and respect from the community as well as a large number of precious memories. Her life story is intertwined with the story of her Mennonite people and life during pioneering days in northern Alberta. She believes that knowing 'where we have been' will help us understand 'who we are.' "

Bill Janzen, B.Ed., M.Ed.

Pushing Through Invisible Barriers is a well researched and well written. It will be a legacy not just for the Mennonites in the La Crete area of Alberta, but a valuable addition to the history of Mennonites in Canada. The time for documenting this history is slipping past us as this generation ages.

This book will be a reference not just for current historians, but is sure to be referenced well into the next century. I look forward to reading the first edition."

Lorraine Funk, publisher.

"Tena Friesen and I shared seventeen years as colleagues at Ridgeview Central School in La Crete, Alberta. I was the principal and she was the librarian. It was very apparent on the day of her interview for the position that our school would be enriched by her dedication to excellence, her wealth of knowledge in the field, but most importantly, her desire to see the lives of our students enriched by reading. She was always committed to acquiring the best material for our school. I was also impressed with her vast knowledge in a variety of areas. It was not a great surprise that one day she would put some of these thoughts into print and share these insights with others. As I read through her autobiography, I was touched by the unique ways she made each of her experiences come to life. You cannot help but be stirred emotionally as she vividly recounts the chapters of her life and how her faith has shaped it. She has also masterfully interwoven her cultural history in this fascinating story. Although this story will likely be more meaningful to her family and friends, it will also engage all those that read it. I look forward to reading it in the final form with all the pictures and documents. I highly recommend it for all who enjoy reading about personal journeys."

Ed Dyck, DipEdAdmin., B.Ed., M.Ed.

"In her memoir, Tena provides a poignant and insightful look at Mennonites, some of Alberta's last pioneers, who by, and for, their faith endured the hardships of Alberta's north."

Ron Joch, B.Ed., B.Sc.

"This book is remarkable in a number of ways. It is a chronicle of the author's life, but it also records a part of Canadian, Alberta and Mennonite history. Follow along as you are taken from the established farms and towns of Saskatchewan to the last agricultural frontier of Canada in the wilderness of northern Alberta. You will also see the courage of a family and neighbours as they pull together to make a new life as Twentieth Century Pioneers.

Woven throughout this book are the three fundamental beliefs of the Mennonite people: reliance on God, importance of family, and respect for the land. As well, Tena Friesen clearly shows us the changes Mennonite communities deal with as the world around them changes.

This book is not just for Mennonite readers. However, it is also helpful for those of us who want to understand these unique and wonderful people in a clearer way."

Dr. Dick McLean, Ed.D., MA, BPE, Pd Ad, REF

"Tena's book had me hooked after the very first page. Vividly descriptive, emotionally charged, intelligent, humorous and riveting, this highly personal account reads like a novel. You won't want to put it down."

Tracy Krauss, best-selling author and playwright

Pushing Through
Invisible Barriers

A Canadian Mennonite Story

How hope transcended adversity

An autobiography by

Tena Friesen

Published by Tena Friesen©
Box 1168, Tumbler Ridge, BC, Canada V0C 2W0
Phone: 250-242-3636
Email: tenafriesen@gmail.com

Produced by Peace photoGraphics Inc.
Design and Layout by Barbara Swail
Additional design by Trent Ernst
Illustrations by Abe Dyck
Cover design by Greg Wasell
Digital photo restoration by Don Pettit
Edited by Rebecca Jean Hefty, LaDawn Dyck,
Dick McLean and Tracy Krauss

Bible quotes are from the NIV Study Bible New International Version, Zondervan, c1985.

The production of this book was funded in part by the D. F. Plett Historical Research Foundation, Inc. and the Gerhard Lohrenze Publication Fund.

Library and Archives Canada Cataloguing in Publication

Friesen, Tena, 1940-
    Pushing through invisible barriers : a Canadian Mennonite
story : how hope transcended adversity-- an autobiography / by Tena
Friesen.

ISBN 978-0-9867064-1-7

    1. Friesen, Tena, 1940-. 2. Mennonites--Canada--Biography.
3. Frontier and pioneer life--Alberta--La Crête. 4. La Crête (Alta.)--
Biography. I. Title.

BX8143.F765A3 2011   289.7092   C2011-906454-5

Peace photoGraphics Inc.
1204 - 103rd Avenue, Dawson Creek, BC, Canada, V1G 2G9
Phone: 250-782-6068 Toll Free: 1-866-373-8488
Email: info@peacephotographics.com
www.peacephotographics.com

Printed and bound in Canada by Friesens Corporation, Altona, Manitoba.
Second Printing September 2012.

In Memory

To Mom and Dad who sacrificed every comfort they knew, blazing a trail to provide a more promising future for their family.

To Pete and Jake, who came along side as I struggled through many trying situations in those very difficult years. I cherish the memories of all the good times we shared.

To Harry, my special brother, who didn't make his mark in this world, but who made it on my heart.

They have reached the end of the trail where glory awaited them.

Dedication

I lovingly dedicate this book to my family who has given meaning and purpose to my life.

Carl, my companion for almost 50 years; you have given me the greatest gift anyone could ever have given me – allowing me to be an individual. I was able to pursue my dreams and discover my giftings with your love and blessing. Without this freedom, I would have lived life always in view of the horizon, but never being able to reach it. You are the kindest, the most understanding and considerate man I know. Thank you for being my friend.

To LaDawn, Craig and Louise. You are all precious gifts from God and very special. I am grateful that you are such an important part of my life and I feel honoured to be your mother.

CONTENTS

PART ONE

My Childhood on the Prairies of Saskatchewan

1940 – 1953

PART TWO
My Youth in the Boreal Forest of Northern Alberta
1953 –1962

PART THREE
A New Beginning
1962 – 1990

PART FOUR
Our Sunset Years

Foreword

Every person's life tells a story. Tena Friesen's life is no exception! Her life story is easy to follow as her parents and siblings leave a settled farming region in Saskatchewan for the rugged homestead lands of northern Alberta. Pioneer life with all its possibilities and heartbreaks is fully displayed, and the reader can appreciate what it was like on the homesteads of the 1950s in northern Alberta.

If the northern forests were to be cultivated, a strong and persistent people would be required. The migration that led Tena and her parents to an unyielding new land showed them to be family people who looked for a better life with God as their guide, protector and provider. Decades later, it is clear that the trust these early pioneers placed in their God was not in vain. The wilderness is now settled and is one of the best northern farming areas in Canada.

Special foods make up an important part of the Mennonite culture. The author has provided favorite recipes to allow each of us to try some of the foods that Tena and her family have enjoyed for decades. When Mennonite people gather to enjoy special events, there is always enough for everyone and the food is delicious. Some of these time-honoured recipes are sure to be there!

References to Mennonite history have been carefully researched before being included in this book. Many of the important details of Mennonite history and heritage have also been checked with Mennonite scholars to ensure their accuracy. As well, current Mennonite history is included. The author has relatives and friends who have migrated to other countries in an effort to meet their needs. As a result, we see an international web of family and friends all connected by family ties, culture and beliefs.

One of the things that really stands out as one reads this book is that Mrs. Friesen continually provides her thoughts about life, her dreams for the future and how she copes with difficulties. Simply put, she is a real person who is not afraid to let others share her thoughts and get to know her better. This transparency also allows each of us who read the book to remember similarities in our own lives, and perhaps, answer some of the unanswered questions that we have about life.

Three of the most important cornerstones of Mennonite culture; Faith, Family and the Land are in ample evidence as the reader is led through the various stages of the author's life. As well, the author addresses the importance of Christianity in her roles as a daughter, sister, wife, mother and community member. It is clear that she wants others to know that she has a relationship with a Saviour who loves her and will care for all who trust in Him.

In conclusion, this is a book that is well worth reading. I have learned much from it, and I know you will too!

Dr. Dick McLean, Ed.D, MA, BPE, PdAd, REF

Introduction

What began as a creative idea to put a few stories on paper has become a legacy memoir.

As I've read and watched Mom's manuscript evolve, I've come to a deeper understanding of how her life has been intricately involved in a recent era of very interesting Mennonite history. I've also gained a deeper appreciation for our very rich Mennonite heritage.

The birth of this book did not come easy for Mom. While reliving events of her life meant fond memories and laughter, it also meant reliving the pain accompanying them. Many of Mom's generation will identify with her stories while we younger stand to learn from her example of how hardship helps develop character.

Perhaps the greatest inspiration she leaves us is her can-do approach to life which, shaped by life's experiences and necessity, has moulded her into the woman of wisdom and faith in God she is today.

The reader will gain respect for her courage to dream and her perseverance to push through the challenges and obstacles that lay in her path. Through it all, her steadfast conviction to live life with integrity to her values and beliefs speaks of her character and gives authority to this work.

I am proud of Mom's accomplishment as an author, but it pales in significance to her roles as my mother, mentor, confidant and friend.

LaDawn Dyck

Prologue

When I shared some of my life's experiences with my children and grand-children, I occasionally got the impression they didn't believe me, especially when I got that questioning look and only silence followed. They couldn't comprehend or begin to imagine life in pioneering conditions - no roads, electricity, telephones, schools, post office or businesses except for one small country store – where entertainment was home-made and you were confined to living in a community where tradition ruled. This was the inspiration I needed to write my story.

They asked questions like, "Grandma, why did you have to wear black on your wedding day?" I still ask the same question and the answer still is, "I don't know." When I started to write I found it impossible to recount only the stories when my whole life was so intertwined with religion, culture and tradition which have shaped the very person I have become.

I knew I would need to try to explain some things about Mennonites in order for the reader to get a clearer picture so I decided to record bits of their history. I found it difficult, however, to write only about their history when the whole culture is so deeply rooted in tradition. As I started to relive my life, I had many questions of my own, there were so many things I didn't and still don't understand. That said, I have been cautious through-out my life not to discard the positive qualities in my culture, especially, the very foundation on which it was founded.

My memory, no doubt, cannot recall all my experiences in the 70 years of my life, but some are permanently stamped like they happened only yesterday. Often, tears clouded my eyes, fell and smudged my paper as I resurrected and relived so many painful experiences: the death of my three brothers and Mom and Dad; the emotional anguish of an uncertain future in my teen years when deep inside me stirred an incredible determination to accomplish a life's dream – to name a few.

As I continued to write and the memories surfaced, there were times when it appeared I couldn't type fast enough. They took me to times and places where I also relived all the good experiences in life when laughter was a stress reliever and was also the medicine that softened the hard times. My mind didn't always rest when I retired for the night. I had a pen and paper on my night table and often, after I'd gone to bed and sleep wouldn't come, I sat up and recorded yet another incident that my memory triggered.

Sometimes, I wonder who will really be interested in my personal life story. But I hope that whoever reads it will gain some insight into a people whose faith is rooted in the Bible. As I was searching the Web I came across a definition of the Mennonite religion: *"The Mennonite religion is international and is not limited to a race or an ethnic group. To be a Mennonite means to be a Christian and a member of a church which is based on the teachings of the Bible. It is a form of life, not a race or nation."*

I wrote my life story, initially, with my children and grandchildren in mind, that they might get a glimpse into their heritage, but also, that they might understand and learn some of life's lessons from it – that the world does not owe them anything, instead, that they may ask the question, "What can I contribute to make this world a better place?"

I pray that this ordinary story may serve as an inspiration, encouragement and understanding that the difficulties in life, combined with laughter, a positive attitude, faith and hope and love, can overcome all obstacles and build strong characters.

Tena Friesen, July 2011

MENNO SIMONS

"For no one can lay any foundation other than the one already laid, which is Jesus Christ."

I Corinthians 3:11

This is a brief overview of Mennonite history. It is only a thread of their history but I have traced my roots back to Russian Ukraine and I trust it will give the reader a picture of how I fit into the larger scope of Mennonite life. I have focused on the migration of my family from Russia to Canada which is but one of the many migrations that have taken place throughout the history of the Mennonite people. Later on in the book, I address other migrations from Canada to other countries that I can relate to in one way or another.

An Overview of Mennonite History

The Reformation was a religious movement of 16th century Europe that began in an attempt to reform the Roman Catholic Church and resulted in the establishment of Protestant churches. It had an effect on political life as well. Martin Luther, John Calvin and Ulrich Zwingli were the forerunners in the Reformation. The movement had already begun with Martin Luther posting the "95 Thesis" on the church doors in Wittenberg. He had 95 grievances with the church and the manner in which it operated. Luther was particularly upset about the sale of indulgences – paying money to have sins pardoned. Once Luther began to look at the operation of the church, Ulrich Zwingli from Switzerland also brought about some reform, but within his church there were a group of men who thought Zwingli wasn't taking the reform far enough. They thought the city council had no right to tell the church authorities what they should do. This was the beginning of the debate about the separation of church and state.

Menno Simons was a Catholic priest, born in Witmarsum, Friesland in 1496. After thoroughly studying the scriptures, he did not agree with infant baptism, so many people who had been baptized as infants were re-baptized and were then referred to as re-baptizers or Anabaptists. The Mennonites had their religious roots in the Anabaptist wing of the Reformation. This Anabaptist movement in the south of Switzerland and Germany resulted from their stand on believer's baptism. They believed

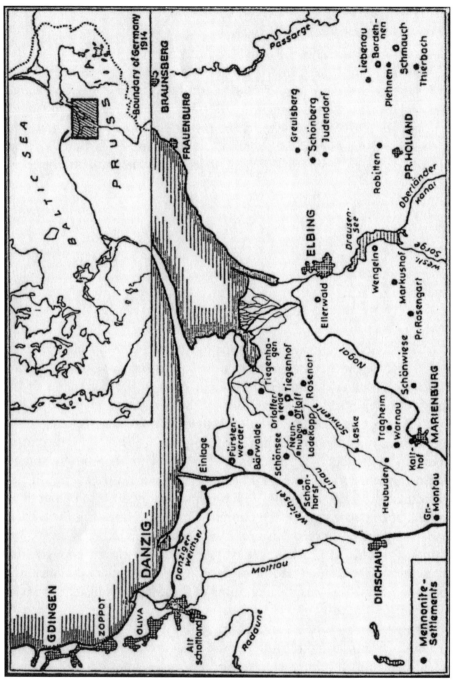

Mennonite Settlements in Poland.

people were to be baptized upon their confession of faith as taught in the
Scriptures by the Apostle Paul and by the example of Jesus Christ when

he was baptized as an adult.

Menno Simons, like many others, already had doubts about the validity of infant baptism. After diligently studying the Bible, he came to accept the Anabaptist view. His aim was to preserve the true Christian gospel. In 1536, Menno Simons made known his new commitment, broke away from the Catholic Church and went into hiding for a year, fearing for his life. To go against the teachings of the Catholic Church was considered a crime and punishable by law. He narrowly escaped death.

As he continued studying the Scriptures, strengthening his faith, he came to the realization that the Church was out of step with scripture. He was also influenced by other strong believers who were reading and interpreting the Bible, modifying their daily lives to live in a way they believed would reflect the Biblical teachings.

Menno Simons was fundamentally dissatisfied with the theology of the church in Rome, so he taught and preached a simpler, more direct way to worship God. The Catholic peasants and urban workers he touched coalesced into a unified congregation, who recognized his spiritual leadership. Menno Simons saw that the Anabaptists were in desperate need of a leader and he was soon ordained to lead them in Holland. After a short while they became numerous enough to be recognized as a group called Mennonites.

Upheavals brought about by the Reformation profoundly affected many societies in general, and especially many of the dissenting Protestants, prominent among them the people who had become Mennonites. And while the movement of the Mennonites from Friesland (Menno Simons-Holland) and from Switzerland (a second front of the Mennonite reformation) was neither simple nor straightforward, it can be said that generally the Swiss Mennonites (Ulric Zwingli) moved west and ultimately to the New World (United States) and the Mennonites of the lowlands of Friesland (Menno Simons) moved east to East and West Prussia (Poland) in the period beginning in the second quarter of the 1500s. It is through this latter group that the Neudorfs and the Friesens trace their origins.

Migrations during the 16th and 17th centuries were undertaken due to the Roman Catholic Church's punishment of dissenters pushing the Mennonites out of the lowlands of Friesland. And while some Mennonites always remained behind, it was a strong cohesive religious group fervently dedicated to the worship of God that forged ahead into new territory, ever seeking relative isolation and separation that they might live religiously, according to their group's and Menno Simons' interpretation of God's Holy Word. To these ends, they took with them not only their religious beliefs, but strong traditions and a material culture with which to build a new life at the end of each of these migrations, ultimately and intrinsically holding to their traditions to set themselves apart and act as a bulwark against the corrupting influences of the world.

The Anabaptists, or Mennonites, believed strongly in adult baptism upon the confession of faith, the separation of church and state, non-resistance, and non-conformity to the world. This clashed with the directives of the combined Church and State and was considered a capital crime. The Anabaptists were the radicals among the reformers; they defied the State law and a great persecution arose in Holland and throughout Europe. Over the next 50 years, thousands of men and women gave their lives for their faith. Many sought refuge in Poland in northeastern Europe. The government in the Vistula Delta, near Danzig of northern Poland, welcomed these Dutch pilgrims, as they had heard that the Mennonites were an industrious, hard-working people and would be an asset to their country.

The Mennonites had learned to drain the marshy land that lay below sea level by building dykes, thereby restoring the deserted, swampy and unusable land and making it productive. With great effort and cost they cleared out the underbrush, built windmills to pump water from lower to higher lands, and built dams to hold back the waters from the Vistula and other rivers. Draining the marshy land was very difficult, so the windmills on the dykes became the symbol of Mennonite contribution to the area.

The Danzig region remained under Poland until 1772, and, under the Polish regime the Mennonites developed a distinct way of life; a cultural and spiritual tradition that is still evident today and which has had a direct effect on the character of Mennonites around the world. They were given relative freedom to practice their faith in exchange for becoming pioneers.

From the 16th to the 18th centuries the Mennonites were not allowed to build church buildings. They met in homes, barns and sheds. The greatest change that happened to them in Poland was the shift from being an energetic, evangelistic people, to a more reserved people. There were exceptions, but in general, spiritual life was at a low ebb. It was also in this early period, when Mennonites were no longer allowed to evangelize, that they became known as *Die Stillen im Lande*, "the quiet in the land." [1] They

---

1 Another interpretation of "Die Stillen im Lande" is found in *Preservings*, December 2005, by Royden Loewen: "The Mennonites were meek and humble and refused to defend themselves" thereby being labeled 'The quiet in the land.'

became like the Dead Sea where the 'Water of Life' could flow in, but it could not flow out. In some respects this may reflect some conservative Mennonites to this day in Canada, Mexico, Belize, Bolivia and Paraguay and, perhaps, in other parts of the world.

In the mid-18th century the Polish government gave the Mennonites permission to build very modest church buildings. They emphasized simplicity because the civil authorities did not allow the Mennonite churches to resemble the Catholic churches in the region. This still reflects the simplicity of church buildings in many conservative Mennonite churches today. They believed in plain dress and were often referred to as 'The Plain People'. During the 16th, 17th and 18th centuries the Polish government did not allow Mennonites to become citizens, and since they were a religious minority, they were always in jeopardy of exploitation or eviction.

A significant cultural change for the Mennonites came about in Poland due to the influence of the German culture around them. To please the noblemen they gradually began to use the High German language instead of the Dutch.

"In Danzig, Dutch as the language of the church disappeared about 1800. As a written language, and the language of worship they took up High German. As a spoken language the Mennonites took up the Vistula Low German vocabulary, which they themselves had already influenced. The Mennonite Low German or Plaudietsch was originally a Low Prussian variety of East Low German, with Dutch influence, which developed in the 16th and 17th centuries in the Vistula Delta area of Royal Prussia, today Polish territory. It was this Vistula Low German that the Mennonites took with them and kept while migrating to Russia, Canada, United States, Mexico, Paraguay, Bolivia, Belize and elsewhere." [2]

There was a mixed attitude within the Mennonite groups toward higher education. Many came to mistrust higher learning when it became evident that the universities, and the clergy trained in them, were largely responsible for the persecution they experienced. Resisting higher education is still reflected in the mind set of many conservative Mennonites to this day.

The Mennonites refused to let their young men serve in the army, and when Prussia took over the Polish region, which the Mennonites had made their home, they had more difficulty negotiating exemptions from military service. They were finally granted exemption on the condition

---

2 Wikipedia

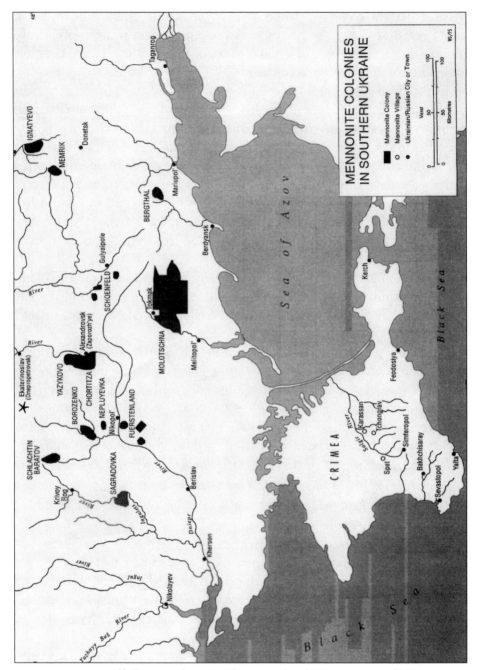

My grandfather was born in Ekaterinoslav (Dnepropetrovsk) *.

that they not purchase land from non-Mennonites. They accepted this arrangement reluctantly, as it resulted in many landless families while others became landlocked – they could not obtain more land to add to the land they already owned. They were also required to pay large fees to support the officer's training schools.

For more than 200 years the Mennonites prospered in northeastern Europe, Poland/Prussia, before the complex political and religious reality of these most tumultuous times forced another migration eastward. Specifically, they traveled more than a thousand miles to the southeast and out of Europe onto the Ukrainian Steppe by invitation of Catherine the Great of Russia who needed settlers to occupy and populate her recently acquired lands.

It was in this expansive, fertile, flat land that the Mennonite agriculturalists settled their families, establishing their communities, their culture and their religious way of life during the last quarter of the 18th century. These new villages and communities, isolated from the Russian Catholic population by Russian law, were based on the patterns already established in northern Europe. In Russia, however, the Mennonites developed a distinct form of village settlement. The government allowed each family to receive about 175 acres of land and the unsettled frontier situation made it necessary for them to live close together for protection. They thus developed the single street village, with the farmland and pastures around the village. By the middle of the 19th century a very orderly village pattern had developed.

The unoccupied lands were suitable for agriculture and the Russian government promised the Mennonites complete exemption from military service, freedom of speech and the liberty to establish their private schools. Although they were allowed their religious freedom they were banned from evangelizing among members of the state church. To persuade a Russian Orthodox Church member to leave the state church was considered a criminal offense and punishable by law.

The first Mennonites to leave Prussia left because they were not able to pay the tax required to exempt the young men from serving in the military. In the late 1700s the first group of 228 families left for South Ukraine. They established the first villages near the small Chortitza stream which flowed through the colony and into the Dnieper River. Since it was the first of the settlements in South Ukraine, it came to be known as the Chortitza Old Colony.

This first group of settlers arriving from West Prussia did not have a minister with them. It had been a practice that ministers were elected from the wealthier class, but since only the landless were involved in the move there was no one among them that was considered qualified to be ordained. In 1794, however, Elder Cornelius Regier and Cornelius

Warkentin came from West Prussia and ordinations took place.

In the early 1800s, Frederick the Great, the King of Prussia, increased pressures by placing more taxation on the Mennonite people because they refused to serve in the military. In 1804, 365 families from the wealthier class also left for South Ukraine and settled in a region about 150 kilometers southeast of the Chortitza Old Colony. This settlement became known as the Molotschna Colony, as it was established on the eastern shore of the Molotschna River.

Since the Russian Government did not allow the subdivision of farms, the inevitable problem of landless families occurred again. To lessen the pressure, both of the original colonies established daughter colonies. The Chortitza founded its first daughter colony in 1836, naming it Bergthal. It wasn't until 1862, that the Molotschna colony established a daughter colony in the Crimea. In 1864 the Chortitza began another major settlement closer to home, naming it Fuerstenland. By 1910, there were thirty six daughter colonies established as the immigrants eventually reached a total of eight thousand families. The Mennonites that immigrated to Manitoba, Canada, from 1874 to 1876, primarily came from the Bergthal, Fuerstenland and Chortitza Old Colony settlements.

Politically, the scene had changed in Russia since the time when Catherine the Great invited the Mennonites to settle in South Ukraine, but culturally, they had not been greatly influenced by the Russian environment. They retained their German culture and Mennonite traditions and most of the people were still not speaking the Russian language. When the Czar visited the Colonies he could not communicate with the Mennonite people which marked the beginning of change. He ruled that the study of the Russian language be mandatory in all schools. For many, this was a strong indicator that they would lose other privileges as well, and they feared government interference in Colony affairs. The Mennonites were in charge of their own local governance and most internal administrative matters, such as taxes and finances, were also left in Mennonite hands but the winds of distrust had started to blow.

In the early 1870s, Russian Mennonite delegates visited both Canada and the United States to explore potential locations for settlement. After negotiations, the delegates were impressed with what Canada had to offer and received a letter from John Lowe, Secretary of the Department of Agriculture, listing fifteen conditions regarding Mennonite immigration. His letter reads as follows:

DEPARTMENT OF AGRICULTURE

Ottawa, 25th July, 1873

Gentlemen:

I have the honour, under the instruction of the Hon. The Minister of Agriculture, to state to you in reply to your letter of this day's date the following facts relating to advantages offered to settlers, and to the immunities offered to Mennonites which are established by Statute Law and by orders of his Excellency the Governor-General-in-Council for the immigration of German Mennonites having intention to emigrate to Canada via Hamburg.

1. An entire exemption from military service is by law and Order-in-Council granted to the Denomination of Christians called Mennonites.

2. An Order-in-Council was passed on the 3rd March last to reserve eight townships in the province of Manitoba for free grants on the condition of settlement as provided in the Dominion Lands Act, that is to say, "Any person who is head of a family or has obtained the age of 21 years shall be entitled to be entered for ¼ section or less quantity of un-appropriated Dominion lands, for a purpose of securing a homestead right in respect thereof."

3. The said reserve of eight townships is for the exclusive use of the Mennonites, and the said free grants of ¼ section to consist of 160 acres each, as defined by the act.

4. Should the Mennonite Settlement extend beyond the eight townships set aside by the Order-in-Council of March 3rd last, other townships will be in the same way reserved to meet the full requirements of Mennonite immigration.

5. If next spring the Mennonite settlers on viewing the eight townships set aside for their use should decide to exchange them for any other unoccupied eight townships, such exchange will be allowed.

6. In addition to the free grant of ¼ section or 160 acres to every person over 21 years of age on the condition of settlement the right to purchase the remaining ¾ of the section at $1.00 per acre is granted by law so as to complete the whole section of 640 acres which is the largest quantity of land the Government will grant a patent for to one person.

7. The settler will receive a patent for a free grant after three years residence in accordance with the terms of the Dominion Lands Act.

8. In event of the death of the settler, the lawful heirs can claim the patent for the free grant upon proof that settlement duties for three years have been preformed.

9. From the moment of occupation the settler acquires a "homestead right" in the land.

10. The fullest privileges of exercising their religious principles is by law afforded to the Mennonites without any kind of molestation or restriction whatever, and the same privilege extends to the education of their children in schools.

11. The privilege of affirming instead of making affidavits is afforded.

12. The Government of Canada will undertake to furnish passenger warrants from Hamburg to Fort Garry for Mennonite families of good characters for the sum of $30.00 for adult persons over the age of eight years, for persons under eight years half price or $15.00 and for infants under one year, $3.00.

13. The minister specially authorizes me to state that this arrangement as to price shall not be changed for the seasons of 1874, 1875, or 1876.

14. I am further to state that if it is changed thereafter the price shall not up to the year 1882 exceed $40.00 per adult and children in proportion, subject to the approval of Parliament.

15. The immigrants shall be provided with provisions of the portion of the journey between Liverpool and Collingwood but between other portions of the journey they are to find their own provisions.

I have the honour to be, Gentlemen, Your obedient servant,

John Lowe
Secretary, Department of Agriculture [3]

The Mennonites agreed to the conditions and began to prepare for the mass movement to Canada. The lack of adequate land for the Mennonite community in Russia and the desire by all Mennonite families to own their own land provided another motivation for emigration when the Canadian government offered free land to the immigrants. Approximately 7,000 people immigrated to Manitoba, Canada, while about 10,000, mostly from the Molotschna Colony, immigrated to the United States (Kansas, Nebraska, South Dakota and Minnesota). Other groups migrated to various other countries. The first group of Mennonites from the Bergthal

---

3 Francis, Dr. E.K. *In Search of Utopia, The Mennonites in Manitoba.* p44, 45. Steinbach, MB: Crossway Publications, 2001.

Mennonite Landing Site, Winnipeg, Manitoba, from 1874 to 1876.

Colony arrived in Winnipeg in the summer of 1874, and the first group from the Chortitza and Fuerstenland Colonies arrived in 1875.

At this time, research indicates there was very little difference in religious and cultural views between the two groups, but that gap has widened considerably over the past 100 years. The more conservative group adopted the name "The Old Colony Mennonite Church." The Bergthal people who were among the first Mennonites to pioneer a settlement along the Saskatchewan River in the Northwest Territories took on the name "Bergthaler."

The large block settlement in Manitoba, which was given to the Mennonites by the Canadian government, was filled up by the turn of the century, and the Mennonite leaders were again faced with looking for more land for their people. By 1877 the East Reserve consisted of thirty-eight villages occupied by seven hundred families. Free land was still available for settlement in Western Canada, so the Mennonite leaders began to look west. In the mid 1890s, twenty years after they had migrated from Russia, many resettled in Saskatchewan, on the vast track of virgin prairie between the two Saskatchewan Rivers. Again they organized their little villages, endeavouring to remain a distinct, compact social unit in order to preserve their political and religious traditions. Two daughter colonies were established – the first was the Rosthern Reserve in 1895 and was extended shortly thereafter to include Hague and Osler. The second reserve was established at Swift Current in 1906. In the spring of 1895, shortly after the first group of settlers arrived on what is known as the Hague-Osler Reserve, the villagers gathered together to decide on a name for their new village. They named it Neuanlage, meaning "New Settlement." The village of Neuanlage is where my dad grew up.

Another wave of Mennonite migration from Russia to Canada took place in the early 1920s. Approximately 70 per cent of Mennonites stayed back in Russia when the first group emigrated to Canada and the United States. They had hoped that the winds of "Russification" would blow over and that perhaps a better future lay ahead, and for a time they did. For the next 50 years they prospered greatly – economically, culturally and intellectually – but their Golden Era came to an explosive end with the Bolshevik Revolution of 1917. They experienced much opposition from the Orthodox Church, which regarded them as a sect. The fall-out from World War I (1914–1918), in which Germany was Russia's enemy, was difficult. In the eyes of the Russians there was little to distinguish the Mennonites from the Germans, as they spoke the German language. The Bolsheviks found other reasons to dislike the Mennonites. They represented capitalist success and another point of contention was their religious faith.

In the years that followed, hundreds of Mennonites were brutally murdered, and thousands were sent to labour camps in Siberia, and were never heard from again. Between 1923 and 1929, approximately 21,000 Mennonites emigrated to Canada and another 2,600 to Paraguay. This group that came to Canada was there to stay, unlike their predecessors, who were forever on the move to separate themselves from the influences of the world. In the 50 years between the two migrations, these Mennonites were very much what the years of prosperity and cooperation with the Tsarist state had made them. They were culturally sophisticated, more progressive in their outlook, and they were, for most part, better educated. New occupational pursuits had opened with the expanding Golden Age in Russia and many went into the teaching profession or business.

The Mennonites that migrated to Canada in the 1870s were progressive in nature as well, but were suppressed by a conservative mind set. They encouraged only agriculture or anything related to it, like blacksmithing, machine work and metal fabrication, as a lifestyle. This no longer holds true for the majority of Canadian Mennonites with a conservative background. Mennonite farmers still dot the Canadian prairies and have become increasingly sophisticated, using the most up-to-date implements

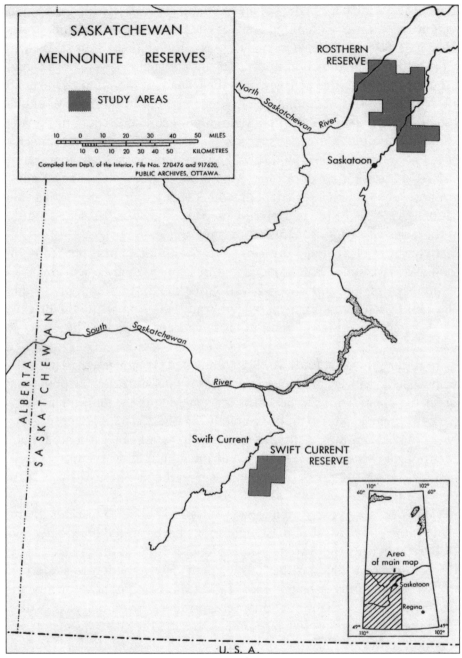

Map courtesy of Richard J. Friesen.

and modern technology.

Regardless of background or when they came, Mennonites have made their mark in Canadian history. They set up their own financial institutions; the Steinbach Credit Union in Manitoba and the Niagara Credit Union in Ontario are among Canada's ten largest credit unions today. Hospitals were started in various cities, among them today's thriving Concordia Hospital in Winnipeg. Educational facilities were born – high schools, colleges, Bible colleges, and, the Canadian Mennonite University in Winnipeg. The Mennonite Collegiate Institute in Gretna, Manitoba, established in 1889, was the first Mennonite secondary school in Canada. Russian Mennonite professors also populate the ranks of major universities. Radio broadcasters, publishers and printers made their appearance. Friesens Corporation of Altona, Manitoba, is one of Canada's leading printers. The Canadian Food Grains Bank was set up largely through the vision of C. A. DeFehr. The DeFehr Company, known as Palliser Furniture, is the largest case goods manufacturer in Canada.

In politics, Jake Epp, the son of a Mennonite minister from the Molotschna Colony in Russia, served in Canada's parliament for more than 20 years. Gordon Thiessen was Governor of the Bank of Canada, the country's leading financial officer. Brad Wall is presently the Premier of Saskatchewan. Many Mennonites have been awarded the Order of Canada.

In the arts, novelist Rudy Wiebe, a renowned Canadian writer, has twice won Canada's Governor General's Award for Literature. Ben Heppner, one of the top opera tenors in the world, is also a Mennonite descendent.

Winnipeg, a city of approximately 675,000, is the largest urban Mennonite community in the world. There are an estimated 1,000 Mennonite owned businesses in Winnipeg, as well as countless social institutions. Most areas of enterprise have been pursued by descendents of Russian Mennonites.

For over 500 years, Mennonites have migrated to various points around the globe. Most of these migrations have centred on the freedom to live their lives the way they interpreted scripture. They were always ready to make a new start because of their determination to stand firm in their convictions – the two most significant being nonconformity and pacifism. Many of the migrations were, however, involuntary departures from the countries they lived in, and, as a result, they have been scattered around the world. Since the migrations to Canada, numerous migrations from Canada to other countries have also taken place. Only in recent years have Mennonites migrated for economic reasons. Many emigrated from Mexico to Ontario and Manitoba, and from Bolivia to La Crete and southern Alberta, as well as to various other locations.

SOURCES

Friesen, Richard J. *Saskatchewan Mennonite Settlements. The Modification of an Old World Settlement Pattern.* Canadian Ethnic Studies IX, No.2, 1975.

Friesen, John. *Mennonites through the Centuries: From the Netherlands to Canada.* Steinbach, MB: Mennonite Heritage Village, 1985.

Global Anabaptist Mennonite Encyclopedia Online, www.gameo.org, 1996–2011.

Hague-Osler Reserve Book Committee. *Hague-Osler Mennonite Reserve: 1895–1995.* Hague, SK: 1995.

Kroeker, Wally. *An introduction to the Russian Mennonites.* Intercourse, PA: Good Books, 2005.

Schroeder, William and Helmut T. Huebert, *Mennonite Historical Atlas.* Winnipeg, MB, Springfield Publishers, 1996.

Pushing Through
Invisible Barriers

A Canadian Mennonite Story

PART ONE

My Childhood on the Prairies of Saskatchewan

1940 – 1953

One

The Familiar Landscape

Excitement filled my soul as the familiar landscape and buildings came into view. Instantly all the memories of my childhood came flooding back. My husband Carl and I were traveling the last stretch of dusty gravel road that led to the old home place where I had spent my childhood. Telephone poles, rubbed silvery grey by the years, still stood single file along the dirt road; a summer breeze was blowing, strumming the wires and I remembered how I would press my ear against the posts and listen to their song.

It was a beautiful day, the sky a cerulean blue with only a few puffy white clouds floating in the air. The prairie wind was stroking the dust covered weeds, wildflowers and grasses along the roadside, giving them life. Ditches overflowed with black-eyed Susans, goldenrod, wild roses, bluebells, pig weed, stinkweed, and thistles; all obeyed the wind and mingled their scents with the sage grasses and the golden wheat bowing down in the fields. A meadow lark perched on a fence post near the garden sang its sweet melody; the grasshoppers snapped and jumped and whirred through the air in the hot afternoon sun adding to the familiar scene. This was Saskatchewan, and only someone who has experienced the sights, scents and sounds of the Saskatchewan prairies can truly identify with it.

The big maple tree, in matronly fashion, still stood in the corner of the garden, and Mom's treasured baby's breath, white with fragrant blossoms, continued to grow beside it just as it had when I was a little girl. The original buildings were still there, only weathered by time. I roamed the yard, reliving where I used to run and play. How my sisters and I enjoyed running barefoot through mud puddles after a rain, making mud pies, playing hop scotch, skipping rope, making whistles out of grass blades and climbing trees. On warm summer days we enjoyed swinging as high as we could go, reciting Robert Louis Stevenson's famous poem:

THE SWING

How do you like to go up in a swing,
Up in the air so blue?
Oh, I do think it the pleasantest thing
Ever a child can do!

Up in the air and over the wall,
Till I can see so wide,
Rivers and trees and cattle and all
Over the country side –

Till I look down on the garden green,
Down on the roof so brown –
Up in the air I go flying again,
Up in the air and down!

Behind the house were rows of maple trees that resembled a small forest. We spent much time here fabricating play houses using old blankets and cardboard boxes. We played for hours, sometimes raiding Mom's garden and making a cold vegetable soup with potatoes, carrots, beans, peas and salt. We enjoyed the birds singing in the maple trees; the brown thrushes, orioles, warblers and robins uniting in jubilant chorus, and occasionally we unexpectedly spotted their nests in the trees. The killdeer made its nest on the ground, and one day when we discovered a nest in Mom's garden, we marked it to make sure no one would step on it. As I stood there, the birds were sweetly singing and their familiar invisible chorus added to the sights and sounds of my childhood memories.

Two

Collecting the Bounty

About 100 yards behind the maple grove was a coulee which filled up with water in the spring. This small body of water was in the cow pasture surrounded by a few scraggly trees, some willows and silver berry bushes. The gophers, awakened by their biological clocks, emerged from their winter homes early in the spring when, once again, they stood straight and tall, whistling their famous morning song and claiming the territory as though it rightfully belonged to them. Here they were content to live and multiply their population. The fields were infested with these curious creatures and they could be seen everywhere, sticking their heads out of their holes, checking for danger, not realizing the danger lay in retreating to their burrows. Their holes in the pasture resembled a cribbage board; their underground tunnels having one front door for about five or six back doors.

Oh, but that gopher field gave us many hours of entertainment! My sisters and I, together with Pete and Jake, carried water from the coulee

Drowning gophers.

in small lard or syrup pails and drowned them out. One of us poured water down one of the tunnels while several others waited at different holes with baseball bats or large sticks, and clubbed them to death. This was teamwork, as we never knew which burrow they would emerge from. The poor creatures didn't even resemble a gopher when they popped out soaking wet. They appeared dumbstruck and bewildered and their small beady eyes pleaded for mercy. At times, a gopher, too young and curious to know danger, came close and no water was needed to collect the bounty.

Now I consider it cruel, but that's what everybody did then and we didn't think much of it. After all, gophers were labeled as pests and the government had put a bounty on the vermin in an attempt to eradicate them. We were paid two cents a gopher tail, which was incentive enough for us to go on the kill. Sometimes we caught fifteen to twenty gophers in one day. That was a lot of money when an ice cream cone cost five cents and soda pop seven cents a bottle.

The Saskatchewan government also put a bounty on crows and magpies paying one cent for a pair of legs. Jake and I spent many hours roaming in the bushes looking for nests. The trees in our area were short and scraggly and crow's nests were big, making them quite easy to spot. Jake usually climbed the trees and handed the baby crows down to me. On one occa-

Robbing crows' nests.

sion we found a nest and discovered the unhatched babies were pecking and the shells had started to crack open. We helped the process along a bit and took four baby crows out of the eggs. Our teacher collected the bounty and we had to bring the evidence to school. I felt a bit uneasy about what we had done, so I asked the teacher if we could claim the legs of the babies we had taken out of the eggs and he said, "No." There must have been some instruction regarding this but I hadn't remembered what it was. Four eggs – four pairs of legs – four cents. LOST! But I was honest and at least felt good about that.

Grasshoppers were another pest we endured, but the government put no bounty on them. Black clouds of grasshoppers landed in the fields, driveways and gardens, and devoured everything in their path. This was before pesticides came on the scene; therefore, other methods of eradication had to be taken. Dad tied rags around long sticks, soaked them with diesel fuel and put a match to them. He gave each of us older siblings a burning stick to try to burn as many of the pesky things as we could. The grasshoppers jumped up only to land a little ahead of our burning sticks, but the hope was that perhaps their eggs were destroyed. Dad also spread poison called Paris Green – a poisonous arsenic mixture – on the driveway and garden to try and keep them away from the house and yard. If you were defeated, and with the grasshoppers you always were, there was a small feeling of satisfaction that at least you had tried.

Three

The 1940s

The terrible stock market crash of 1929 ushered in the Great Depression, which lasted almost a decade. Those years were often referred to as the "Dirty Thirties." A series of drought years set in; unemployment was at an all time high and grain prices had reached their lowest levels. After a few years, the price of grain didn't matter anymore – there was none to sell. The drought and grasshoppers had ruined all farmers' livelihoods, putting the Saskatchewan rural population in very desperate straits. The average wage for anyone who could find a job was about 50 cents to $1.00 a day. The effects of these hard times carried over well into the 1940s. The world was at war, Canada having joined in September, 1939. A great number of families were living on relief – "government handouts" they called it.

Despite the difficult times, life went on. In 1940, Vivien Leigh won an Academy Award for her role as Scarlet O'Hara in *Gone with the Wind*. Eight Oscars were awarded to the sweeping epic that was released in 1939. The six teams of the National Hockey League kept going, despite the hard times. The Liberals were back in power under W. L. Mackenzie King, who held the post of Prime Minister off and on from 1921 to 1948. He attempted to make life easier for Canadian citizens by introducing numerous social programs, some as a result of the drought years and others due to the war. These were desperate times when prices seemed high because there was no money. In 1940, the price of sugar was 21 cents for a 5 lb.

bag, gasoline sold for 18 cents a gallon and a first class postage stamp cost 3 cents. It was at this time that Dairy Queen made its first appearance, as did McDonalds, when Richard and Maurice McDonald opened the first hamburger stand in San Bernardino, California, on May 15, 1940, selling burgers for 15 cents – establishing the principles of modern fast-food restaurants.

In 1940, the British Parliament made a change to the British North America Act (BNA Act), allowing the Canadian government to bring in the Unemployment Insurance System, which created some security for workers.

In 1942, food rationing went into effect due to the war, creating extra hardships – although some items like coffee, tea, sugar and gasoline had already been rationed by circumstances for a number of years. It was implemented to control consumption and also freed cargo ships for wartime duties. Ration books were issued by the Wartime Prices and Trade Board and were essential to survival. They contained coupons for staples like sugar, flour, coffee, tea, butter, etc. It was permissible to trade coupons with others if you chose to do so. I don't know when rationing came to an end, but one day Dad gave us the books to play with saying he wouldn't need them anymore.

In 1944, the Family Allowance, or "Baby Bonus," was introduced to ensure adequate nutrition and clothing to all children under the age of sixteen. All families were eligible. In the summer of 1947, the government also introduced a bill designed to adjust and increase pension payments for senior citizens. Seniors received a cheque of $28.00 a month and the proposed incremental increase was up to $32.75 by the age of 70.

It was during these difficult times, while Mom and Dad, like most parents, were struggling to make ends meet, that another baby arrived. That was me, the seventh of sixteen children. The first six children had already been born to Mom and Dad during the difficult '30s. John, Helen, who died just prior to her fourth birthday from *Somma'krankheit*, a 24 hour flu with diarrhea, Margaret, Pete, Annie and Jake preceded me. I was born on November 7, 1940, in an old farm house about four miles south of Hague, Saskatchewan, on the night of one of the worst snow storms the prairies had seen in many years – so Mom and Dad told me.

Although life was difficult, it equipped men and women with a survival spirit, producing generations of hard-working citizens who had learned to get by with very little. Perseverance and a positive attitude were key qualities, as these hard times lasted for many years. Mom and Dad learned many of life's lessons during these difficult years which prepared them for the hardships that lay ahead.

Taken in November 1940 when I was just a few weeks old and didn't make it into the photograph. In the back row, Mom, and Dad holding Jake. In the front from left to right; Annie, Margaret, John and Pete.

My great-grandparents, Jacob and Anna Peters, with
my grandmother, Margaret (Peters) Klassen.

Four

My Mennonite Heritage

I was born Tena Neudorf on November 7, 1940. The birth place on my birth certificate reads: NE ¼, Sec.11, Tp.40, W of 3, Sask. – the land location where I was born. My parents both descend from a Mennonite heritage dating back approximately 500 years. My mother, Anna, was born to John and Margaret Klassen on March 5th, 1911, at Schoenfeld, Saskatchewan, and my father, Jacob, was born to Peter and Helena Neudorf on October 23rd, 1910, at Reinland, Manitoba.

My maternal grandfather, Mr. John P. Klassen, was six months old when he was brought over from Ukraine, (Russia) during the first Mennonite migration to Canada in 1874–1876. He was born in the province of Ekaterinoslav, (old name) now called Dnepropetrovsk and both sets of my great-grandparents were part of this migration as well. [4]

A Catholic priest by the name of Menno Simons broke away from the Catholic Church when he diligently started studying the scriptures on his own. His motto was, as it is for all Christians, *"For no one can lay any foundation other than the one already laid, which is Jesus Christ."* 1 Corinthians 3: 11. He emphasized evangelism and pacifism. He taught that a Christian's highest allegiance was to Christ and His teachings and thus emphasized

---

4 The Mennonites migrated from Poland to Ukraine (Russia) by invitation of Catherine the Great, along with many other beleaguered Protestants from Europe. When my grandparents migrated to Canada they came from Ukraine which was under Russian control. The terms, Russia and Ukraine are used interchangeably throughout the book.

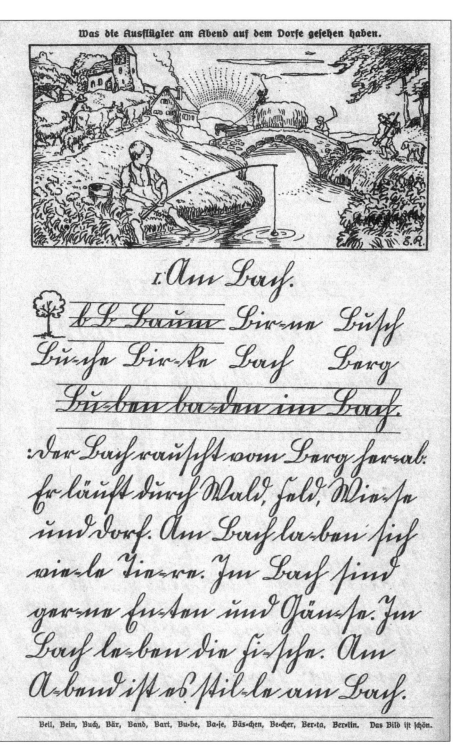

Children were taught to write German in Gothic script. From the *Kinderweldt*.

discipleship, which meant expressing one's faith in daily life – living a life that reflected Biblical teachings. His followers were called Mennonites.

In order to fulfil this teaching, the Mennonites felt a need to separate themselves from any outside influences, or "the world." Therefore, they were adamant about educating their children in private schools in the German language. Their curriculum through the years has been based on the Bible. The first books they used were the arithmetic text book, and the grammar text book, the *Fibel*, or "primer," from which they were taught to read and write in Gothic script. They then progressed to the Catechism, New Testament and the Bible which laid a solid foundation for the Christian faith in the lives of their young children.

The Mennonites were determined that their young men would not serve in the military in keeping with their pacifist stance. For more than 200 years they prospered in northeastern Europe (Poland/Prussia) where they were exempted from military service and allowed educational freedom. These same privileges were granted to them when they accepted the invitation of Catherine the Great to populate and farm the great sweeping plains of the Ukrainian Steppe.

Many years later, when the Russian government, during the time of Czar Alexander II, no longer honoured the *Privilegium*, the "charter of privileges," which the Mennonite delegates from Russia had made with Catherine II, negotiations to retain their earlier exemptions began. When this proved fruitless, delegates were sent to investigate the possibilities for group emigration to North America.

On July 1, 1867, the Dominion of Canada was established by the British Parliament under terms of the British North America Act (BNA) forming the first four provinces of Canada, namely Quebec, Nova Scotia, New Brunswick and Ontario. *"In 1870, Canada acquired title to the northwest territory of North America, which had until then been under the jurisdiction of the Hudson's Bay Company. This was but one of a series of steps undertaken by the John A. Macdonald government of the young Dominion of Canada to ensure that its dream of a continent-wide national state would be realized. Paper jurisdiction over this huge prairie region with its 1,500 kilometers of undefended border meant little without a settled population occupying the land. The Dominion government considered the colonization of the Western plains as one of its most urgent concerns.*

"Under considerable pressure from its small settled population, Ottawa gave Manitoba provincial status in 1870. However, the federal government retained control of Crown lands in order to use them to lure settlers and compensate railroad construction companies. The Dominion Lands Act of

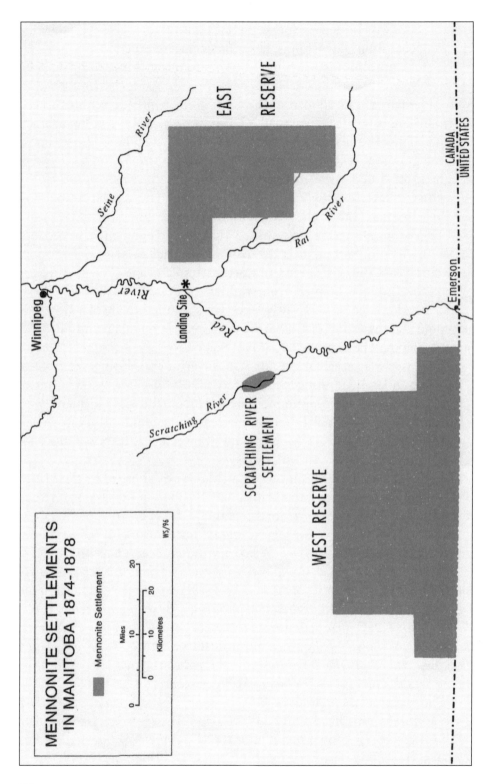

MENNONITE SETTLEMENTS
IN MANITOBA 1874-1878

Mennonite Settlement

Miles
0   10   20
0   10   20
Kilometres

WS/96

EAST RESERVE

WEST RESERVE

SCRATCHING RIVER SETTLEMENT

Winnipeg

Landing Site

Seine River

Red River

Rat River

Scratching River

Emerson

CANADA
UNITED STATES

My Mom and Dad on their wedding day, July 19, 1931.

1872 provided for homestead grants for settlers. In 1873, the Royal Northwest Mounted Police was created to ensure law and order in the West. Good transportation was promised in the form of a transcontinental railway agreed to in the negotiations, to bring British Columbia into Confederation." [5]

5 Ens, Adolf. *Subjects or Citizens*, c1994 pp 11–12

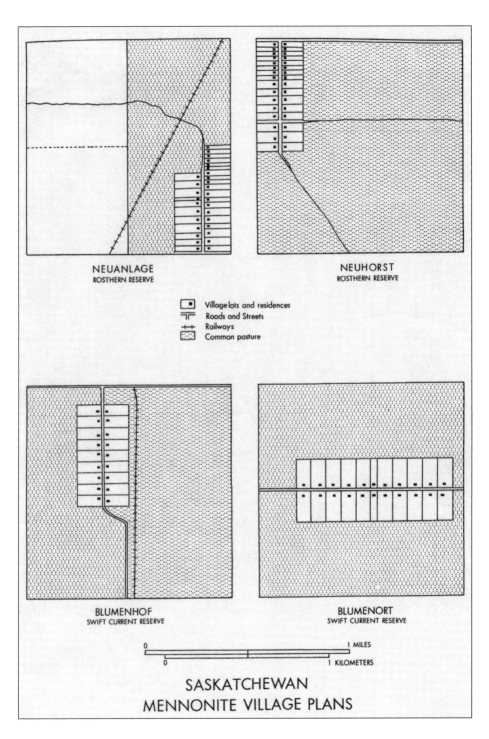

NEUANLAGE
ROSTHERN RESERVE

NEUHORST
ROSTHERN RESERVE

■ Village lots and residences
Roads and Streets
Railways
Common pasture

BLUMENHOF
SWIFT CURRENT RESERVE

BLUMENORT
SWIFT CURRENT RESERVE

0   1 MILES
0   1 KILOMETERS

SASKATCHEWAN
MENNONITE VILLAGE PLANS

Map courtesy of Richard J. Friesen.

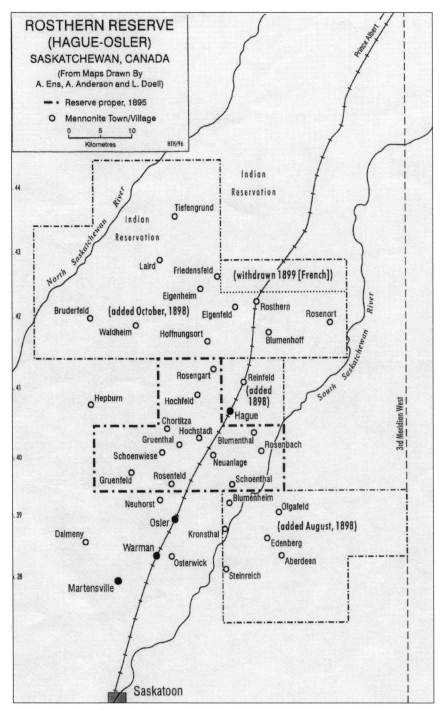

A map of Rosthern reserve (Hague-Osler). Mom grew up in
Hochstadt, Dad grew up in Neuanlage. Our farmstead was at Osler.

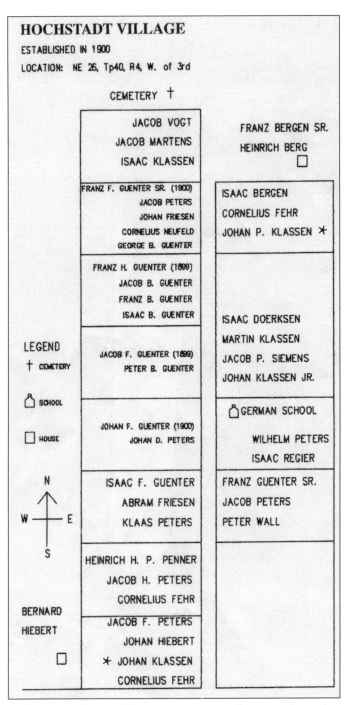

Hochstadt village. *Johan P. Klassen is my grandfather, Johan Klassen is my uncle. Compiled by Leonard Doell, computer drawn by Victor R. Peters.

NEUANLAGE VILLAGE

ESTABLISHED IN 1895

LOCATION: SE23, Tp40, R4, W. of 3rd

⌂ OLD COLONY CHURCH ALT. JACOB WIENS (1899)	REV. PETER KLASSEN (1895) FRANZ GUENTER REV. JOHAN WALL REV. JOHAN P. WALL CORNELIUS SCHMIDT
JACOB TEICHROEB (1895) JULIUS KLASSEN CORNELIUS FEHR	GERHARD HEIN (1895) FRANZ PETERS ISAAC WALL JOHAN FEHR
JOHAN TEICHROEB SR. (1895) PETER KASPER JOHAN PETERS SR. AARON PETERS JOHAN HEPPNER	GERHARD REMPEL (1895) DIEDRICH REMPEL SR. HEINRICH BRAUN PETER MARTENS □ JACOB NEUFELD PETER D. PETERS
JOHAN MARTENS (1895) JOHAN U. PETERS JOHAN ANDRES CORNELIUS UNRAU	ABRAM GIESBRECHT (1895) PETER ENS JACOB PETERS SR. □ CORNELIUS FEHR JACOB MARTENS
JOHAN TEICHROEB JR. JACOB PETERS PETER NEUDORF SR. ✶ REV. JOHAN P. WALL	PETER MARTENS HERMAN NEUFELD (1895) □ ABRAM ZACHARIAS ✶ JOHAN NEUDORF JACOB LOEWEN JR. □ JACOB LOEWEN SR.
GERMAN SCHOOL ⌂	ISAAC SCHMIDT (1895) PETER KLASSEN JACOB KLASSEN JOHAN P. KLASSEN FRANZ HARDER
CORNELIUS UNRAU (1895) ABRAHAM FRIESEN ISAAC JANZEN	PETER MARTENS (1895) JACOB PETERS BERNARD KRAHN JACOB KLASSEN
ISAAC GUENTER SR. MARTIN KASPER □ ABRAM J. PETERS JOHAN PETERS	PETER WOELKE (1895) JACOB KLASSEN PETER BUECKERT
PETER DRIEDGER (1895) ISAAK DRIEDGER JACOB NEUFELD PETER JANZEN	JOHAN F. PETERS (1895) PETER TEICHROEB

Neuanlage village. * Peter Neudorf Sr. is my grandpa, Johan Neudorf is my uncle. Compiled by Leonard Doell, computer drawn by Victor R. Peters.

After negotiations were completed, the Canadian government drew up an agreement that satisfied the demands of the Mennonite delegation. They were granted the privilege to live according to the principles of their faith which they had enjoyed in Russia. The two most important were to exempt the young men from serving in the military and the freedom to educate their children in their own private German schools. Free homestead grants were available to further encourage settlers, which satisfied their agricultural and economic interests. Approximately 7,000 Mennonites made the decision to immigrate to Canada while about 10,000 immigrated to the United States.

The Canadian government set aside large blocks of land in Manitoba, initially eight townships, in what came to be called the East Reserve, and later another seventeen townships in what was called the West Reserve. These reserves were located east and west of the Red River respectively. This land was for the exclusive use of settlement by the Mennonites, not only to occupy the West, but to create a land base sufficient to establish a community large enough to support the desired culture and society.

Once on the Canadian prairies, the Mennonites settled in villages. They copied the village patterns and their names which had been part of their communities in Russia. They brought with them the distinct European

Grandma and Grandpa Klassen's house-barn.

architecture of house-barn units, which originated in the Vistula region of Polish/Prussia, now Poland. The Mennonite farmers constructed their house-barn dwellings on long (about one-half mile in length) narrow, individually owned yards or village lots of variable size and shape. These yards and their unusual houses were positioned on either side of a wide village street. Generally, the street was planted with maple or poplar trees which, in due course, became stately, lending a distinctly European flavour to the look of the villages. For the first settlers, this exclusive village pattern took on mythic, almost sacred, dimensions.

The house and barn were connected by a *Gang*, which was either a breeze way or a passage way. This arrangement offered conveniences, and perhaps the primary advantage was caring for the livestock during the extremely harsh winters they experienced on the Canadian prairies. The connected house-barn and its associated street village proved to be adaptive, effective and successful in its transfer to the Canadian prairies. Apart from the practical reasons for the barn being attached to the house, house-barns were, along with the villages, an attempt to remain separate, and preserve a physical environment in which their religion and culture could thrive.

Most importantly, however, combined with the village system, the

A house-barn identical to that of my Grandma and Grandpa Neudorf's.

59

Grandma and Grandpa Klassen, circa 1946.

house-barn created a familiar setting for the establishment of the essential social and religious organization of Mennonite culture. The re-creation and retention of this familiar environment helped maintain the cultural traditions of the beleaguered, often persecuted, religious migrants in a land that, while it looked like the plains of southern Russia, was uncultivated and only sparsely populated, but would with time and hard work produce prosperous farms.

Both my parents grew up in an organized village in a house-barn unit. Dad grew up in the Neuanlage village and Mom in the Hochstadt village

Grandma and Grandpa Neudorf with their four oldest sons, taken in 1910, shortly before my dad was born. Grandma is wearing her *Kruzhel'metz*.

only two miles apart. My paternal grandfather had attained a homestead outside the village, as did most of the village settlers. When Mom and Dad were married, Dad purchased one quarter of land from him, they moved onto it, and never went back to village life.

Mom's parents' house and barn were separated by a breezeway (a few feet of platform without a roof) between them. The breezeway had one door leading into the house and another door that led into a small room which was attached to the barn. It had a cement floor and this is where

Grandma did her cooking in the summer. My Grandpa Klassen's barn was as clean as it could possibly be, except for the odours, which could be controlled but not avoided. He swept the barn floors as religiously as Grandma swept the house floors. In the winter, when the animals were confined to the barn, he diligently cleaned up after them. Throughout the history of the Mennonite people, cleanliness has been seen as a virtue second only to godliness. This rang true with both sets of my grandparents, although it was a constant battle due to the house-barn arrangement.

Dad's parents' house and barn were separated by a passageway (an enclosed room between the house and barn). The room had one door opening into the house and another into the barn so the odours were ever present – more so in the winter when the animals were kept indoors.

The village families did not have fenced pastures, so they shared a common cattle pasture. Often, when Dad reminisced, he told us how he and his brothers and other young fellows from the village had to take turns herding the cattle. They were kept in a small fence behind the farm buildings over night and every morning a herdsman walked down the village street ringing a bell, alerting the farmers to chase their cattle onto the street. They were then collectively herded to the common pasture. Dad said even though they weren't allowed to play cards, they did anyway, often forgetting about time, and the cattle, and then getting into serious trouble.

Both my grandmothers dressed in traditional Mennonite clothing, which was the dress code in Europe over the centuries. The women wore long, dark, long-sleeved dresses without collars completed by an apron. The married women wore a dark-coloured head covering, usually a shawl with fringes, embroidered in very bright coloured flowers. For church services they wore a *Kruzhel'metz*, "lace cap," under this shawl. This lace cap was a delicate piece of art work made from black lace, sewn together, layer upon layer, and shaped into a head covering. My Grandmother Klassen did not adhere to strict dress code, but my Grandmother Neudorf wore the *Kruzhel'metz* most of the time and always wore dark, long sleeved dresses that reached to the floor. I don't recall ever seeing her dressed any other way. After more than 125 years since the migration, the conservative Old Colony Mennonite women scattered around the globe still dress in traditional clothing, although wearing the *Kruzhel'metz* is, for the most part, an option.

The Governor General of Canada, Lord Dufferin, paid an official visit to the Mennonite settlements in August of 1877. He addressed a large crowd of Mennonites and emphasized, *"It is with great pleasure that I have passed through your villages, and witnessed your comfortable homesteads, barns and byres, which have arisen like magic upon this fertile plain, for they prove that you are expert in agriculture, and possess a high standard of domestic comfort.*" Upon his return to Winnipeg, he summed up his impressions of the tour through the province in a public speech saying,

"*Although I have witnessed many sights to cause me pleasure during my various progresses through the Dominion, seldom have I beheld any spectacle more pregnant with prophecy, more fraught with promise of a successful future than the Mennonite settlement (Applause). When I visited these interesting people, they had been only two years in the province, and yet in a long ride I took across many miles of prairie, which but yesterday was absolutely bare, desolate, untenanted, the home of the wolf, the badger, and the eagle, I passed village after village, homestead after homestead, furnished with all the conveniences and incidents of European comfort, and of a scientific agriculture; while on the other side of the road, cornfields ripe for harvest, and pastures populous with herds of cattle stretched away to the horizon (Great applause.) Even on this continent – the peculiar theatre of rapid change and progress – there has nowhere, I imagine, taken place so marvelous a transformation.*" [6]

William Hespeler was a special immigration agent of the Canadian government who was instrumental in bringing the Mennonites from Ukraine to Canada from 1874–1876. When news came that the Governor General was to visit the Mennonite settlements, Mr. Hespeler came from Winnipeg to help plan the event.

Margaret Epp describes the Governor General's visit to the Mennonite settlement in her book *The Earth is Round*, c1974 pp 208–210;

"*A flat top rise was chosen as the meeting place. From the summit you could see twelve comfortable villages.*"

"*Long ago the Mennonites had become good judges of horses. There were handsome horses in the cavalcade. The whole mass of people watched with laughing interest as the fifty riders set off, their horses cutting fancy figures as they tossed their manes and snorted. The boys shouted, waving their hats as they thundered over the knoll and out of sight.*"

"*The crowd waited, patiently yet expectantly. Now … now … you could hear voices and the jingle of bridles and the thud of hooves. The visitors came in a knot, looking very fashionable and lively and interested. The Mennonite guard of honour had gone wild. They kept racing round and round the visitors in a wide circle.*"

---

6 Francis, Dr. E K. *In Search of Utopia*, pp 78 and 79

"*Someone had erected an arbour on top of the rise. The word Willkommen (Welcome) was spelled out in big letters. The Mennonites sang German hymns of praise and thanksgiving to God for leading them to their new homeland. There were speeches of thanks to the Canadian government, too, for welcoming them. The visitors smiled and applauded when the children sang. They smiled again, the ladies especially, when the girls in white came to hand over their bouquets of garden flowers.*"

"*Lord Dufferin's speech was long and flattering. An old lady, who took it all in with a smile, was heard muttering, 'Not so flowery, not so flowery, Herr Dufferin. We are people, only people. Without God's help we could have done nothing.' But she smiled at the man who seemed to love her people so greatly.*"

Other groups of settlers also came to settle in the West – although not all of them as prosperous as the Mennonites. Many were lured by free land, but it was another one in the series of steps undertaken by Prime Minister Sir John A. Macdonald's government to ensure that its dream of a continent-wide national state would be realized.

My great grandparents Jacob and Anna Peters in Gnadenthal (Plum Coulee), Manitoba, celebrating Thanksgiving in their new homeland in 1900. Back row L - R: Jacob 15, Heinrich 10, Peter 11, Margaretha (my grandmother) 14, Front row: Johan 12, Anna 6, David 5, Anna 39 (my great-grandmother) holding Klas 1, Jacob 42 (my great-grandfather) holding Katherina 3.

Aerial view of the farmstead Mom and Dad purchased at Osler in May 1945.

Five

My New Home

My family moved about fifteen miles south from my birth place to the Osler district in May of 1945 when I was five years old. I don't remember very much about my first home but I do recall the house and a few things inside the house; where the table and cook stove stood and a small porch which had shelves in it. There was a small coulee close to the house where Mom fetched her water in the summer. Sometimes, Mom gave me a small syrup pail or lard pail and said I could help her carry the water, which made me feel very important.

The property Dad purchased was a homestead consisting of one and a half quarters of land. The new place was exciting. The house was a two story frame structure with a verandah. The main floor had a roomy kitchen and dining area which was finished with light blue Congo Wall, a smooth and easy to clean wall covering that extended halfway to the ceiling. It didn't have kitchen cabinets, although there were cream coloured shelves with sliding doors along the west wall that served as cupboards. The main floor also had a large living room, one bedroom, a pantry, and a porch – and I can't forget the dirt cellar underneath the floor. The second story had three bedrooms. It was a fairly big and classy house in those days.

A summer kitchen with a cement floor had been built close to the house. On hot days the cooking was done here in order to keep the house cool for sleeping. Since cooking was done on a wood cook-stove, the

The house on the property Dad bought at Osler, 1945.

house heated up very quickly.

Not too far from the house stood a big red barn which was infested with rats. They were big, fat and so tame they ate alongside the pigs from the feed trough. Not many years later Dad and John tore the barn down, salvaging whatever good boards they could to build a machine shed. There was a garage and several other outbuildings where the barn swallows made their nests under the eves. We watched as they built their nests with mud, swooping up time and again, their short legs, forked tail and pointed wings aiding them in their rapid flight. In the spring we could hear the baby birds chirping, begging for food.

The privy was situated fairly close to the house and winter visits there made few good memories. Snow crunched under our boots, and the hinges creaked with frost as we opened and closed the out-house door. The walls and seat were covered in hoar frost, but we had no choice in the matter when relief was needed. During the night we were allowed to use a chamber pot. I was always afraid of the dark, and when nature called in the evening I waited as long as possible, always begging someone to accompany me on this dreaded trip. In the winter, no one ever wasted any time there.

This new place had a big yard and a pasture where we could roam freely, picking wild flowers, silver berries and rose hips, which were very tasty after a frost. We went for walks and explored the countryside. I recall our walks in late summer when the scent of silver sage mingled with the fragrance of the odd wild rose bush that still bloomed along the roadside. Beautiful maple trees surrounded the garden and yard – two huge maples shaded the house and summer kitchen. Lush green grass grew in front of the house, while the rest of the yard was covered in "poor man's lawn," which grew regardless of moisture or soil conditions and never needed mowing. A white picket fence surrounded the house. It was a nice farmstead, well-suited for a large family.

Six

Radio was King

We had some connection with the outside world through newspapers and radio. Dad subscribed to *The Western Producer* and *The Free Press Weekly Prairie Farmer*. Both were weekly newspapers which later merged and went by the name of *The Western Producer*. Whenever Mom and Dad went to Saskatoon they picked up *The Saskatoon Star Phoenix*, a daily newspaper. *The Family Herald* also found its way into our home regularly. I eagerly waited for this newspaper to arrive every month as it usually ran a story with one chapter of the story being printed with each edition. One year it ran a story called *The Little Kingdom* by Hugie Call. The story was about a little girl who loved animals, but caught a virus from an animal and died when she was six years old. This story was so real to me that it felt like I was experiencing it right along with this family. When the final chapter was printed it had a footnote saying, "This book is hard cover and may be purchased for $1.50." I asked Mom and Dad if I could order it and they said, "Yes." I treasure this book, as it was the first of my library collection.

Circumstances demanded recycling out of necessity rather than for environmental reasons. After the newspapers were read, we had to cut them into squares and take them to the toilet for recycling. When the squares ran out, well guess what? The Timothy Eaton mail order catalogue with its glossy smooth pages had to do. We gave the pages a good crumpling treatment but they still couldn't compete with the relative effectiveness of newspaper. Oh, but then came Christmas and how thankful we were when Dad brought home many boxes of Japanese Mandarin oranges which came individually wrapped in those soft mint coloured papers. For a short while we lived in style!

The radio was KING! Many times the static on the shortwave radio was so bad and the reception so poor that the voices from other stations would blend in with the crackling, often going in and out. Only two people could comfortably have their ear next to it at any given time. Occasionally there was a toss-up as to who would listen to what. Dad, of course, listened to the news as he had to know what was happening in politics and sports. The radio kept Dad up-to-date with happenings in the war, and, until the day he died, he remembered the times and dates of the major events that had unfolded. My older brothers listened to *The Cisco Kid, Roy Rogers,* and the *Gene Autry* programs. Another favourite was the crime drama *The Shadow Knows.* The famous opening of the program went like this: 'Who knows what evil lurks in the hearts of men? **The shadow knows!**'

Most of our family enjoyed listening to *The Hit Parade,* the top 10 in country music. We were always guessing which song would be added to the top 10 and which one would be dropped. Some hits of the '40s were, "You Are My Sunshine," "Candy Kisses," "Tennessee Waltz," "When My Blue Moon Turns to Gold Again," "The Wabash Cannon Ball" and others.

Comedies were also favourites. Listening to *Fibber McGee and Molly, The Pepper Young's Family* and *Ma and Pa Kettle,* were times when we all laughed together. Sometimes we listened to Jack Benny and Bob Hope which Mom didn't always agree with as they occasionally threw in an off-coloured joke – nothing like the ones you hear today though, that need to go through the washing machine first!

On Saturday evenings during the winter months, Foster Hewitt was heard across the airwaves announcing *Hockey Night in Canada* and there was no question as to which station we'd be tuned into. There was something about those Saturday nights that created a cozy atmosphere. Mom was always cooking and baking, preparing food for Sunday, as Sunday was a day of rest. The aroma of her freshly baked bread, cakes and cookies, a pot of *Borscht*, "soup" simmering as the wood crackled in the cookstove, and the water kettle humming a low, contented tune, completed the homey feeling. The dog lying on the rug by the door would perk up his ears as Foster Hewitt shouted, "He shoots, he scores!" Sometimes my mind drifts back to these times when I smell my own freshly baked bread, soup simmering on the stove, and the TV Channel is tuned in to a hockey game.

It wasn't difficult to keep up with the happenings in the National Hockey League as there were only six teams in the League at the time – the Toronto Maple Leafs, Montreal Canadiens, Chicago Black Hawks, Detroit Red Wings, Boston Bruins and the New York Rangers. I was more interested in the Western Hockey League as Dad would occasionally take us to hockey games in Saskatoon, so, of course, the Saskatoon Quakers became my favourite team. I knew every player by name and later, when Dad bought a herd of cattle, Annie and I named them after the Quaker players – names like McCullough, Kalita, Bentley, (Bev, Doug and Max), Lorn "the Gump" Worsley and others. We thought we were honouring the players but I doubt if they would have been impressed had they known. Eventually many of these players were traded to the Montreal Canadiens which then became my favourite team in the National Hockey League.

One day Dad came home from an auction having purchased a gramophone. It was in a tall cabinet and had to be hand cranked to get the right speed. The needle needed changing after every song. We had no records, but one day John surprised us when he brought home a recording by Wilf Carter, who was nicknamed "Montana Slim." One side played "The Smoke Went up the Chimney Just the Same" and on the flip side was "The Little Blue Shirt My Mother Made for Me." John became our hero!

Did we ever wear that record out! When we ran out of needles we re-used them although we had strict orders not to. We wanted to listen so badly that we did it anyway. This was very hard on the record and when the needles got too dull, the record would start to wobble and go "whoa, whoa" but we listened until it quit. Later we got more records by various artists including Kitty Wells, Roy Acuff, Hank Williams and others. I felt sad when Hank Williams died very suddenly at a young age on January 1, 1953.

Telephone service was available and we were able to communicate locally and even long distance. Our ring was two long and two short. When the phone rang five consecutive rings it was a message for all thirteen families on our line, usually to announce a meeting or some topic of interest to everyone. With that many families using the same line it was often difficult to find it free when it was needed. Frequently it was used as a pastime for some folks to catch up on the latest news. When we wanted to phone outside our party line, we needed to ring Central and they connected us to whomever we needed to call.

Seven

Planting and Reaping

The shrill whistle of the gophers, the cawing of the crows and the frogs croaking in unison in the coulee let us know that spring had arrived and seeding the land was not far behind. Dad made sure the tractor, one-way, seed drill and other machinery were repaired, greased and ready to go when the land was dry enough to be worked. Dad and my older brothers prepared the soil, sowed the seed – often in the dust – and prayed that the rains would come. Only too often the rains did not come on time resulting in another crop failure; another lean year in desperate times, but there was always the hope that next year would be better.

Many times, late at night when the distant rumble of thunder accompanied by small flashes of lightening appeared in the west and came ever nearer, there was a sign of hope. As the storm progressed and lightning flashed across the sky with loud crashes of thunder following, Dad would go outside trying to figure out which way the storm clouds were moving and maybe, just maybe, they would open up and water the thirsty land. Some years dry thunder storms swept away all hope of a harvest.

Lightning storms in Saskatchewan were often severe, and as a young girl I was absolutely terrified of them. When the storms came in the middle of the night Mom and Dad woke everyone up and we all sat around the kitchen table until the storm passed. I still don't understand the reason for this. Sometimes the lightning bolts were extremely bright and lasted long enough for us to see the neighbour's buildings. The deafening noise of thunder scared me more than the lightning.

One evening, when a storm was raging, we were concerned for Dad's safety as he still hadn't returned home from a trip to Saskatoon. We watched the lights of every vehicle to see if one of them would turn into our driveway. Suddenly a bright flash of lightning lit up the night sky and we recognized Dad's truck coming down the highway some distance before the turn-off into our yard. We were relieved and thankful when Dad was safely home.

We inherited rocks and Russian thistle with the purchase of the land. There was a gravel pit on this property, and the borders were dotted with rock piles inhabited by gophers, rabbits and mice. The job of picking rocks was endless and sometimes we wondered if they were equipped to reproduce. In the winter, rabbit and coyote tracks told their own story, and the birds left their prints in the snow, ever in search of food.

Much of the top soil had been blown away by dust storms during the drought years. Russian thistle and other weeds thrived in the dry, dusty soil and rain or no rain, they always produced a bumper crop. There were no death-dealing chemicals then to make us weed-free, therefore the farmers followed God's instruction in the Bible for weed control: Lev. 25: V 3 & 4 reads, *"For six years sow your fields, and for six years prune your*

The fence lines on the property were lined with rock piles.

vineyards and gather their crops, but in the seventh year the land is to have a Sabbath rest, a Sabbath to the Lord. Do not sow your fields or prune your vineyards." The farmers' summer fallowed their fields to keep the weeds down.

The tumble weeds grew to a very large size. During the late summer and early fall, the tough prickly weed ripened and broke away from its roots. The prairie winds started the prickly balls of Russian thistle rolling, piling them high against the barb wire fences. In early spring Dad, together with my brothers, pitchforks and matches in hand, started to burn the detested weeds. All around us in the neighbourhood puffs of smoke went up as farmers proceeded with the first task of spring.

When the rains did come on time and produced good crops, there was great joy and satisfaction in bringing the harvest in. The grain was cut and made into sheaves or bundles with a binder pulled by a tractor. The sheaves were stooked to dry; eight bundles to a stook. There was always a wait for the threshing crew to arrive as it moved from farm to farm until everyone's crop was in.

We were excited when the threshing crew arrived, usually about five or six teams of horses with their hay racks as well as several field pitchers who stayed in the fields to help load the bundles. The threshing machine was parked wherever Dad wanted the straw stack to be. Its location was

Cutting grain and making it into bundles.

A stooked field.

of great importance, as it served as a shelter for the pigs and cattle in the winter. The pigs would dig a hole in the straw stack, crawl in and be quite cozy. The cattle stood near the entry of the pig domain, which provided shelter from the icy winter winds.

The teams headed for the fields loading and hauling all the sheaves to the threshing machine. We waited for Dad to fire up the tractor to watch the machine go into chewing motion. The first two hay racks to get loaded took their place on either side of the threshing machine where the men fed it bundle by bundle with their pitchforks. The rest of the teams followed, loading and re-loading until all the sheaves were threshed. The straw shot out from a huge spout, building the straw stack; a small stream of golden grain ran into the grain wagon underneath. The grain was stored in granaries or hauled directly to the elevator, four miles away in Osler. In those years, elevators dotted the landscape, as most every small prairie town had their own.

The new straw stack held a lot of meaning for us as well as for the pigs and cattle. It meant fresh straw in our mattresses for our trundle beds, or *Schlop'beintj*. Mom opened up all the mattresses and shook out the oat straw – crushed fine by a winter of sleep. When the covers were washed

78

Threshing the grain and building the straw stack.

and ready, we raced to the straw stack to fill them up. How I enjoyed going to bed at night, with the smell of the new straw lingering in my nose until I fell asleep. The first few nights the newly-filled mattresses were so high that we couldn't close the lid of the *Schlop'beintj*. When open it served as a bed and when closed it served as a bench to sit on.

Mom sewed flour sacks together for mattress covers. Flour came in dingy, 100 pound, off-white coloured cotton sacks. Mom dyed the sacks different colours with the old-fashioned Diamond Brand dyes, usually mint green and a hot pink which later turned into a dusty rose. It was a small improvement from the original colour, but it was a change and made life a little more interesting. These sacks were also used for sheets and tea towels. In later years, the flour company had advanced considerably – the sacks now boasted printed and floral designs which Mom used for pillow cases, dresses and aprons. Our generation and the generations before us were definitely the forerunners of recycling.

Feeding the threshing crew was the responsibility of the household where the threshing was done. This was a big assignment for Mom, feeding approximately 15 hungry men as well as her own large family. Mid-morning and afternoon coffee breaks required lots of extra baking.

The *Schlop'beintj* served two purposes; seating and sleeping.

She usually made 15 to 20 loaves of bread at a time as well as cakes, cookies and big pans of delicious cinnamon rolls. I felt so important when I could carry the baked goodies and the steaming hot coffee to the workers. Mom usually made one special meal. Most often it was pot-roasted chicken with *Bobbat* – a steamed dumpling she put on top of the chicken.

Recipe for Bobbat

2 cups flour
2 tbs. sugar
1 tsp. salt
4 tsp. baking powder
1 egg
Enough milk to make the batter firm enough to hold
1 cup raisins
1 cup dried prunes

Put cheese cloth or any other thin cloth on top of the chicken, then spoon the Bobbat on allowing it to steam for about one hour.

Mom needed to prepare at least five or more chickens, big pots of

Mom holding Babe. This photo was taken in 1949 when Mom was 37 years old.

potatoes, plus vegetables and coleslaw to feed everyone. The ten or so fruit and cream pies she baked for dessert had a way of disappearing rather quickly even after a heavy meal. When the crop was in, Dad was thankful for the bounty and Mom was thankful that the crew had moved on.

Dad in his early '40s.

Eight

The One-Room School

The farmstead Mom and Dad bought four miles west of Osler was located in the Altona School District. The school opened its doors in 1904 when Saskatchewan was still a part of the Northwest Territories. School districts in the NWT were numbered in the order in which they were formed. The Altona School District was the 859th district organized in the area which, in 1905, became Saskatchewan and Alberta.

The one-room school was located one-half mile south of our farmstead. There were 53 enrolled students in grades 1 through 9 when I started grade one. All the students, except for the Opheim family, were of Mennonite origin, as were most of the teachers who taught at Altona during the lifetime of the school. The rest of the country schools in the surrounding districts consisted mainly of Mennonite students as well. This was due to the fact that very few other people had settled here when the Mennonites came to settle this part of the west.

The opening exercises included roll call, reciting The Lord's Prayer in unison and singing "God Save the King." The flag was raised before the exercises began. When I started school Mr. Hein was the teacher and I was anxious to learn how to read and write. We were taught by repetition in all three R's – 'Reading, Riting and Rithmetic'. The Dick and Jane books with Spot the dog were our first readers. I felt it quite the accomplishment when I quickly mastered:

Come Dick.   Come, Jane, come.
Come and see.   See Spot and Baby Sally.
Come, come.   Come and help. Look Dick.
Come and see.   See Jane help Spot.
Come and see Spot.   Oh, see something funny.
Look Spot.   See little Spot.
Oh, look.   Funny little Spot.
Look and see.
Oh see.

Multiplication tables were also taught by repetition and we had to recite them to the teacher. Much of our school work was done on the chalkboard under the teacher's watchful eye. At the end of the school day several students were assigned to clean the chalkboards and felt erasers. The brushes were cleaned outside by knocking them against the wall of the school leaving white powdery marks on the school building.

We were required to memorize poetry which all the students in the class recited as a group. One poem we memorized still remains vivid in my memory.

TREES

I think that I shall never see
A poem as lovely as a tree

A tree whose hungry mouth is pressed
Against the earth's sweet flowing breast

A tree that looks at God all day
And lifts her leafy arms to pray

A tree that may in summer wear
A nest of robins in her hair

Upon whose blossom snow has lain
Who intimately lives with rain

Poems are made by fools like me
But only God can make a tree

Joyce Kilmer

Altona school where I attended from 1947 to 1953.

Our school supplies were provided by the school board. The five cent scribbler had a ready reference of the arithmetic tables on the back cover including the multiplication tables, tables of time (seconds up to one year), weights, measures and others.

The school offered outdoor plumbing; two "two-holers," one for the girls and one for the boys. Our water supply came from a well located a short distance from the school yard and was carried into the school house with buckets by the students. A water dispenser in the form of a pail and dipper stood at one end of a small table and an enamel wash basin at the other. A bar of 'Lifebuoy' soap sat in a saucer beside the basin so we could wash our hands when necessary. As I recall, all the students used the same dipper for drinking, but to my knowledge no one ever got sick because of it.

Once we were past the first few grades in school, we were allowed to write with a straight pen which had a detachable steel nib. A small bottle of ink was needed for writing. All the desks had a circular opening in the top right hand corner to accommodate the standard round bottle of ink. The pens had to be dipped into the ink for every few words written. The nib could only hold a drop or two at a time, making writing tedious and very time consuming. The pen was scratchy, prone to blotting and it was difficult to keep the ink flowing freely, especially when too much pressure was applied. On occasion, I removed the bottle from the ink well to speed up the process, only to waste time when I had to scamper to find an ink blotter after it spilled on my desk or exercise books.

Our school desks were designed for two students per desk. The varnished desk tops were plain, but over the years many of them acquired individuality as students would invariably scratch or carve initials, names, designs or drawings on their shiny surfaces. They were slightly sloped with a storage space directly underneath the writing surface. A sudden jolt sent everything flying to the floor; pencil boxes, crayons, pencils, rulers, geometry sets and books. A common prank, usually played by the boys, was to put a thumb tack on the seat of the desk so the student would jump up and scream when she or he sat down, resulting in a lot of butt-rubbing. I quickly got into the habit of checking my seat before I sat down.

For most students, the mode of transportation to and from school was horse and buggy, or cart in the summer. We usually walked on warm days, but occasionally we caught a ride with the Klassen family. I can still smell the horses blowing hot air and the steam from the horse apples rising to meet our noses as we drove against the wind heading for home.

Bunks on the school yard.

Horse and bunks were used to travel in the winter. The bunks had a small, home-made heater with a narrow stove pipe running through the roof. There was a small glass window in the front and the horses reins passed through two small holes beneath the window. We were snug in the stove-warmed bunk, listening to the music of the creaking runners beneath it as they slid over the crusted snow. In good weather we walked to school and on mild winter days we hitched the horse to the stone boat.

One time, when Annie and I had hitched the horse to the stone boat and were driving across the field, the horse got spooked and we were in for a ride at a galloping pace. We were so scared we jumped off and tumbled into the snow. The horse finally slowed down and found its way back home. A barn, located on the far corner of the school yard, sheltered the horses. At noon the students fed them with feed brought from home. The boys had the responsibility of cleaning the horse barn, usually at recess or noon hour.

When Mr. Hein resigned from teaching at our school, Mr. Peter Paul Lepp replaced him. I believe every student he ever taught remembers him for his music and penmanship programs. He spent many hours trying to perfect in us a beautiful, legible handwriting, and he was for the most part successful. Whenever I see attractive handwriting, my mind automatically takes me back to my school days – wondering if perhaps, that person was also rigidly trained in penmanship.

Mr. Lepp loved music and thought all his students should be interested in music as well. Whoever was interested in learning to play a musical instrument was given the opportunity. We could choose to play guitar, mandolin, rattle bones or organ. Mr. Lepp played the violin. Annie and I were overjoyed when we received a brand new guitar for Christmas one year! It certainly boosted our enthusiasm for music classes. Mr. Lepp taught us many songs which I still appreciate as much today as I did then. "The Old Rugged Cross," "Old Black Joe," "My Grandfather's Clock," "Hold Fast to the Right" and "When the Saints Go Marching In" are a few.

Mr. Lepp read to us from the Bible every morning and then assigned our work. I discovered that learning can be a very painful experience when he asked our class to write a report. Either I had not heard the instructions or perhaps wasn't paying attention, but I didn't dare say, "I can't" as Mr. Lepp had settled that account earlier in the school year. He got very annoyed when he asked the students to do an assignment and the response was, "I can't." To make his point, he wrote "I can't" on a piece of paper, and asked all the students to come outside with him. He got a shovel, dug a hole, put the paper in and buried it. He made it very

Altona School Orchestra, May 11, 1952. In the back row is our teacher, Mr. Lepp, then Erma Boldt, then me.*

Annie holding the guitar we got for Christmas. I am holding the dog.

clear so that everyone understood. "I can't" was dead; "I can" was alive! Therefore, I attempted to do the assignment and wrote something down. I didn't know how to end it so I ended it like a letter: "Please write soon, Goodbye, Love Tena." I was so humiliated when Mr. Lepp laughed and read what I had written out loud. In this one-room school all the students in the other grades couldn't help but hear it. I ended up crying, but was determined to learn exactly what he meant by writing a report.

Annie wasn't particularly fond of literature classes but was quite proud of a short poem she wrote as an assignment. Her pride didn't last long after Mr. Lepp finished reading her well thought-out poem.

> *This book is dead*
> *As dead can be*
> *It killed a man of long ago*
> *And now it's killing me.*

Mr. Alfred Friesen, a traveling missionary, visited our school regularly. He read Bible stories to us and asked us to memorize Bible verses. If we had done so, upon his next visit he rewarded us with a prize, usually a book mark or a picture of Jesus or other Bible characters with a Bible verse underneath it. This is when I first started to memorize Bible verses.

On cold or rainy days we were allowed to stay indoors at recess and play games on the chalkboard. Tic-Tac-Toe and X's and O's were favourites. Outside games we enjoyed playing were Fox and Goose, Prisoner's Base, Pump Pump Pull-away, Kick the Can and Drop the Handkerchief. Many times when I thought recess or noon hour had just begun, Mr. Lepp would shake that hand-held school bell and it was time for more work.

Practicing for Track and Field events took up most recesses and noon hours as soon as the school yard was dry enough in the spring. Most surrounding schools participated in the big competition at the annual Warman Sports Day which was the highlight of our school year. The events included races, running long jump, standing broad jump, high jump, ball throw, pole vault and, of course, softball. Dad usually took about 20 to 25 students in the back of the pickup truck and we were off to the races – of course seatbelt laws were nonexistent.

The Warman Sports Day was a special day – a fun day, when we were treated to ice cream, soda pop, bubble gum, and sometimes a hot dog. Hot dogs sold for ten cents a piece, so we didn't always get one, but Mom packed us a good picnic lunch which we enjoyed eating together with other students who had also brought a lunch.

Usually the Altona School students came home with many red, blue and white ribbons – 1st, 2nd and 3rd prizes. For three consecutive years, Annie brought home the championship trophy, known as "The Cup" for winning mostly 1st in all the events. We were all so proud of her. I usually came home with quite a few ribbons, but I never won "The Cup."

Mom packed our lunches in Roger's Golden Syrup pails or small lard buckets with holes punched in the lid for ventilation. After a good breakfast, usually consisting of porridge, or cream of wheat and toast, and not to forget the cod liver oil we had to take faithfully every morning, we were off to school. A few students at our school, who already had store-bought lunch kits, considered themselves superior to the rest of us, sometimes teasing us about our lunches. No matter how much I got teased, I still appreciated the lunches Mom packed for me; her tasty home-made bread spread with *Brohd'fat*, the grease left in the pan after frying home-cured sausage or ham. I still enjoy it to this day, only now it's my husband that laughs at me. Sometimes Mom made a sandwich spread with flour, sugar and cocoa and mixed it with milk. It resembled the Nutella spread we now buy in the grocery store. Mom also packed cakes, cookies, apples and oranges in my lunches and she usually had a good snack, often

Roll'küake or *Pan'küake*, waiting for us when we returned home from school. Other times we spread our bread with butter and sprinkled it with sugar which was also a treat. Here's the recipe for *Roll'küake* taken from *The Mennonite Treasury of Recipes* cook book.

Roll'küake

1 cup heavy cream
2 eggs
2 cups flour
1 teaspoon salt

Sift flour and salt into mixing bowl, add other ingredients. Mix well. Add a bit more flour if dough is too soft to handle. Roll out, fairly thin, on a floured board and cut into strips. Cut one slit in the center then pull one end of the Roll'kuak through this slit. Fry in deep, hot fat. Lard is best.

We ate these with watermelon when hot, and after they had cooled off we spread them with Roger's Golden syrup – a snack we thoroughly enjoyed after school.

In winter the students made a skating rink in the school yard. The water was hauled in barrels from a nearby well with horse and sleigh. This was usually done in the evenings and on Saturdays. One year Mr. Lepp insisted on making the ice rink in front of their house, which was on the school yard. This way he could keep an eye on us when we went skating on Friday or Saturday evenings, which we often did. Mr. Lepp didn't approve of girls and boys holding hands while skating, or any other time for that matter. This was the measure he took to try and prevent it. There was one advantage to his strategy – the light from their living room window would shine on the rink and give us some light on those dark, dark nights. When Mom and Dad came home from Saskatoon one day, they had bought me a pair of black, second-hand boy's skates – several sizes too big – but I felt so special!

Styles in clothing were simple as there wasn't much choice in those days. My sisters and I wore mostly blue jeans with cotton shirts, saddle shoes and bobbi socks, although some students wore dresses to school. The fad for girls was to wear neckerchiefs, which are similar to a handkerchief but with permanent pleats resembling an accordion and big enough to tie around your neck. I felt so grown up when I got two of them in

Altona School teacherage with the school in the background.

different colours, one in hot pink and the other in fluorescent green.

Preparations for the Christmas concert started in November when we began to practice our parts for the program and sing Christmas carols. Mr. Lepp planned a good program with exciting plays, poems and lots of singing accompanied by musical instruments. He always managed to get a real Christmas tree and the students were assigned to decorate it. What really stands out in my memory is that Christmas trees were decorated with real candles which were designed as a decoration. They were mounted on a gadget that slipped onto the tree branch. What a fire hazard that must have been, but the tree was so beautiful when all the candles were lit.

Mr. Lepp, with the older students, built the stage in early December and time seemed to pass relatively quickly after that. When the night of the concert arrived we all got dressed in our Sunday best and headed for the school. About half an hour before the program started, one of the girls played the organ while the older students gathered around and sang Christmas carols as the guests were arriving. The candles on the tree were lit and the spirit of Christmas radiated throughout the school house as parents and community came together to share in this very special evening. After the program, all the students and preschoolers received a candy bag prepared by the school board. I was excited to receive such a treat before Christmas. We usually didn't get any Christmas treats until Christmas morning.

FORM X

(School Act, Sections 32, 76 and 77)

Declaration Re Naturalization

I, ... do solemnly declare:

1. That I am a British subject by birth (or naturalization);

And I make this solemn declaration conscientiously believing it to be true, and knowing that it is of the same force and effect as if made under oath, and by virtue of the Canada Evidence Act.

Declared before me at.... Altona S.D. 857

this ....15.... day of ....Jan....

A.D. 194.9....

Chairman (or J.P. or Commissioner for Oaths.)

FORM Y

(School Act, Sections 32, 76 and 77)

Oath of Allegiance

I, ... do swear that I will be faithful and bear true allegiance to His Majesty King George VI (or reigning sovereign for the time being), his heirs and successors according to law. So help me God.

Affirm/Sworn before me at.... Altona School

this ....15.... day of ....Jan....

A.D. 194.9....

Chairman (or J.P. or Commissioner for Oaths.)

(This form, when completed, should be retained on the files of the S.D.)

(Over)

The last event of our school year was the annual year-end picnic. Parents came and joined the students, bringing all the preschoolers for a fun-filled day. This was one time when every student got to enjoy hot dogs, candy bars, soda pop, ice cream and bubble gum, all provided by the school board. Our teacher presented us with the free coupons. Oh, what a treat! Mr. Lepp organized races, ball games, and other activities for all ages from preschool to grandmothers. I always enjoyed watching

Revised Form No. 123—23sp-556

Nomination Paper

We, the undersigned resident ratepayers of The ...... *Altona* ......

School District No. *859* , hereby nominate ...... *J. J. Neudorf* ......
NAME

as a candidate at the election of a trustee now about to be held.

Witness our hands this *15* day of *Jan.* 194*7*

Moved by ...... *J. B. Boldt* ......

Seconded by ...... *P. D. Friesen* ......

Signatures of Resident Ratepayers

No nomination shall be valid unless the nomination paper is accompanied by the candidate's acceptance which shall be in the following form:

CANDIDATE'S ACCEPTANCE

I, the said ...... *J. Neudorf* ...... named in the foregoing nomination, hereby state:

1. That I am of the full age of twenty-one years;

2. That I am a resident ratepayer of The ......

   School District No. ......

Strike out one of these paragraphs (3) but not both

3. That I am able to read and write in the English language, and to conduct school meetings in the English language;

   or

3. That I held the office of trustee prior to the first day of July, 1930, and have obtained a certificate from the school superintendent of this district that I am capable of performing the duties pertaining to the office of trustee, which certificate is attached hereto;

4. That my declaration respecting naturalization (form X) and my oath of allegiance (form Y) are attached hereto;

5. That I will accept the office if elected.

Signed in the presence of

...... *J. P. Boldt* ......

Signature of Witness

(Over)

Signature of Candidate

(This form, when completed, should be retained on the files of the S.D.)

the grandmothers play ball and competing in the races. This special day marked the end of the school term, and I looked forward to summer holidays. Two months free to run and play and not worry about studying. I attended the Altona School from 1947 until 1953.

Dad served many years on the Altona School Board, first as the

GOVERNMENT OF THE PROVINCE OF SASKATCHEWAN
DEPARTMENT OF EDUCATION

(To be made in triplicate,
one copy to be forwarded to
the department as soon as
the teacher takes charge.)

AGREEMENT

BETWEEN BOARD AND TEACHER
(FOR SCHOOLS ORGANIZED UNDER THE SCHOOL ACT)

This Memorandum of Agreement Between the Board of Trustees of the .... _Altona_ ....
Name of district

.... School District No. ..... _859_ ...., of Saskatchewan, herinafter called "The Board"

and .... _Jacob D. Hein_ .... hereinafter called "The Teacher," holder
Name in full of teacher

of a valid Saskatchewan certificate of qualification to teach in such school, is made pursuant to a resolution

passed by the Board at a meeting held on the ..... _24_ ..... day of ..... _Sept._ .....
Date   Month

194_7_, in accordance with the provisions of _The School Act_ and in particular, Sections 109, 110, 111 and 212
thereof, and provides as follows:

1. The Board hereby contracts with and employs the teacher from and after the ..... _1st_ ..... day
of ..... _Sept._ ...., one thousand nine hundred and forty-..... _seven_ ...., at the yearly salary
of ..... _1600.00_ .... dollars, to be computed
and paid in accordance with the provisions of _The School Act_ and further agrees that it and its successors in
office will exercise such powers and perform such duties under _The School Act_ and the Regulations of the Department of Education as may be requisite for the payment of such salary.

2. The Teacher agrees with the Board to teach and conduct the school according to _The School Act_ and the
Regulations in that behalf.

3. This agreement is subject to the condition that the teacher shall continue to be the holder of a valid
certificate of qualification as a teacher in Saskatchewan.

4. The Board hereby agrees to increase the salary of the teacher by the sum of ....

dollars each year until a maximum of .... dollars per annum is reached.

5. This agreement shall continue in force until terminated in accordance with the provisions of _The School
Act_, or replaced by a new agreement.

6. The vacation periods shall consist of: Summer vacation ..... _July & August_ ..... ;
(Dates)

Winter vacation ..... _Xmas Dec. 23 to Jan 1_ ..Easter vacation ....
(Dates)   (Dates)

Dated this ..... _24_ ..... day of ..... _Sept._ ...., 194_7_

Signed on behalf of the Board   (Corporate)
                                 (Seal   )

Peter D. Friesen   _J.T. Neudorf_
Witness to Chairman's Signature   Chairman

Peter D. Friesen   _J.D. Hein_
Witness to Teacher's Signature   Teacher

Stoon San August 1945   Class and number of
Date and place of last anti-tuberculosis X-ray   Saskatchewan certificate _Int Jr High School 113-49_
examination of teacher.   Class   Number

                                 Issued ..... _24_ ..... _Sept._ ..... _1947_
                                        Day   Month   Year

Teacher's P.O. Address ..... _Osler_

Note.—1. The teacher must sign this agreement with christian names in full and give the number as on certificate held.

2. Except with the consent of the Minister, the minimum salary shall be at least $1,200 per annum for
teachers with permanent certificates and at least $1,000 per annum for all other teachers.

3. This agreement will not be accepted by the department unless complete in every detail.

4. Section 127 of _The School Act_ requires the agreement to be completed by the board and the teacher
before the teacher enters upon his duties or within seven days thereafter.

Form 27

Secretary Treasurer from 1946 until 1950, as well as serving for a number
of years as Chairman of the Board. In order to qualify as a nominee, Dad
had to sign a Declaration of Naturalization affirming that he was a British
subject as well as signing an Oath of Allegiance promising to be faithful
and bear true allegiance to King George VI and/or his successor.

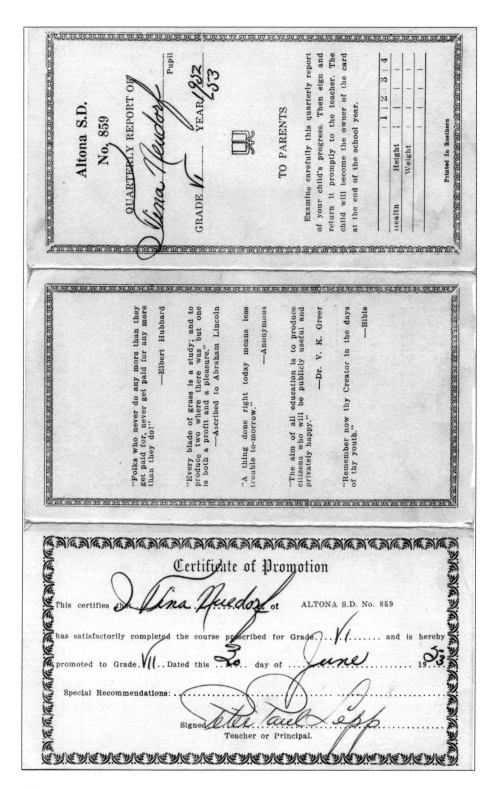

Altona S.D. No, 859

QUARTERLY REPORT OF *Tina Neudorf* Pupil

GRADE *VI* YEAR 19*32-33*

TO PARENTS

Examine carefully this quarterly report of your child's progress. Then sign and return it promptly to the teacher. The child will become the owner of the card at the end of the school year.

Health	1	2	3	4
Height				
Weight				

Printed in Rosthern

"Folks who never do any more than they get paid for, never get paid for any more than they do!"
—Elbert Hubbard

"Every blade of grass is a study; and to produce two where there was but one is both a profit and a pleasure."
—Ascribed to Abraham Lincoln

"A thing done right today means less trouble to-morrow."
—Anonymous

"The aim of all education is to produce citizens who will be publicly useful and privately happy."
—Dr. V. K. Greer

"Remember now thy Creator in the days of thy youth."
—Bible

Certificate of Promotion

This certifies that *Tina Neudorf* of ALTONA S.D. No. 859

has satisfactorily completed the course prescribed for Grade.... *VI* ...... and is hereby

promoted to Grade. *VII*.. Dated this ... *20*.. day of .... *June* ...... 19.*53*.

Special Recommendations:...

Signed *Peter Paul Epp*

Teacher or Principal.

96

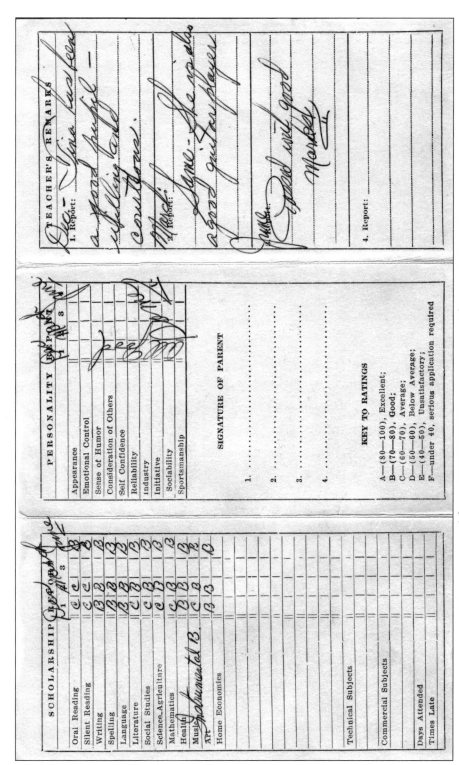

My report card from 1952/1953. I was promoted from grade six to seven.

Setting out the bowls on Christmas Eve.

Nine

Christmas Traditions

For several weeks before Christmas, Mom was very busy preparing food for the holidays. The Mennonite tradition is to celebrate three consecutive days at Christmas, Easter and Pentecost. The tradition was brought over from Russian Ukraine when the Mennonites migrated to Canada in the 1800s. It is practiced in Ukraine, Canada, Bolivia, Mexico, Paraguay, Belize, and in other countries where Mennonites live to this day.

Traditional Christmas food at our house was *Süakomst'borscht*, "sauerkraut soup" usually made with pork hocks or other pork. Mom always made her own sauerkraut, giving it that homemade flavour. She also added dill, onion, parsley and ketchup. *Plüme'moos* was another favourite – a tasty cold fruit soup made with dried fruit; usually prunes, raisins, apricots and apples, that we normally had only at Christmas time. This Christmas special was made with a water base. All the other *Mooss* we enjoyed during the rest of the year was made with a milk base and was made with canned fruit – any fruit would do. Home-cured ham, bread, buns, *Tjrinjel*, cakes and cookies completed the Christmas menu. *Tjrinjel* are made from a sweet dough using milk instead of water. When the dough had risen and doubled in size, it was rolled into a thin rope and then twisted to form a fancy flat bread.

Mom made a variety of cookies. Gelatin cookies were a favourite, but oh, it was a trying experience. After Mom made the dough and baked the cookies, the time consuming task of getting the gelatin onto the cookies began. Mom boiled the mixture of sugar, water and gelatin. We brought in a big galvanized tub of snow, placed the pot with the mixture into it and took turns beating it with the hand-held egg beater – almost wearing it out – until it stood in peaks. Sometimes it took several hours until the mixture was firm enough to spread. Often we had to bring in a second tub of snow as it melted rather quickly in the warm kitchen with the hot gelatin sitting in it. Mom crushed corn flakes with a rolling pin, then, after the cookies were spread with the white marshmallow topping, she sprinkled the tops of the cookies with the crushed corn flakes. A cheap and easy way to decorate cookies, but they were so good.

Mom made thin, flat oatmeal cookies that were held together with jam, and she also baked jam jams which had a date filling. We had no special dishes or decorations to brighten up the table, only special food.

We had a Christmas tree in our home but the gifts were never wrapped or placed under the tree. Our tradition was to set up bowls on Christmas Eve. Early in the day we started gathering them, making sure there would be one for everybody. Sometimes Mom or Dad used Mom's big bread pan when there weren't enough bowls to go around. We couldn't set them up until after supper. Then we placed them on the table in order of our ages with our names written on a piece of paper and placed at the bottom in hopes that Santa Claus wouldn't get mixed up.

Many times I had a very difficult time falling asleep on Christmas Eve, and sometimes I wonder if I slept at all. Mom always kept a small coal oil lamp burning at night. The first one to wake up in the middle of the night took the lamp, woke up the others, then we all tip-toed into the kitchen to find out what Santa Claus had brought us. Then we headed back to bed. One year just before Christmas, I discovered there was no Santa Claus. When I realized it was Mom and Dad who bought all the gifts and put them in our bowls, I was utterly disappointed.

Our bowls were always filled with peanuts, nuts, candy, Japanese Mandarin oranges, a Delicious apple and sometimes a candy bar. There was usually a colouring book, crayons, a story book, a drawing book, pencil, notebook, puzzle and a main gift. When I was quite young, my sisters and I usually got a doll and my brothers got trucks and other boy things. One year Margaret and Annie each got a dresser set which consisted of a hand held mirror, comb and hair brush which came in a silk-lined case. A gift like that made any young girl feel grown up because it was a popular gift that girls got from their boyfriends when they were dating. At 8:00 a.m. on Christmas morning the King delivered his speech to the nation. I don't ever remember what the speech was about, but he was royalty and that was enough to spark an interest.

Here are the recipes Mom always used:

Maltj Mooss

Pour about one gallon of milk into a pot that will not easily burn in the bottom. Sprinkle approximately ¾ cup sugar into the milk and place on medium heat. Do not stir until it comes to a boil. In the meantime, mix about ½ cup cornstarch and enough water to make a slurry. When at boiling point, slowly add the slurry to the milk, stirring constantly. When this comes to a boil remove from heat and cool. Cover with saran wrap to avoid film from forming. When cold, add any kind of canned fruit.

Gelatin Cookies

1 cup brown sugar
2 eggs
2 tsp. baking soda
1 tsp. vanilla
6 tbs. syrup
Flour to make stiff dough

Roll out to ¼ inch thickness
Bake at 350 F for about 10–12 minutes

Gelatin Topping

1 ½ cups water
2 tbs. gelatin
2 cups sugar
1 tsp. vanilla

Cook until thick. Remove from heat. Set in ice water or snow and beat until it stands in peaks. Crush 2 cups of corn flakes and sprinkle on the gelatin topping.

Ten

Royal Visit

The spring of 1951, in most respects, was like any other spring. Crocuses were peeking through the earth when there were still patches of snow left in shady places. The red-breasted robins were singing and hopping in the front yard, preparing to make their nests in the maple trees. The frogs presented us with their croaking competition; many nights the tune of croaking frogs lulled us to sleep. Our pests, the gophers and crows, also gave notice that winter was over.

Spring was always an exciting time of the year for me, bursting with new life, new ideas and adventure. My siblings and I spent lots of time playing outside; often the icy winds cracking the skin of our hands until they started to bleed. For bedtime, Mom greased them with Vaseline and wrapped them up. By morning our hands felt much better, but in the evening it was the same thing all over again.

This spring held extra excitement for me. The radio announcements and newspaper reports proclaimed that Princess Elizabeth and Prince Philip were coming to Canada on a six-week tour and they were scheduled to visit Saskatoon. With great anticipation, I waited for my dream to become reality. Was there even a remote chance that Mom and Dad would take us to see them? I didn't know, but I kept asking. The reigning monarch and their families were highly respected by most families and ours was no exception. Was our country not flying the "Union Jack," the national flag of the United Kingdom which was officially called the

British Union Flag? Every morning several students were assigned to raise the flag before school exercises began and to take it down when the school day was done. Each morning our teacher, with all the students, would stand to sing,

"God save our gracious King,
Long live our noble King,
God save the King.
Send him victorious,
Happy and glorious,
Long to reign over us,
God save the King."

We were taught to be loyal to the British Royal Family. King George VI was the reigning monarch at this time and Princess Elizabeth was heir to the throne. King George VI and Queen Elizabeth had toured Canada in the spring of 1939, becoming the first of the 17 sovereigns who had ruled Canada to cross the ocean.

Occasionally there were photos of the Royal Family in the newspapers. If I could get hold of the newspaper first, I cut them out and pasted them into a scrap book which became one of my few treasures. What an exciting day when Dad told us that he and Mom would take us to Saskatoon to see the royal couple. I was disappointed, however, when I realized they were not bringing their children, Prince Charles and Princess Anne, as they looked so adorable in the pictures in the newspapers.

June 10, 1951, the scheduled date for their visit, finally arrived. My sisters and I arose earlier than necessary that morning. To add to our excitement we were allowed to wear our best clothes. We left home fairly early and, therefore, were fortunate to see the royal couple close up. Many who arrived later did not get such a good view. Princess Elizabeth and Prince Philip walked by only a few yards from where we were standing. There were thousands of people, and I'm positive the population of Saskatoon doubled that day. I had never seen so many people gathered in one place before. Someone had parked a small car a short distance from the street where the royal couple was walking. Many young people climbed on top of that car for a better view and totally crushed the top of it. Princess Elizabeth was very pretty in her beautiful clothes and radiant in real life compared to the black and white newspaper photos.

All that excitement for only a few minutes ... the time it took for the royal couple to walk down the street where we were standing and watching. Mom had packed a picnic lunch which was also a treat. We ate our lunch beside the truck as there were no campsites, and later Mom and Dad treated us to an ice cream cone and other goodies. Going to bed that night I felt so privileged. I was grateful to Mom and Dad for taking the interest and time to do special things for us. My dream had come true – I had actually seen members of the Royal Family. I was saddened when the announcement came on February 6, 1952, that King George VI had died in his sleep. Little did I know that only eight months after I had seen Princess Elizabeth, she would become our Queen. She was crowned on June 2, 1953.

Eleven

Winters on the Prairies

When the winter winds started howling and we were safely sheltered from the storms inside our cozy home, I felt a sense of security with Mom and Dad sitting at the table reading or writing letters and all of us children playing games or doing some other fun things. Mom and Dad made sure the fires kept burning as we watched the snow pile up underneath the windows. Gusts of wind swirled the new falling snow around and around, at times darkening the windows.

Many times winters were harsh on the Saskatchewan prairies. Blizzards frequently blew in very suddenly, piling up huge snow drifts in a very short time. During one storm in particular, I didn't feel this security. This notable evening, Mom and Dad had gone to visit Uncle John and Aunt Sara Klassen who lived only three miles from our place. The howling wind and blowing snow were relentless, causing the drifts to pile higher and higher. Oh, how we waited for them to come home, but they didn't come. The raging storm worried us, and we were afraid that perhaps they would be stranded and freeze to death in the bitter cold.

When Mom and Dad realized a storm was in full force, they had made an attempt to come home but couldn't make it through the snow drifts. They managed to turn around and return to Uncle John and Aunt Sara's place. The telephone lines were down due to the storm so they couldn't call to let us know they were safe. It was a consolation for them that we were all safe at home. Mom and Dad couldn't come home until the next afternoon when the snow plough opened the road. We were extremely relieved when we heard the snow plough coming and saw Mom and Dad's truck following close behind.

Another blizzard that is recorded vividly in my memory did not affect the safety of our family, but the safety of many others. Again the storm came with all its fury and hit suddenly. It was a spring storm which came in the evening on April 19 in 1951. The gravel road ran east and west about 300 yards south of our yard. A vehicle got stuck in a snowdrift right across from our house, and two men came knocking on our door and asked for shelter. Of course, Mom and Dad took them in. A short while later another vehicle got stranded, and this time a few more people needed shelter. Several couples from near Hague had taken the young people from their church to a retreat in Saskatoon; a group of 44 people. There was not a question what Mom and Dad would do. Our custom was, and is, as it is with most Mennonites, that our doors are always open to anyone in need; there is always room for one more and the food on the table is always shared.

This was in the evening, and sleeping arrangements created a problem. For many I'm sure it was the first time they slept standing up! The floors were wet from all the fresh snow and people couldn't take off their boots as there was no place to put them. Mom put blankets underneath the table, on the floors upstairs, in the living room and wherever a dry spot could be found. Some of us had to give up our beds for the older folks, and by morning I was very tired and sleepy.

Mom was well-experienced in cooking large quantities of food. I'm sure her expertise and ingenuity served her well this time as she served breakfast and lunch for all these people. I don't recall what foods she prepared, but there were no complaints. It is safe to assume that they had a good supply of staples on hand, as we were stranded as well and couldn't go for groceries.

Our house was a very noisy place with 58 people sharing space, when suddenly, above all the chatter, someone heard the snow plough coming. The leaders of the group were very relieved and grateful for the Lord's faithfulness in His protection and provision. He had supplied sufficiently for their needs. We were watching from the window as the snow plough opened the road and were surprised when we noticed that the snow was piled so high it was hiding the telephone poles.

Whenever these storms came during school hours, our teacher dismissed us immediately in order for us to get home before the fury of the storm hit. Thinking back, I wonder how safe it was to send all those students into that snowstorm to get home safely. I don't recall anyone ever getting lost or stranded as the horses always seemed to find their way home.

When the storms let up and the drifts were piled high around the house, I had much fun playing outside with my sisters. We scooped the snow out of the drifts to make snow tunnels and we played in them for hours. Sledding down the big, hard drifts gave us much entertainment. We made snow angels by lying down in the loose snow, moving our arms and legs as far as they could go, leaving an imprint that resembled an angel. We also played Fox and Goose and other games.

We usually played Fox and Goose after the first snowfall. We traced a large pie-shaped design in the snow by shuffling our feet, exposing the dried-up brown grass. Someone volunteered (or was chosen) to be the fox. He chased anyone he thought he could tag and the tagged one would then become the fox. Everyone – fox and geese – had to stay on the lines of the wheel, or pie. It was hard to pass anyone without falling into the snow and whoever fell into the snow was disqualified. Home was the hub of the wheel, and there the geese were safe.

Many times, when soft snowflakes were gently coming down, we lay on our backs in the snow and enjoyed the snowflakes melting in our faces. We had our mouths open to catch the big, juicy flakes as they came spiraling slowly downward. With cheeks glowing, we returned to the house at the call for supper. When we opened the door, a flood of light and warmth, and the aroma of mouth-watering food greeted us. Our outer clothes and home-made woolen slippers "Socke" were packed with snow in every crease. We shook the snow off our clothes before we came in, and then hung them over chairs or the wood box, while the Socke were placed on the open oven door to dry. Winter and its storms could be an enemy, but often proved to be a gentle friend as well.

Waiting for Tom.

Twelve

We Killed the Cat

Our big tom-cat was a nuisance, always bothering the chickens in the hen house. I don't recall if Tom was an egg-sucking cat, but he was after the hens sitting on the nest. Perhaps he had a better chance at whatever his intentions were if the hen was sitting relaxed.

One day Mom decided to catch him in the hen house. She did! She kept watching and when he went in, she followed him. When he was sitting near the nest she grabbed him, but oh, what a mistake! Tom scratched her up so badly she bore the scars on her arms for the rest of her life.

Tom was, for the most part, a gentle cat and made his abode underneath the porch step. After this incident, Jake got a bright idea and persuaded me to take up arms. Jake took a hammer and handed me a piece of wood; a 2 x 4 about four feet long. Once we knew Tom was underneath the step we decided to lay in wait and punish him on Mom's behalf. He was taking his time coming out, so we started calling him, "Kitty, kitty, kitty … " We always called him when there was food, so it is likely he figured it was mealtime! He wasted no time in coming out and appeared where Jake was keeping watch. Jake didn't hesitate. Wham! He hit him with the first blow. Poor Tom just lay there. It looked like he'd pretty much had it, so together we finished the job. Mom couldn't believe what we had done. She never scolded us, but I believe to this day she was thankful for a job well done, although she never said that. After all, it wasn't our intention to kill the cat; we only wanted to punish him. Perhaps we did!

Thirteen

Fun and Exciting Times

Summer times were fun times on the farm. As a young girl, I spent endless hours playing outside with my siblings. On rainy days we kept busy with activities in the house. Special times included swimming trips to the Lake Resort at Watrous. We didn't have our own swim suits but were able to rent them for twenty-five cents apiece. The right sizes weren't always available but that didn't seem to matter. One day Uncle Jake and Aunt Margaret Klassen and our cousins also came to spend the day at the lake. It was always fun to be together with family. Dad gave each of us children five cents to buy an ice cream cone. I usually clung pretty tightly to any money that was given to me, but somehow this time I lost it. I was sitting beside the water crying when Uncle Jake noticed me. He asked me what the problem was. No sooner had I told him that I had lost my five cents when he dug into his pocket and gave me a nickel. I wiped the tears from my eyes as I made my way to the ice cream stand. It was such a small act of kindness, but as a young girl it meant the world to me, and, even today, sixty years later, it still touches my heart.

Sometimes Mom and Dad took us to Saskatoon to see the Circus and Exhibition. I was fascinated with the clowns and thrilled to see the wild animals live. I had only seen black and white pictures of elephants, lions, tigers and other tropical animals. I didn't experience any fear with the elephants as they appeared very content and laid-back, but the lions and tigers, with their agitated behaviour, frightened me. Fear stabbed my heart when I watched the acrobats performing. At night after I had gone to bed, I couldn't get the performance out of my mind.

Visiting relatives and friends was the heart of our social life. My best friends were Erma Boldt and Helen Klassen. We were friends in and out of school. Mom and Dad were good friends with Erma and Helen's parents, enabling us to spend much time together.

We had to create our own entertainment as these were the days before television or any modern technology. We never had bicycles, but in pretense we pushed old truck tires all over the farm bumping into anything and everything. My cousins, John, Ben and Harold Klassen often dropped by our house on their way home from school, sometimes staying for the evening. Frequently we played hide-and-go-seek until long after dark, hiding in the manger in the barn, the grain fields, in the garden among the corn and behind buildings. One time I was hiding in the grain field close to the house but no one came to find me. The sun had already set and it was getting darker by the minute. I got very scared when I realized everyone had gone inside and no one was looking for me. I ran to the house as fast as I could and never played hide-and-go-seek after dark again.

I loved to go with Mom and Dad to visit my aunts and uncles. My uncle, Pete Doell, was the town cop in Hague, and one evening when we were visiting at their house, he was on duty. He had arrested a man and put him in the cell. Later that evening when he went to check up on him, he asked Dad to go with him and they allowed me to come along. I was disturbed when I saw this man lying on a hard wooden bench, shivering. I felt sorry for him when there were no blankets available but Uncle Pete covered him with the flag. The poor man had failed to realize he wasn't thirsty anymore, kept on drinking, and fell into a deep sleep. This was my first introduction to alcohol abuse.

There was always some excitement when we went to Grandma and Grandpa Klassen's house. They didn't own a car and Grandpa hadn't learned to drive one. On one occasion when he attempted to drive Uncle Jake's car he had trouble finding the brakes. He started yelling, "Whoa! Whoa!" but the car wouldn't stop like the horses had. This incident frequently comes up when we reminisce with family and cousins. At Christmas time Grandma gave us a candy bag and sometimes a small gift. In the summer we spent time in their garden enjoying the fruits and vegetables. At family gatherings we and our cousins were always looking for things to do. The train track ran across their land, and when we heard the rumbling of the passenger train which echoed across miles of open prairie, we ran to the railroad track to watch it go by. The ground shook from its vibrations. Usually, the conductor blew the whistle and the passengers waved to us.

On one occasion I was staying at the home of my friend, Erma Boldt. Circumstances made it necessary for me to travel on the train all by myself and I was frightened. Mr. and Mrs. Boldt took me to the train station in Osler to board the train for Hague. It seemed like a very long trip to me although it was only a few miles. I was relieved to see Mom and Dad waiting for me at the train station in Hague.

One incident that will forever be seared in my memory took place on a summer evening. I don't know that I have ever been more scared in all my life. Mom and Dad and John were away visiting when we discovered that Mary was missing. We searched everywhere; the yard, every building, the bushes and the well. We knew if she had fallen into the well we would not be able to see her. Our neighbours, the Clarence Peters, who lived nearby, had a dug-out so we went to check there. We thought perhaps there would be some evidence; maybe footprints near the water if she had ventured that far. We couldn't find any clues. We were all terrified and couldn't wait for Mom and Dad to come home. We couldn't contact them as Grandma had no telephone. Only when they returned home did we discover what had happened.

Mary, just a little girl, had been determined to go along. Mom had said no, but Mary hadn't accepted no for an answer and snuck onto the back of the truck. When Mom and Dad dropped John off at a friend's house he noticed some blond hair sticking over the truck box. He checked it out and discovered the little stowaway. What a relief we experienced when they returned and had Mary with them.

Different times in the winter, grouse and prairie chickens came close to the house in search of food. Dad and my brothers built a wooden trap and set it up outside, placing it in front of the kitchen window. They raised the front of the trap, tied a string to it then led the string into the house. They spread wheat along the path leading to the trap and placed a small pile of wheat inside of it. We would watch and wait. Sure enough, the birds discovered the wheat that led into the trap. When there were quite a number of birds assembled, enjoying their bounty, someone would pull the string and the birds were trapped. I don't know if this was just a pastime or if Mom and Dad actually butchered the birds and used the meat.

On winter evenings we often sat around the table entertaining ourselves. Some of our favourite pastimes were colouring, puzzling, playing with pick-up-sticks or paper dolls. The Eaton's catalogue was a source of entertainment. We used it as a picture book and dreamed of all the things we would like to have. When the new catalogue came, we used the dog-eared pages from the old one to cut out paper dolls and dressed them in paper clothes. Mom taught us to embroider. What patience she must have had! We spent many hours embroidering tea towels and pillow cases. She saved her empty thread spools and we used them to braid either store string or wool. We pounded small nails around the hole in the center of the wooden spools and kept weaving the string through the nails until we had a long braid. When it was long enough, Mom attached it to our mittens, one on each end; then pulled it through our parka sleeves to avoid losing them.

Rarely, as a child, did I have nightmares, but one night when I was sleeping upstairs a bad dream woke me up. I was terrified and went downstairs to lie down on the couch, which was close to Mom and Dad's bedroom. I wanted to be close to them but I didn't want to wake them up. Mom noticed me and asked, "Who's there?" I said it was me. She asked me why I had come down and I told her about my bad dream. She said, "Come into our bed." I can't ever forget the warmth, security and protection I felt climbing into that warm bed, nestled between Mom and Dad.

Fourteen

Grandma, Self Appointed Medical Doctor

Growing up brings many experiences with it, and as a child I experienced an especially traumatic one. Uncle Abe, Dad's brother, had been sickly all his life. Going to the doctor was not a pastime in those days, at least not in Grandma Neudorf's household. They did take Uncle Abe to the doctor, however, and he was diagnosed with a heart condition. Whenever he exerted himself his fingernails and lips would turn a bluish colour. There didn't seem to be any medical treatment available for his condition at that time. Grandma, the staunch matriarch in the family, always took matters into her own hands when medical treatment was needed. She would never have been a burden to the health care system. Her motto was, "If a little bit helps, then lots helps more." I can only guess that she treated Uncle Abe with Wonder Oil (the cure-all remedy in those days) and various homemade remedies, but whatever she treated him with was to no avail. He passed away at the age of 34 years on July 27, 1947, when I was almost eight years old.

When Mom and Dad took us to see Uncle Abe's body, it left a lasting impression on me. The body had to be kept cold so Granddad dug a shallow hole at the end of the house and lined it with wooden planks. They laid the body on a sheet of plywood and grandma covered it with a white sheet. It was then placed in the hole – covered with another sheet of plywood, and kept there until it was prepared for the funeral. I felt sorry for Uncle Abe lying in that cold, dark, damp hole all by himself, and as a young girl I wished I would never have to die.

Often when the subject of doctor visits came up, Dad would reminisce and tell us some of his experiences with Grandma playing the physician. He told us about the time he had been very sick and Grandma administered something that she thought would cure him. Whatever it was knocked him out for a few days, but he said he felt much better after he woke up.

Another time Dad accidentally cut his finger. Part of his finger was still dangling when he came in crying. Grandma came to the rescue, cut it off completely, poured Electric Oil on it, bandaged it up and told him to go outside and play.

Dad also told us of the time when Grandma's legs were aching badly. She went to the cupboard and took out a bottle, likely thinking it was liniment or some other pain reliever. She gave her legs a good treatment and in no time her legs were burning as though on fire. Since Grandma couldn't read English she wasn't able to read the labels on the bottles. She had used paint remover. My guess is that, next time, perhaps, she would have recognized the bottle. I believe, that after a while, Grandma must have concluded that making medical decisions had either relaxing or painful results.

Granddad's personality surfaced now and then, and, although he was a man of few words, he wasn't easily swayed. He was gentle in nature, but it seemed like we couldn't get to know him very well. On one occasion Mom and Dad were traveling with Granddad and Grandma to Saskatoon when suddenly Grandma was alarmed and said, *Foud-a-que* (her pet name for Granddad), "Father, you're driving on the wrong side of the road." Granddad replied, "It's nobody's business where I drive." In his opinion the road was his to drive on as he pleased and the lack of highway patrol did nothing to convince him otherwise.

Fifteen

A Pig-Butchering Bee

Early in the morning, when we saw a string of lights coming down the highway and turning into our yard, we knew it was the beginning of a very important and exciting day. A pig-butchering bee was about to begin.

It's a Mennonite tradition. In late fall when the days grew short and the frost came to stay, friends and neighbours gathered to butcher about four or more hogs in one day. It required five or six couples to get all the work done. Mom and Dad were both busy for several days prior, preparing for the big day. Mom was responsible for getting all the food on the table, and Dad made sure he had all the equipment, some of which he had to borrow from the neighbours.

The equipment included a scalding trough, block and tackle, meat grinder, sausage maker, several meat cutting tables, a ladder and three cauldrons or *Mieagropes* as we called them. This big iron kettle had a metal skirt around it and a small door at the bottom for firewood. It was used to heat water for scalding the pigs, and later, after much scrubbing and cleaning, to render the lard. Dad filled the *Mieagropes* with water the night before and loaded them up with firewood. The first task in the morning was to light the fire, making sure the water would be boiling when daylight came. He had already sharpened all the knives the day before.

Mom and Dad invited the same couples every year if possible, as they

Scraping bristles off the pig.

had learned to work well together. This same group usually helped each other until every family had their hogs butchered. It was a great social event and we children thoroughly enjoyed it, too. This was one day we were allowed to stay home from school. We loved to listen to the men and the women tell stories and joke around. Sometimes I didn't know where I'd rather be, with the men or with the women. My siblings and I had to run many errands, therefore missing out on some of the stories.

The custom was that all the people who came to help also came for breakfast, which was served between 6:30 and 7:00 a.m. This meant we had to get up early, making sure the beds were made and the house was neat and in order before the helpers arrived. It was also customary that

Nieuw Azië"

.Nr: 1 T.Nr: 64

Peking Eend met zoet-zure EUR 17.50
    saus
    (1 Bami a EUR 1.00)
Hoi Sin Po   EUR   21.50
    (1 Bami a EUR 1.00)
Sieuw Ah   EUR   18.80
    (1 Witte Rijst)
Koffie   EUR   1.90
Bier   EUR   3.80
Tonic   EUR   1.90
Rode wijn   EUR   3.20
                    =============== +

otaal: EUR   68.60

BTW 19.0% EUR   1.12
BTW 6.0% EUR   3.49

Bedankt voor Uw bezoek
  en graag tot ziens !
多謝　再見！

washing.

w... ...ne few times that I remem-
b...

...he breakfast table. When
d... ...iant cast iron cookers, the
...work had begun. The pigs
were scalded in the scalding trough then put on a ladder, which was
placed on top of the trough. After the bristles were scraped off the hogs,
they were hoisted up with a block and tackle. Several women appeared
with knives and buckets of warm water to give them another scraping and
a good washing. When they were done, one of the men skilled in gutting
appeared with a sharp knife; then two women brought a big galvanized

My brother Pete gutting the pig.

tub, held it under the pig, and the butcher dropped the guts into it. The warm, steaming innards were then taken into the house.

The worst job of the day was about to begin. All the intestines had to be emptied and cleaned to be used as casings for the sausages.

I am stirring lard in the *Miea'grope*, still butchering pigs the old fashioned way.

The small intestines were turned inside out which required two people as someone had to pour warm water into the guts to rinse out the guck in the process of turning them inside out. How I detested this smelly job! One time Aunt Helen Neudorf got this job going, and knowing how

Cutting up the meat.

Separating the lard from the cracklings.

Preparing cracklings and lard for the deep freezer.

Our daughter, LaDawn, making sausage.

much I hated it, looked around the room until she spotted me, gave me a sheepish grin and said, *"Na, Tena, kohm hoohl dit fe mie,"* which means, "Now, Tena, come hold this for me." We didn't say "no" to an adult! I struggled the entire time to avoid losing my breakfast. After they were emptied, turned inside out and rinsed, they were scraped, rinsed again, put into warm water, then set aside until it was time to make the sausage.

The large intestines were used as casings for *Läwa'worscht* or "liver sausage." They were emptied and cleaned, usually with bran and salt; then set aside to be filled later. *Läwa'worscht* was made with ground pork, liver, salt and pepper.

The men cut up the meat, trimmed the hams of fat, and then put them aside to be salted later in the day. The hams were stored and kept frozen during the winter, then smoked in the spring. The fat meat was separated from the lean by sliding the knife between the *Schwiens'schwoat* "pig rind" and the fat. It was put on a pile to be ground and rendered later while the lean meat was put on another pile to be ground into sausage meat.

Before electricity came in, Dad removed the crank of the meat grinder and attached a pulley to it. He then removed the tire from the back wheel of the pick-up truck, jacked it up and attached a belt from the meat grinder to the rim of the wheel. With the motor running, power was generated and the grinding did not have to be done by hand. While the ground fat was being rendered, people took turns stirring constantly with a *Rea'holt*, "a long wooden paddle," to avoid settling and burning at the bottom of the *Miea'grope*.

When the lard was liquefied, some of the spare ribs were tossed in and cooked together with it. *Rebspaa*, we called it. We all enjoyed eating the ribs for supper and again for breakfast the next morning. When the lard was ready, it was put through a big sieve to separate it from the *Jreewe*, "cracklings," the small bits of fat which had turned a golden brown. We enjoyed eating the cracklings the next morning. We didn't use a fork, but instead we tore small pieces of bread and used it to pick up the cracklings. *Jreewe'schmolt*, the sediment that settled in the large tubs of rendered lard, was used to spread on bread instead of butter and was very tasty.

Salt and pepper was added to the lean ground meat before it was put into the sausage maker; a very simple recipe as no other spices were used. A short pipe extended from an opening at the bottom of the sausage maker onto which the casings were slipped. Someone slowly turned the crank, pushing the meat into the casings. Another helper stood near by and coiled the *Worscht*, "sausage," as it made its way out. After the sausages were made, the meat for the liver sausage was put into the sausage maker and the casings were filled in the same way.

Large vats of pork sausages were then carried to the smokehouse to be hung and cured. They were smoked, preferably with wheat straw, as it gave them a unique flavour. The timing was important and the right amount of straw was needed to get the flavour of the sausages to perfection. Once in the smoke house, they had to be watched very carefully because there was always the danger of fire as the smoke houses were built of wood. Usually the sausages stayed in the smoke house for several days.

In the meantime, the head, feet, hocks, tongue and ears were cleaned. This was all boiled in the *Miea'grope* together with some rind and the liver sausage after the lard was rendered. All the meat was then taken off of the head and, together with the boiled rinds, was put through the meat grinder and made into *Sill'tjees*, "head cheese." The feet, hocks, ears, tongue and heart were made into *Sill'fleesch*, "pickled pork." In those days, Mom used whey for this, but in later years she used pickling brine. A wooden barrel was placed in the cellar, and then the cooked meat was placed in it and covered with brine.

The pig skin that wasn't used for head cheese was used to make soap in the spring. Mom's recipe called for lye, making the job very dangerous. We couldn't be nearby when she and Dad made the soap. It was also made in the *Miea'grope*; then poured into shallow pans to set. The next day Mom cut it into squares. On wash day, she shaved some of it into a small enamel bowl to melt on the stove before adding it to the water in the washing machine.

After all the work for the day was done, everyone looked forward to a well-deserved supper. Dad again served wine before the meal. Mom usually cooked a big pot of *Borscht* and served it with *Mooss*, fresh *Rebb'spaa, Läwa'worscht* and bread. It was customary that each family took home a liver sausage as well as some of the ribs. Often they sat around and reminisced until midnight. Much had been accomplished in one day and everyone was tired but happy. It's rather unfortunate that this tradition is all but lost.

Sixteen

Providing for the Family

Proverbs 31 describes the virtuous woman, which describes my mother well. V13: *"She selects wool and flax and works with eager hands."* V15: *"She gets up while it is still dark; she provides food for her family."* V27: *"She watches over the affairs of her household and does not eat the bread of idleness."* V28a: *"Her children arise and call her blessed."*

Mom planted a large garden every year, and whoever was big enough had to help hoe the garden, pick the vegetables and dig potatoes and carrots in the fall.

Potato and bean beetles were pests, so my siblings and I had to pick them off the plants – an assignment I wasn't particularly excited about. Mom canned many jars of peas and beans to last through the winter. The abundance of produce was preserved in various ways, as Mom abhorred wasting food. She experimented with many pickle recipes, often creating her own. Her cellar shelves were lined with bread and butter pickles, dill, mixed vegetable, mustard, green tomato and onion pickles and relish made with cabbage, onion and cucumbers. She grew a small variety of watermelon which had an orange-coloured flesh. In the fall she put them into a wooden barrel down in the cellar and covered them in pickling brine. Since they were left whole, it took a while for them to get pickled; but we enjoyed them all winter. A barrel of apples also found a place in the cellar.

I detested going down into that dirt cellar, as some friendly salaman-

Hoeing in Mom's garden in Saskatchewan, 1952.
From the left are Betty, Margaret, me, Helen and Mom.

ders also called it home. If we took a light down with us, they disappeared. However, during the day, when we had only the light from the pantry window to guide us, they would not run for cover. We were always in bare feet, and occasionally I would step on one of those cold, clammy creatures and scream. They were totally harmless, but oh, how I despised them.

All the canned goods were stored down there along with the potatoes and carrots. Mom also grew raspberries, strawberries, choke cherries, red and yellow currants, sand cherries and rhubarb, which we enjoyed eating in the garden. She mainly made preserves from all this fruit. Along with all the peaches, pears and cherries she canned when in season, there was a good variety of fruit to choose from when making *Mooss*.

Mom and Dad often went visiting in the evenings, leaving Annie and me to look after the younger children. On one occasion it was getting rather late in the evening, and we felt like having a snack. With apprehension, we went into the cellar and brought up a jar of peaches. We weren't really free to do this without permission. Right after we opened the jar, Mom and Dad drove into the yard. We quickly hid the peaches in the back corner of the cupboard and waited for an opportunity to eat them. The next afternoon, Annie proudly informed me that she had eaten all the

130

peaches. She told me she was thankful she hadn't been caught; relieved that we escaped getting into trouble. I, on the other hand, was very angry with her because I wanted some of those peaches, too.

In the winter evenings Mom sewed our dresses and hooked all our *Socke*. These high slippers were made from sheep's wool, which she carded and made into a string just the right thickness for the hook. She covered the bottom of the *Socke* with pieces of old blue jean material to keep us from getting holes in them so quickly. When we went outside we wore overshoes over our *Socke* to keep them dry. Often times she would sit up until two or three o'clock in the morning, knitting, sewing or mending our clothes.

Wash day wasn't pleasant either. Mom pre-washed the very soiled clothing on a glass scrub-board in a big, round galvanized tub. She used a wooden washing machine that had a ribbed bottom with a big handle on top which had to be pushed back and forth to get the clothes clean. Everyone big enough for this job took turns. The machine leaked for the first while until the wood had swelled enough to stop the draining. Mom put a bucket under each leg to save the soapy water. The wringer was cranked by hand; therefore, getting enough exercise was not a problem on wash day.

Power washing machines had made their debut, and Dad decided to bring one home. The noise was deafening and a cloud of blue smoke filled

The old, man-powered, wooden washing machine with hand-cranked wringer.

the house as the exhaust system wasn't designed for comfort. A long hose was attached to the machine and had to be led outside either through an open door or window. The house, depending on the temperature outside, was often very cold on wash day, especially in the winter. In the summer the washing machine was moved outside onto the grass, making wash day a bit more comfortable. This new power washer wasn't ideal, but it was easier physically than the old wooden model. We weren't used to this awful noise all day, and it interfered with our listening to the Hit Parade. We couldn't possibly all listen at once so we took turns digging our ears into that radio. At least we got to hear some of the music.

Since clothes dryers were not yet introduced into our world, laundry was hung outside to dry on warm summer days. Mom strung lines near

Grandma Klassen bought this stove from Eaton's many years ago. It is a family heirloom now owned by a great-granddaughter.

the ceiling to dry clothes on cold or rainy days, resulting in much humidity in the house. In the winter, she hung the tea towels, pillow cases and sheets outside to "freeze dry," which was also a bleaching process. Sometimes bluing was added to the rinse water to whiten the whites.

Sad irons were heated on the wood cook stove to iron all the clothes. Sheets and towels were run through the mangle to soften them. Most of our clothes were cotton and often dried very hard when there was no wind to help the process, resulting in a lot of ironing.

Whenever there was extra milk and cream, Mom made *Glomms*, "cottage cheese," and butter. She also set milk on the counter at room temperature in order for the milk to thicken quickly. The *Ditje'maltj*, "thick milk," was like unsweetened yogurt, and we ate it with vinegar, cream, salt and pepper; a real thirst quencher on hot summer days. Cucumbers, hard boiled eggs or cooked noodles were often added as well. Buckets of *Ditje'maltj* were slowly heated on the back of the cook stove and after some time it turned into cottage cheese.

Mom was very creative in cooking, baking and running the household. She often made something very tasty out of leftovers or a limited supply of groceries. She even turned dry bread into bread pudding. She soaked the bread in milk, added cocoa, sugar, eggs, and sometimes raisins, and baked it. I disliked it and could never eat it, but some of my siblings thoroughly enjoyed it.

At different times the Rawleigh and Watkins dealers, who were competing for business, went from farm to farm and Mom bought their special vanilla, black pepper and pudding mixes, which had more flavour than the store bought variety. She also bought Wonder Oil, Electric Oil, Camphor Ointment and Carbolic Salve. We used the Carbolic Salve to soften the cows' teats at milking time when they were dry and cracked.

One day another salesman came to our door to show Mom and Dad all the stuff he was selling, and they were immediately interested. He was trying to sell a children's walker, one like we had never seen before. It had a big table, large enough for toys and books. Harry, my youngest brother who was almost two years old, was slightly handicapped and still hadn't learned to walk. Dad bought this walker for $32.00. Harry was a much happier boy, making it easier for everyone as he didn't have to be carried so much. Dad also bought a very heavy cookware set – "Wear-ever" they called it – from this salesman for $49.00, and today, almost 60 years later, it's still in use. Mary became the proud owner when she paid $300.00 for it at Mom and Dad's auction sale.

Food was never wasted. Mom saved all the fat drippings and used it to bake bread. She saved water from cooking noodles to starch clothes. When this wasn't available, she cooked a starch by adding a flour mixture to boiling water. Before the starched clothes were ironed, she sprinkled them with water and rolled them up to dampen, which helped to get good ironing results. Mom used the whey from making cottage cheese to pickle the pig's feet and other meat. Buttermilk was used to make *Somma'borscht,* "summer soup." This soup was best when made in the summer when all the greens were available from the garden, hence, the name. Potatoes, dill, onion, beet leaves and *Süa'ramp,* "sorrel," (sour leaves, we called them), were added to a smoked meat broth. Often she made a buttermilk pie, consisting of two crusts almost like cake dough with a jam filling in between.

Mom seldom had a break from running and overseeing the household. She had the mental stress of pulling it all together, although my older sisters, Margaret and Annie, helped her a lot. There were times when she was unhappy about different things, but I can't recall ever hearing her complain about her role as a housewife and mother.

Seventeen

Berry Picking Time

Saskatoon berry picking time was one of the highlights of my summer. Our whole family went on this one-day excursion. Mom prepared a lot of food to last the whole day. She fried home-cured ham, made potato salad and *Mooss*. She also packed bread, cakes and cookies which made us eager for lunch time to roll around. We brought drinking water, and Mom made cold coffee for the adults. To make cold coffee she added several scoops of coffee grounds to half-gallon jars filled with cold water. By noontime it was a deep caramel colour and had good flavour. A simple recipe that was likely enjoyed more then than any fancy latté today.

Early in the morning we headed for the North Saskatchewan River, about 25 miles away. The banks of the river were loaded with Saskatoon bushes and, most years, berries grew in abundance. We – my brothers and sisters and I – piled onto the back of the truck while Mom and Dad and the younger children rode in the cab. I remember our hair flying and our eyes watering as we faced the wind, looking over the cab while driving.

Mom and Dad made sure each one of us had our own bucket to pick berries, and extra containers – cream cans, tubs, and cardboard boxes – were brought along to cart all the berries home. When we arrived at the river bank, we all got our buckets and tied them around our waists with a belt or binder twine allowing us to use both hands for picking. Everyone made their way to the bushes and soon, the sound of the berries hitting the bottom of the buckets could be heard all around. Dad was always scouting out good berry patches to make sure no one would waste any time. Mom and the younger children stayed near the truck where Mom started sorting berries as soon as the first full buckets arrived.

Uncle Frank and Aunt Mary Hiebert and Uncle Pete and Aunt Elizabeth Doell joined us on one of these trips. We were always fascinated by Uncle Pete's storytelling and other forms of entertainment. One afternoon, when we were all in the bushes picking berries, we heard a rooster crowing. Impossible! Unless a rooster had ventured far away from a farm yard and ended up near the river bank. Interestingly, the rooster was only crowing when Uncle Pete was by himself somewhere. It took Dad a little while to figure it out until he remembered that Uncle Pete was always up to something. When Dad asked him later if he had heard the rooster crowing, he just laughed. Then we all knew it was him.

On one of these berry picking trips, Betty, who was three years old at the time, had ventured away from the truck and got lost in the bushes. It was a terrifying experience. All the berry-picking stopped and everyone started searching and calling for her. We were all relieved when she was found, crying and bewildered, but safe.

Mom kept sorting berries throughout the day as they arrived at the truck. When all the containers were full, we headed for home. Once there, she only needed to wash them and they were ready for baking or canning. We ate the fresh berries by the handful and couldn't wait for Mom to bake fresh Saskatoon pies the next day. As deep freezers were only a dream at this time, all the berries had to be preserved in one way or another. Mom made delicious jam and canned the berries to make pies, add to *Mooss*, or eat with *Pan'küake*. We had spent a good day together as a family and had all these luscious berries to enjoy throughout the winter – until next year's berry picking season arrived again.

Eighteen

Chores

My siblings and I were assigned duties in and around the house at a young age. We were a large family and we were all expected to help until all the chores were done. For the most part, we didn't question Mom and Dad's authority or the responsibility they gave us.

In the winter, Mom had a 45 gallon barrel sitting beside the wood heater, and as soon as there was enough snow on the ground, we had to fill that barrel with snow. We carried it into the house in buckets, although sometimes two of us would join forces and use a galvanized tub as the job got done faster that way. The barrel was expected to be full at the end of each day. Wash days needed extra water, that's when the *Miea'grope* came in handy. We built a fire under it and kept melting snow until it was filled with water, then carried the hot water inside and poured it into the snow filled barrel. Mom also heated water on top of the kitchen wood stove in big pots as well as in the large oblong galvanized wash boiler, which was used mainly to boil clothes to whiten them. The stove had a built-in water reservoir that Mom tried to keep full at all times. The hot water from the reservoir always came in handy. After wash day was done, all the used water was carried out. In the winter, the water was always carried to the same place, close to the house. After some time it turned into a nice little ice rink where we enjoyed skating in the evenings.

Extra water was also needed on Saturdays; it was bath time whether we needed it or not. The story of one incident that happened circulated many times. Two young fellows went to the city and stayed over night in a motel room. They saw the nice big bathtub and the running water and one of them remarked, "Too bad it isn't Saturday, then we could have a bath."

On bath nights, one or two of us carried the big, round-bottomed galvanized bathtub into the house; on cold days it was placed beside the wood heater in the kitchen while one person stood guard; in the summer we used the back room, which provided a little more privacy. In either case, a guard was needed to make sure no one entered the room when someone was in the process of bathing. Privacy was not taken for granted when there were no locks on doors or when curtains served as a substitute.

The detested job of shoveling manure from the cow, pig and chicken barns had to be done. This was usually the boys' job, but sometimes we girls helped as well. The stench would stay in my nostrils long after the job was done. We made a big manure pile beside the cattle barn which was spread on the land to fertilize the soil come spring – a completely organic operation that enhanced the land rather than depleting it, as is the case with all the chemical fertilizers, herbicides and pesticides in use today.

Milking and feeding the animals, chickens, ducks and geese was a

The galvanized bathtub was our best friend on Saturday evenings.

twice-daily job. For several years Mom raised ducks and geese, and at one point she had a flock of about 30 ducks, all hatched by sitting hens. Mom gathered as many duck eggs as possible, and when a hen (chicken) started to brood she placed the eggs under her. When it was nearing the time for the eggs to hatch, she took a container of warm water and placed the eggs in the water, one at a time as the eggs had to stay warm. If the water moved that meant there was life inside the egg. She marked the egg with an X to avoid testing it a second time, than returned it to the nest. It was always interesting to watch the baby ducks follow the mother hen and to watch the mother hen, most bewildered, when the ducklings headed for and enjoyed the mud puddles after a rain. She ran after the ducklings and stopped short at the edge of the puddle.

Late one afternoon Mom was waiting for Dad to come home, as she was going to butcher several ducks. The water had been boiling for quite some time and she was getting a bit anxious to get the job done. Annie looked at me and quietly said, "Let's you and I go and chop those ducks' heads off." Without a second thought, we headed for the barn yard, caught two ducks which we thought were the biggest ones and took them to the chopping block. Annie handled the axe while I held their heads and in short order we had the job done. Mom couldn't believe her eyes when we brought them into the house, as Annie and I weren't very old yet. Experience is the best teacher, and we were learning!

We faithfully milked the cows morning and evening. There was no one happier than the cats at milking time. When they heard the milk hitting the bottom of the pail, their dinner bell had sounded. They loved the attention as we took aim squirting warm milk into their mouths. The buckets of milk were taken into the house to be separated. It was poured through a strainer into the large stainless steel bowl that was attached to the separator. The separator was cranked by hand and had to run at a certain speed to get the cream the desired thickness. A bell went off, announcing that the speed was right to open the valve, and the separation process began; skim milk coming out of one spout and the cream out of the other. Many times Pete and I enjoyed catching the warm milk in a cup and drinking it on the spot.

Carrying the fuel in to heat the house and carrying the ashes out were continuous jobs. In the summer the house was heated with wood, and in the winter, with coal. We carried the wood into the house with a sled pulled by a rope, and the coal with a coal bucket, which had a scoop near the top so the coal slid quite easily into the stove. The ashes were spread on the garden plot to control insects and worms that were always ready to devour the tender green shoots as they sprouted in the spring. Firewood was scarce, therefore we roamed the maple grove and pasture for dead branches or other pieces of wood – anything that would burn and give off heat. Often, when we couldn't find any more wood, Mom instructed us to gather dry cow pies. Recycling at its best!

Duties assigned indoors included washing and drying dishes, sweeping and washing floors, making beds, peeling vegetables and helping with the younger children. I am thankful that at a young age I was taught to work and share responsibilities. Now, I consider it a gift that Mom and Dad gave me, preparing me for all the hard work that lay ahead while raising my own family.

Nineteen

Mennonites on the Move

Religious persecution of the Mennonites in Russia (Ukraine) resulted in the migration of about 7,000 Mennonites to Canada in the early 1870s. They settled first in Manitoba and 20 years later many of them settled in Saskatchewan. Free homestead grants were available in Canada, and the Canadian government promised them religious freedom and exemption from military service. The Mennonites were also allowed to have their own private schools, instructing their children in the German language, which was the solidifying force in the preservation of their religion, culture and traditions. By the turn of the century, most Mennonite families were resisting public education and were not willing to give up their private schools.

In the early 1920s the Mennonites felt their religious freedom threatened when the Canadian government passed new legislation which removed the freedoms granted earlier, especially in the education of their children. English was the language of instruction in the public school system, and it was becoming evident that attendance there would become compulsory. Therefore, in 1922, a mass migration of the Mennonites from Saskatchewan and Manitoba to Mexico began.

In 1931 some of the Old Colony Mennonites from Saskatchewan, concerned about what was happening but opting out on the move to Mexico, checked out a remote area in the northern Canadian wilderness. They had set their sights on Carcajou, a small settlement on the banks of

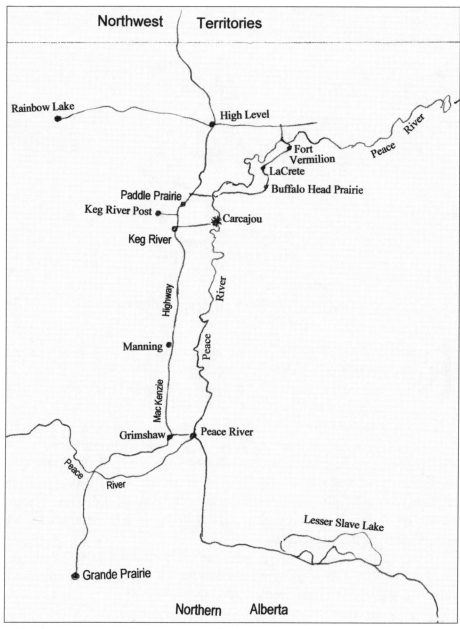

The Mennonites settled at Carcajou before moving farther north to La Crete.
Map drawn by Tena Friesen.

the Peace River in the province of Alberta – about 180 kilometers north of the town of Peace River – and decided to settle and try farming there. They traveled by vehicle as far as Peace River town, then loaded all their belongings onto a scow, or boat, and proceeded downriver to Carcajou.

They settled in the river flat along the Peace River. Although they had been warned by an elderly Cree man that the river had a history of flooding in that area, they did not take his warning seriously. Other families soon joined them, as this seemed to be the ideal place to make a new start.

The region was sparsely populated, mainly by trappers and some native families. After negotiations, the provincial government told the Mennonites not to expect schools to be built for them. This was good news, and again they felt content that there would be no government interference into their way of life.

Nature would have its way and the floods came, discouraging the settlers. More people had inquired about land at Carcajou, but no more land was available and the river was very unpredictable. After some years, many hardships, and several floods, they opted to move again. Three men who had settled with their families at Carcajou went to check out the availability of land further north, which is now La Crete. At this time the area consisted of a handful of scattered residences belonging to Anglo and Metis trappers and homesteaders. It was known that wheat could be grown successfully in this northern region. Records showed that wheat grown on the Fort Vermilion Mission Farm was awarded first prize at the Centennial Exhibition in Philadelphia in 1876. Fort Vermilion is only a few miles north of present day La Crete. The land was suitable for agriculture and was still obtainable under the provisions of the Homestead

Mr. John Peters, Mom's uncle, transported many families
to Peace River to catch the river boat north.

La Crete Landing - waiting for the river boat to arrive.

Act of 1872. The decision was made to move and start over. They set up their private German schools and churches and with no threat of public schools, were able to maintain their religious freedom and continue to live a peaceful life.

When the Mennonite settlers moved from Carcajou to La Crete and other families from the Hague district of Saskatchewan joined them in the 1930s, there was still no highway north of Peace River. The people who moved from Saskatchewan shipped all their livestock, machinery and personal belongings by train to Peace River where it was loaded onto the river freighters for the long journey to the river landing at La Crete. Many people hired Mom's uncle, Mr. John Peters, to drive them from the Hague district of Saskatchewan to Peace River town where they caught the river boat north.

When the new settlers had started their farming operations, all their grain and livestock was shipped to market at Peace River via the river freighters. The boats had schedules and a trip usually took three to four days, but difficulties were often experienced on the river. Heavy drift-wood would pile up, and occasionally mishaps caused delays and the boats could arrive a week to ten days late. The farmers built corrals and a log barn at the landing site to house their animals, and a granary to store the grain until the boat arrived. Feed for the animals was brought along, as they had to be fed while waiting for the boat as well as the days they were in transit. On their return trip, the freighters were loaded with supplies like gas, oil, groceries and whatever else the people needed to

The Weenusk II leaving La Crete Landing for Peace River.

carry on their farming operations. There was no winter transportation, which meant that the farmers couldn't get their grain or livestock to market from river freeze-up in the fall until river break-up in the spring, creating a huge back log.

River freeze-up is a term used to describe the river in late fall when large ice floes make it impossible to safely navigate the river. Building the ice bridge – and being able to cross safely – can take up to a month, depending on snow fall and temperatures. It takes a lot of flooding for the

Ice jam at Fort Vermillion, Alberta.

ice to become thick and solid enough for vehicles to cross, especially the large tractor-trailer units. These ice bridges are common in the north to this day.

River break-up (sometimes referred to as spring break-up) is the term used to describe the river in spring when the warm weather begins to melt the ice, thus making it unsafe for vehicles to cross. The initial cracking and breaking and moving of the ice can be a spectacular experience; the impact and power of the massive boulders creating deafening crashes. Some years, an ice jam delayed the ice from moving out and it could take several weeks until the river was safe for ferry travel.

Road construction from Peace River to High Level was completed in 1948, and in 1950 a road was constructed from High Level to Fort Vermilion, ending the river boat era. Commercial trucking replaced the river freighters although the boats continued to make some unscheduled trips until 1952.

In 1937, three of Mom's uncles and one aunt from the Hague area, together with their families, decided to join this group of Mennonites at La Crete. Good reports were coming back, and it appeared to be the land of opportunity. Bountiful crops were produced with much hard work being the ticket, and people were again able to make a livelihood off the land. In 1949 Mom and Dad made a trip to the Peace River country to visit the relatives and investigate the favourable reports that had been coming back. They were encouraged by their observations. Good farm

Mom's uncles and their families with all their belongings on the "Russian Navy" en route to La Crete Landing from Peace River, May 14, 1937. The river was the only "highway" north of Peace River.

land was not easily obtainable in Saskatchewan, therefore most young men headed to the cities in search of employment. Mom and Dad had their roots in the soil and were envisioning a different future for their large, growing family, as farming was their choice of lifestyle and the way they had always made a living. While they were at La Crete, they made arrangements for Mr. Jacob Peters, Mom's cousin, to keep them posted of any future land sales.

Mom and Dad received word from Mr. Peters in the summer of 1951 that a public land auction was coming up in Fort Vermilion. They made another trip north, taking John with them. Dad bought three quarter sections of land at this sale. He paid $7.50 an acre for two of the quarters and $3.50 an acre for the third quarter. The arrangement was a 10 per cent down payment and 10 years to pay the balance. New economic and agricultural opportunities were on the horizon for Mom and Dad, and dreams of prosperity began to occupy their minds.

In October of 1952 Dad, together with John and Margaret, took the first load of machinery to La Crete. The 44 Massey Harris tractor was loaded on the three-ton Fargo truck, and the Massey Harris Model 16 pull-type combine was loaded on the flat deck trailer. The trip was long and tedious, as the road conditions were very poor. There was no pavement and very little gravel on the roads north of Edmonton. When they arrived at what is now High Level, they unhitched the trailer with the combine and left it there. They unloaded the tractor and used it to tow the truck through

Margaret and John with the first load of machinery
taken to La Crete in October 1952.

The second load of machinery taken to La Crete in January 1953.

the mud holes whenever necessary. After they got to La Crete, John drove the tractor back to High Level – about a 150 mile round trip – to get the trailer with the combine.

Dad, Pete and Jake took a second load of machinery to La Crete in January of 1953. This time they took the threshing machine and other equipment. The trailer had a flat tire at Kinuso, so they left it there. Some

John and Annie shingling the roof of what was to be our new home.

Pete, Annie and John finished shingling the garage roof in May, 1953.

time later, with the help of Mr. Jacob Peters, they got the trailer with the threshing machine to La Crete.

It wasn't until March of that same year that the wheels really went into motion. Dad, together with John, Pete and Annie headed north with a load of supplies, building materials and whatever else they would need to erect several buildings. They stayed for two months and built two structures. One was a 20' x 30' building that would serve as a house when the family arrived, and the other was a 24' x 34' garage, which would serve multiple purposes. Dad rented a small house from Mr. Ben K. Peters for the duration of their stay, and Annie perfected her cooking as well as her carpentry skills during this time.

The bush on this land wasn't heavy as a fire had swept through this area some years earlier, thereby allowing Dad, John and Pete to break and clear about ten acres before they headed for home.

Dad sold the farm at Osler to Uncle Art and Aunt Margaret Moser, and plans got under way for an auction sale. Mom and Dad had difficult decisions to make, as they couldn't possibly take all their possessions and, therefore, had to sell more than they wanted to. As a 12-year-old girl, I didn't understand and couldn't comprehend what this move meant and how it would affect me in every area of my life.

June 10, 1953, is a date permanently fixed in my memory. It was a beautiful afternoon when, only nine days before we would leave, I was sitting together with my classmates reading in the shade of the trees surrounding

My sisters and me shortly before we moved. Margaret and I are in the back. Annie holding Martha, Betty, Babe and Helen are in the front. Mary is missing.

the schoolyard. A spring breeze was gently stirring the pages of my book. I was in deep thought, wondering if and when, I would see my friends again.

The day of the auction sale, June 13, arrived, and I began to get a glimpse of reality when we carried many of our belongings outside. They would soon belong to someone else. What I remember most vividly was when our horse, Joker, was sold. Jake loved that horse and he broke down and cried when the new owner led it away. Much of the sorting had already been done, and shortly after the auction sale, Dad brought home a bunch of cardboard boxes and the packing began.

One evening in June we all dressed in our Sunday best and Mom and Dad took our whole family to Parker Studio in Saskatoon to get our family portrait taken. How special that photo is today! Another evening, just a few days before we were scheduled to leave, our friends and extended family organized a surprise farewell party for our family. People mingled inside and out on the grass, enjoying the refreshments they had brought, as they couldn't possibly all fit in the house. I remember it as a sad evening, as many people were crying when they said goodbye. But it was good to know that they cared and our family would be missed.

I'm sure Mom and Dad must have had mixed feelings about uprooting their large family, although I don't recall them ever verbalizing it. They were leaving behind a reasonably comfortable lifestyle, exchanging it for what they knew would be many trials and hardships. They had lived through the years of depression and I'm certain the difficult question must have been, "Do we really want to do it again?" They were taking a great leap of faith and were willing to make the sacrifice, giving their family the chance for a more promising future. They had a large family and little money, but they were still young and, being equipped with a pioneering spirit, were willing to face the challenge.

On June 19, 1953, after all our belongings were loaded and all our good-byes were said, I took one last look at the house and the yard that held so many precious memories – the place where I had spent a happy and carefree childhood; the big yard where we always played, climbed trees, and ran barefoot through the mud puddles after the rain; the dirt road that led to our school, the pastures and the fields and our neighbours just down the road. Finally, we all got settled for the long trip ahead and waved good-bye to the old home place. We were headed for the wilderness of northern Alberta!

Our family in June 1953, taken just a week before we moved to northern Alberta. In the back row are Jake, Annie, John, Margaret, Pete and me. In the front are Helen, Bill, Betty, Dad holding Martha, Mom holding Harry, Mary and Babe.

PART TWO

My Youth in the Boreal Forests of Northern Alberta

1953 – 1962

Twenty

Our Journey North

The big, three-ton Fargo truck was loaded with all the goods that were not liquidated at the auction sale and would be needed to start life over again. Either John or Pete drove the big truck, and they always had an extra passenger or two. Dad drove the pick-up truck with Mom and the younger children in the cab. Dad had mounted a camper shell on the back of the pick-up to keep us out of the wind and rain, and that's where all the rest of us settled in. It had one small window that we took turns looking out of while driving. We were now thirteen siblings plus Mom and Dad. Betty, Helen, Mary, Bill, Babe, Martha, and Harry had joined the family after I was born.

We also had a passenger on this trip. Sarah Martens, whose parents were friends with Mom and Dad, asked if she could catch a ride to visit her relatives who lived at La Crete. When I reflect back, I shake my head to think they even considered taking a passenger, but their motto was "God first, others next and then myself," which certainly rang true here. This time I don't think God would have held it against them if they would have said no, as the vehicles were already overcrowded – sixteen people in total. We stayed together while traveling and often changed seating arrangements. We all got very tired and restless squished into that little camper shell. Sarah was thankful for the opportunity to visit her relatives and didn't mind sharing limited space.

The narrow gravel road north of Edmonton had turned into mud with

Stopping for a hot meal in Grimshaw, AB, before braving the worst stretch of highway on our journey to our destination at La Crete, another 300 miles away. In the back row are Annie, the restaurant owner, me, Sarah Martens, Margaret, Jake, Mom and Dad holding Harry. In the front row are Betty, Helen, Mary, Bill, Babe and Martha. John and Pete had not caught up to us yet.

all the rain. Traveling was slow and cumbersome with countless pit stops resulting from all the people on board. Perhaps, at times, it was an excuse to get out of that crowded camper shell.

Mom had packed a lot of food, but with sixteen mouths to feed it likely didn't last long. At appropriate times and places Dad picked up food at a grocery store; usually bread, meat, fruit, cookies and something to drink. We had extra blankets in the camper which were spread on the grass beside the roadside at meal times.

One of the vehicles had mechanical problems at Kinuseo causing a long delay. Dad rented a cabin for all of us to sleep in, giving us a good break from the camper shell. After the problem was fixed, and after many more difficult miles and many hours later, we arrived at Grimshaw. It was time to stretch our legs and get refreshed. Mom and Dad took us to a Chinese restaurant for a hot meal. The restaurant owner had never seen such a large family before, so he asked Mom and Dad if they would agree to have a family picture taken with him in the picture as well. Mom and Dad didn't object.

It seemed like the road conditions and mosquitoes got progressively worse the further north we traveled. Late in the afternoon we made it to what is now High Level. There was only a garage and several other buildings at the time. The road from High Level to Fort Vermilion had no gravel and had not dried up after the frost came out of the ground and before the rains came. At one point, when the truck was stuck in the Rocky Lane area, Dad walked to a local farmer who helped us out in our distress.

High Level in 1953.

Eventually we made it to the river crossing at Fort Vermilion. The small cable ferry looked unsafe and frightening in that big body of water and the children clung to Mom in fear. We all vacated the vehicles to stretch our legs and enjoy the beautiful scenery. We marveled at the panorama of colour – the breath-taking beauty of the mountainous hills stretching to the far horizons. These forested river banks boasted many shades of green. Spiraling, deep green spruce trees dwarfed the stands of the lighter shaded, white-barked, poplar and birch trees. The clouds in the sky added to the beauty of the reflection in the water. The river flowed tranquilly – living up to its name – "the mighty Peace River."

After that little bit of excitement it was back into that camper shell to endure another stretch of gumbo, mud holes and mosquitoes that would take us to the future town site of La Crete. There was no more bickering about looking out of that little 10" x 12" window as all we had seen for the last 400 miles was dense forest on both sides of the road. At times I felt these endless miles of northern forests closing in on me, not knowing where the road would lead. Hours later the pickup got hopelessly stuck again. Dad walked to the nearest farmstead, about one-half mile or so, which happened to be the Peter R. Neustaeter farm. Mr. Neustaeter was willing to help even though he was already asleep for the night. He got his tractor going, gathered his chains and came to the rescue. No doubt this wasn't the first time he helped someone out, considering his farm was located right beside the road in the heart of mud hole country.

We crossed the river on this cable ferry on June 23, 1953.

This ordeal took several hours and we were fighting mosquitoes the whole time. No sooner did we close our eyes to try and get some sleep and the buzzing of hordes of the blood-thirsty tormentors in our ears, nose and mouth robbed us of any sleep. This mud hole was in a swampy muskeg area, and with the long, warm summer nights, breeding conditions were ideal; the mosquito season had reached its peak. We were good bait for those blood-sucking, bedeviled pests. I claim to this day that I built up my immune system with mosquito venom on that trip and the years that followed, as they rarely bother me now.

When we were safe on the other side of the mud hole, heading for the next one, it was two thirty in the morning. We were now on the final stretch – another fifteen miles that would take us to the Jake Peters home, Mom's cousin, who lived three miles past our homestead. We arrived there about six o'clock in the morning and Mr. and Mrs. Peters took our whole family in for two days until we were unloaded, unpacked, and settled enough to make it on our own. It was June 23; five days since we had left our home in Saskatchewan. In those days and in those road conditions, distance was measured in days rather than miles.

We had arrived at our destination in this remote and desolate land – this land of opportunity! *"This area and the surrounding townships had been surveyed in 1914 by Mr. J.A.S. King, who stated in his report, 'No doubt, someday, there will be one of the very finest little communities in the northwest in this Buffalo Head Prairie.'"* [7]

This is the area where Dad had bought his homestead. A few miles south of the homestead, the rugged Buffalo Head Hills tower high above the horizon, displaying their beauty which changes with the seasons. About six miles west flows the mighty Peace River, nestled between its high river banks. This mighty river was the highway to the north for the early settlers who came to tame this raw and rugged land, magnificent in all its splendour. This pristine wilderness was home to the many animals from which the early trappers carved out a living and where the first settlers had come to try farming and make a living off the land. It was here that Mom and Dad intended to carve out a living for themselves and their family.

---

7 *La Crete and Area Then and Now Society, Heritage of Homesteads, Hardships and Hope: 1914–1989: La Crete.* 1989.

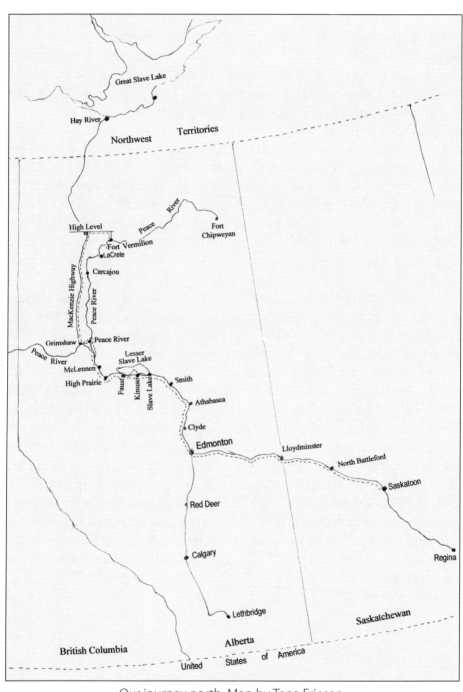

Our journey north. Map by Tena Friesen.

Twenty-One

Starting Over

The big move was accomplished. We had all survived the long monotonous trip without any accidents and in good health, so there was much to be thankful for. It seemed like we had landed on the other side of the world, and many of our acquaintances in Saskatchewan believed just that. The landscape was beautiful; the trees all leafed out in striking shades of green. The road running from our homestead to the Jake Peter's farm was a narrow bush trail framed on either side with dense woods of poplar, birch and spruce – the tops of the tall trees on both sides of the road touched overhead. It was the beginning of a new era for us in an oasis of this forest-shrouded northland – a sharp contrast from the near treeless, windswept prairie we were used to.

The long summer evenings were new to us with many more hours of daylight this far north. We enjoyed the early sunrises and late sunsets of our first northern summer. The dawns and twilights were such gradual blendings, there seemed to be no abrupt transition. Often we forgot to look at the clock and worked much too late; we could read the newspaper outdoors at midnight. Life would be very different from what we had known before without the conveniences we had grown accustomed to. Life would consist mainly of work – hard work – for my parents and older siblings in primitive conditions that would test the faith and strength of character and push the human spirit to the limits.

Dad and my brothers set up the wood cook stove in the garage where most of the cooking was done that first summer. Sometimes we ate in the garage and at other times in the "house." Mom, Margaret and Annie did most of the cooking, while my younger sisters and I got our fair share of the clean up. We all seemed to eat twice as much and sleep twice as long as we had done previously. Mom concluded it was due to the long trip, but people who had experienced this move told her it was due to climate change, and that it lasted approximately three months.

Since the garage wasn't insulated, the sunlight filtered its way in through the knot holes and cracks in the walls, revealing all the dust in the air coming from the dirt floor. The mosquitoes, bugs and other insects also found their way in through the spaces in the walls. John, Pete and Jake slept in the garage that first summer and had to fight the pesky things every night. We stuffed rags into the biggest cracks in the walls to try and keep the mosquitoes out. Several times during the night, someone built a smudge in an old bucket and smoked out the building in order to get some sleep. It kept the mosquitoes at bay for a little while, but as soon as the smoke disappeared, they were back. We did the same in the building where the rest of us slept, and there was no choice in the matter – we were all blessed with a new brand of perfume.

The mosquito remedy didn't work for flies. Dad bought fly stickers and hung them from the rafters. The stickers resembled shot gun shells, only they had a tab at the bottom, which when pulled, released a streamer of heavy, yellowish, sweet-scented sticky paper. The flies were attracted to the sweet smell, landing them on the death trap. On hot sunny days it didn't take long for the yellow paper to turn black. The two feet of trap was moving and buzzing as the flies died in agony.

The deep silent woods surrounding our new home were occasionally interrupted by night noises that sounded strange, and at times eerie. The familiar noise of buzzing mosquitoes or yipping coyotes posed no threat, but there were noises we didn't recognize. The call of the owls echoing through the trees was scary at first, but after a while it got to be comforting – almost like sending a message – don't worry, all is well.

One of the first tasks Dad and my brothers undertook was digging a well, as it was crucial to have a good water supply for such a large family. They dug a very deep well which produced no water. A dry hole! Two more tries at different locations produced the same result, abandoning the idea of a well for our water supply. Discouragement aside, empty barrels were set up to catch the water from the roofs when it rained. Dad and the boys built wooden eves troughs and led them into the barrels. A commune of mosquito larvae and other dancing, diving, squiggling creatures lived happily in the rain barrels but the water was never used for drinking. When the rain lasted for any length of time, the rain barrels overflowed, and Mom scrounged up every large pot or five-gallon bucket she could find to save the precious water. Other than that, every drop was hauled with tractor and wagon from the ditches along the roadside, as long as they held water. When that supply was depleted, it meant a trip to the river six miles away. We got our drinking water from the Jake Peters who had a well that produced good water. In the winter we melted snow or hauled ice chunks from the river.

That first summer Dad and my brothers broke another 50 acres of new bush land. Every one of us who was old enough and strong enough was assigned to pick roots. Dad hitched the big flat deck trailer to the tractor, and someone had to move the tractor forward as we threw the roots on. When the trailer was full, it was hauled to the nearest brush row, unloaded, and then the whole process started all over again.

Breaking this new land had the potential for many delays and hardships. In the midst of making progress, at an unexpected time, Dad discovered a flat tire on the back wheel of the tractor. This would cause a long delay. Mr. Ben K. Peters operated a garage in the community for minor repairs, but this job, however, proved too big for his operation. Dad therefore, had to take the tire to the repair shop in Fort Vermilion, about twenty five miles away, in very bad road conditions. Jake and I went with Dad for the ride.

Repairing the tire was taking an awfully long time, and Dad soon realized that this repair man had not been blessed with speed. After a while Jake and I got restless and informed Dad that we were going for a walk. We walked down to the river just a short distance from the garage and spent a little time by the water's edge. As we skipped stones over the water, threw twigs into the moving stream and watched them sail away, we noticed a motorboat approaching the shore. It was a middle aged Native man. He stopped his boat, started talking to us, and asked if we were interested in going for a ride down the river in his motorboat. He said if we gave him $1.00 he would take us to see the snake pit in the riverbank.

We must have had the money, as we climbed into the boat with him and he took us down the river. We hadn't told Dad where we were going or with whom, but this man proved to be trustworthy. He told us he loved to be on the water and he appreciated some company. Jake and I had our first motorboat ride and a good lesson in history. He explained many things to us; the behaviour of the snakes and why they acted the way they did. He showed us the first Hudson Bay Trading Post site where the trappers came to trade their furs and told us all about hunting, trapping and the Indian way of life. We were glad to be back before Dad was ready to go home. With great excitement we told him about our little adventure only to be reprimanded, thereby learning another lesson: "Never go with a stranger, and always tell someone where you are going."

As there was no refrigeration available to keep the food cold, my brothers dug a hole approximately four feet wide by six feet long by three feet deep on the north side of the garage and built a wooden cover for it. In spring, after river break-up, Dad and the boys hauled ice chunks from the river and put them into the hole. They covered the ice with saw dust and it lasted for a long time and kept the food cold. When this hole was no longer cold enough, Mom poured the milk, cream and other food into large lidded syrup or lard pails and hung them into the well.

More trees were cut down with an axe or power saw to extend the yard, always leaving big stumps sticking out. We always ran around in bare feet in the summertime and frequently stubbed our toes on these stumps for several years to come. On one occasion, Bill, as a young child, noticed that one of our baby chicks was limping. He had it all figured out and told Mom the chick had stubbed its toe on a stump.

Getting food on the table with the limited supply of groceries available was a test for Mom. She cooked large pots of *Borscht* or other soup and served it with either *Pan'küake,* "crepes," *Fat'küake,* "fruit fritters," *Roll'küake,* "a deep fried dough," *Schnetje,* "baking powder biscuits" or bread. Many times Annie and I stood by that hot wood cook stove for hours making the *Pan'küake,* while the younger children stood in line to get them hot out of the frying pan. *Wrennetje,* "perogies," was another meal we thoroughly enjoyed. Mom made them with home-made cottage cheese and served them with cream gravy, home cured ham or sausage, and strawberries or other fruit.

Often times when the fire had burnt too low before we added more wood, we removed the lid of the cook stove and placed the frying pans directly on the fire causing the pans to be covered with a layer of soot. This created another job: trying to clean these pans darkened our dish cloths and dish water, leaving soot particles floating in the water. When we put more wood on the fire, a cloud of black smoke billowed above our heads, escaped to the open beam and added another layer to the smoke darkened rafters. Here's Mom's recipe for *Fat'küake*:

Fruit Fritters

1 cup flour
1 ½ tsp. baking powder
½ tsp. salt
2 tbs. sugar
1 egg, beaten
½ cup milk
1 ½ cups fruit (any kind)
Sift dry ingredients. Beat egg and add milk.
Pour into dry ingredients. Stir until batter is smooth.
Add fruit to the batter and blend together.
Drop by spoonfuls into deep hot fat.
Fry until golden brown.
Makes 15–20 fritters.

We ate them as they came out of the hot fat. We each had a saucer of sugar, dipped the fritters in the sugar and enjoyed them whole heartedly.

Pete knew that Mom would welcome an addition to her menu and, when he spotted a Sandhill crane in the field, he knew what he was going to do. This big bird would definitely help to put a few more meals on the table. Mom butchered it and put it on to cook, thinking there was time enough to cook it for supper. Unfortunately, it didn't get done – that day, or the next. After many hours of cooking it never did get tender enough to eat. It was likely one of those "oldie goldies" who had refused to give up the ghost. What a disappointment that was for Mom.

It was wild strawberry season shortly after we arrived, and one day Mom asked several of us to go pick strawberries, as she wanted to make some *Mooss*. We gathered some jars and headed for the bushes. No sooner had the picking started when we heard a commotion in the bush. We were terrified, thinking it was a bear, and headed for home, hiding in some brush near the buildings. After we thought we had waited long enough, we went to the house and told Mom we hadn't found any. I don't think she believed us, as the berries were plentiful. I don't know why we didn't tell her the truth – likely we were afraid she would send us right back. There was no *Mooss* for supper that day.

That first summer we had no garden. Many people had extra vegetables and shared them willingly, which was a huge blessing. It helped us get through the summer as well as the first winter. Like all the settlers in those early years, we would have to learn to live off the land. Dad and my brothers dug a hole under the house that served as a root cellar. They cribbed the walls with rough boards to keep the dirt from caving in. The snug-fitting trap door was centred in the kitchen floor, with a ladder leading into it. Several shelves lined the walls where the canned jars of food were kept. Potatoes and carrots were stored in bins also built with rough boards. No floor was put in the bins as the vegetables stored better on the earth floor.

The Abe Wieler family had moved and settled on the creek bank at West La Crete the year before we moved; the creek was later named Wieler's Creek. The Jake Friesen family had settled right across the road from the Wielers, and we were all in the same predicament where education was concerned. Mr. Wieler, with much opposition, had the contract to build the Buffalo Head Prairie School the summer we arrived. It was the first public school to be built in the community, but the community was not yet ready for public education. Some families left their established farms and comfortable homes and relocated to lands outside the school district to avoid sending their children to public school. The school was located about five miles from our home and, considering the distance and road conditions, attending there wasn't even an option. Neither was it for the Wielers or the Friesens, who lived even farther away.

Mr. Samuel Nafziger came to teach at this school. The Nafzigers, with their three boys, had left a comfortable life in Alden, New York to answer the call to teach in this northern community. The school wasn't completely ready when they arrived, giving them no other option than to set up house in the school, together with some of the construction workers, until their house would be built. They also found the change in lifestyle extremely difficult and experienced the birth of a baby at home without a midwife. The school opened its doors in November of 1953, with fewer than ten students in attendance, but the winds of change had started to blow, and this isolated community was on its way to big changes.

The Wielers and Friesens had been enrolled in correspondence school the year before and were continuing their education this way. In July, Dad and Mr. Wieler made a special trip to Edmonton, a thousand mile round trip in very poor road conditions, where Dad enrolled us in correspondence school and brought our lessons home. Our education was to continue regardless of the obstacles we faced. Mr. Wieler picked up lessons for his family and the Friesens. I bonded rather quickly with Betty Wieler and Lena Friesen, who were both my age, and we shared a common goal. I was thankful to have friends so soon after we arrived.

In August, only two months after we moved, my Grandpa Klassen, Mom's father, passed away. Despite the primitive communication system, Mom and Dad got the telegram in time to travel back to Saskatchewan for the funeral. This was a major setback time wise, with all the work that needed to be done before winter set in, and, no doubt, it left its mark on their pocket book. Grandpa was very sick when we moved, which made it very difficult for Mom to leave. She hadn't expected the sad news that soon.

In September of the same year, Uncle Henry and Aunt Helen Neudorf, with their family of thirteen children, moved to La Crete from British Columbia. A Mennonite migration had taken place from the Swift Current and Saskatoon areas of Saskatchewan to Cheslatta, BC in 1940. The people were very poor, and the effects of the depression and the Second World War were taking their toll. They were living on relief payments from the government and it appeared that without any help the potential for them becoming a burden to society was very real. Many lived on rented land – not an ideal situation for Mennonite farmers! In the late 1930s, the leaders of the Old Colony churches approached the British Columbia government for land.

The BC government was looking for settlers, and they knew if anyone

Mom on far right holding Harry, together with her siblings and their spouses, taken after Grandpa's funeral. Dad took the picture.

People at the train station in Osler, Saskatchewan waiting for the train to take them to Burns Lake, British Columbia on their move to Cheslatta, June 1940.

could make the land productive, it would be the Mennonites. The provincial governments of Saskatchewan and BC worked together, and the delegates negotiated a deal for land at Cheslatta, in the Burns Lake area. [8]

They were promised free land, and anyone who moved would have all their moving expenses paid and would receive three years of relief payments. Anyone who did not want to stay after the three year probation period would have all their expenses paid to return to Saskatchewan. This plan provided drought stricken families with a new start, cash strapped provinces with a way of decreasing relief payments and a way for British Columbia to increase its northern population.

In the negotiations, they were promised their own private German schools, providing there would be some English instruction on every Friday afternoon. To qualify, the condition was that every family needed $200.00 in cash, two horses, two cows, two pigs and ten chickens. They also needed to bring one piece of farming equipment, which the settlers would share when clearing and working the land. Military tents for temporary housing were provided by the government until their log

---

8 My brother John's wife, Marge, was in this move and her father, Mr. Jacob Petkau, was a delegate negotiating with the government for land. It was Marge and her sister Aganetha Bueckert that provided me with most of the information.

homes were built. Approximately 200 people representing 28 families undertook this move.

Sadly, after all the hard work in breaking the land, much of it was not suited for agriculture. The focus shifted to ranching and forestry, enabling the people to make a living that way. *"In a few years the Mennonites were living in comfortable homes, making a good living and no more assistance was needed. In 1941, another 25 families were relocated from Saskatchewan to the Vanderhoof area of BC. About eighteen years later, in 1958, when outside forces began to exert pressure on the Mennonite community and the BC government insisted that they send their children to public school, Mr. Abraham Peters, the leader of the Old Colony Mennonite Church at Chesletta, lead about half of the Mennonite settlers to Fort St. John, BC."* [9]

Uncle Henry and Aunt Helen were making a living in the lumber sector before they moved north. Since they were landless, they built a log house in the back yard of Aunt Helen's sister's farm at West La Crete, which happened to be the Jake Peter's family, who had also helped us to make a new start. This dwelling was very primitive, with dirt floors. Somehow they cured the floors, making them hard as cement and very smooth, sweeping them like any other floor. The family moved in before the outside door was installed, leaving Aunt Helen no other option than to string heavy blankets as a substitute. One evening, late in the fall, when we were visiting them, we could hear the wolves howling in the distance. At home, in my bed that night, sleep would not come for fear the wolves would get in through that blanket door. I have many fond memories of visits to their log cabin home. I was thankful to have family living nearby. We spent much time together socially and, a few years later, we attended the same school.

School, as we had not known it before, was about to begin. We all had to get used to a new way of studying. All six of us were

We depended on the mantle lamp for light during the long winter evenings.

---

9 Short excerpt from *Preservings*, Issue No. 28, 2008.

eager to begin working on our lessons. Betty, Helen, Mary, Bill, Babe and I worked under the strict supervision of Dad and Margaret, while Mom and Annie cooked all the meals and did all the other housework. Sometimes, Annie helped the younger children with their lessons as well. Procrastination was not a word in our vocabulary at that time. Dad supervised the older ones while Margaret instructed the younger children. Dad had been a bit confused about our grade levels, and registered Helen in grade four instead of grade three but she didn't experience any difficulty with the work. Although Dad didn't have a high school education, he was very capable of helping me with seventh grade arithmetic, science and social studies; the subjects I needed the most help with. Every lesson in every subject was sent to Edmonton for correction. Mail day, once every ten days or two weeks, became very important to us, as we always looked forward to getting our corrected lessons back. In the heart of winter when we had only a few hours of daylight, much studying was done by the light of the mantle and coal oil lamps.

The weather, that first winter, stayed reasonably mild until Christmas. The wood cook stove was moved into the house and a wood heater was set up on the opposite wall. Black stove pipes ran up to the ceiling and out through the roof, and firewood was piled high beside the stoves. The smell of wood smoke, a mixture of spruce and poplar, lingered in the house.

Our winter fuel supply.

Practically every evening before he went to bed, Pete took the big butcher knife and cut kindling to start the fires in the morning. Using crumpled newspaper and blowing into the opening on the side of the stove usually got the fire going. Big pots of water were always sizzling on the stove either for cooking, washing dishes, laundry or bathing. Large, red-rimmed enamel bowls, chipped in many places, were used to wash dishes. The used dish water was poured into slop buckets that stood beside the door. This little 20' x 30' building afforded no privacy when it served as a kitchen, dining room, bedroom, laundry room, bathroom and classroom – each in turn and sometimes all at once.

After the field work and other outside work was done came the task of securing firewood for the winter months. Everyone heated their homes with wood, as it was the only heat source available. Firewood was plentiful and free for the taking, but there was much work involved in getting it home and readied for the stoves. The trees, dead fall or other, had to be skidded out of the bush, loaded onto the flat deck trailer and then hauled home. Dad, John, Pete and Jake set up the saw wheel and sawed the wood into the required lengths for the heater and cook stove. Ours was the daily job of splitting the wood and carrying it into the house. Dad and my brothers built a slab barn that first fall. Dad bought a herd of cattle, some pigs and later chickens. A supply of milk, meat and eggs was essential to the self-sufficiency and well-being of our family.

The nights were getting frosty; a foretaste of the coming winter. Dad and the boys built two small bedrooms onto the north side of the existing building and were able to finish the job before the cold weather set in. Dad banked sawdust around the foundation of the house and the snow-covered sawdust kept drafts out from under the floors. The weather turned bitterly cold after Christmas. The house, if you want to call it that,

Me in front of the house, with the two small bedrooms and a small porch added on.

wasn't insulated and had no ceiling. Dad put a hole near the top of the wall for the heat from the main living area to find its way into the little bedrooms. As we started life on the homestead our days were filled with hard work that left little time for idle regrets over the easier life we had left behind.

Much of the heat escaped and formed icicles that hung from the roof and almost reached the ground. In milder weather we sucked on them until our lips and tongues would freeze. There were no storm windows, and the single paned glass gave off a real chill, especially in the extreme cold temperatures when several inches of ice built up, making it impossible to look through them. The frost painted palm trees and jungles on the windows, and I marveled at the beautiful art work of the Master artist. When the weather turned milder and the ice on the windows began to melt, Mom put rags on the window sills to catch the drip. When these rags were saturated, the water made it to the floor anyway – creating another job.

White polka dots of frost grew thick on the exposed nail heads. Sometimes two rainbow sun dogs escorted the sun, refracting through a frigid haze. We studied at the table with two wood burning stoves going, and when the Fahrenheit thermometer plunged to minus 60 degrees, we sat with our parkas, ski pants and wool *Socke* on, and were still cold; more so when the cold drafts swept about with each opening of

Studying with our parkas on inside, showing the north side wall and east end.

the door – resulting in a heavy fog inside the room when the cold air collided with the warmth inside the house. Mom or Dad got up at regular intervals during the night to keep the fires burning. That first winter was a test of endurance for all of us. One cold day we saw a moose running across the field, and I remember thinking at least we were warmer than he was.

The worst of the worst was outdoor plumbing, especially in minus 40 or lower degree temperatures when hoar frost was an inch thick around the hole, and we had no choice but to plant ourselves firmly. Occasionally the door of the outhouse was left open and the blowing winds formed snow drifts inside and around the toilet so we couldn't move the door, making it difficult for us to get either in or out. We were all afraid of the dark, resulting in much cooperation in accompanying each other on these dreaded trips. Even though no one ever wasted a minute there, it didn't stop the one who was waiting in the frigid temperatures from continually saying, "Hurry up, hurry up." At times we had the flashlight to guide us; at other times we had to find our way in the dark. We were often scared half to death, as we feared there might still be some rabid animal roaming around, a remnant of the rabies epidemic

The inside of the house, showing the south side wall and west end.

that swept the Peace River country the year before we moved.

When there was a need to go somewhere, either to the store or neighbours, it wasn't possible to plug in the truck and wait for the motor to warm up. Dad had a propane-generated flame-thrower, about three feet long, with a shield at the end to protect the flame. Dad hooded the front of the truck with tarpaulins so the heat couldn't escape, then lit the flame-thrower and mounted it underneath the truck. Depending on temperatures, it could take many hours until the motor had warmed up enough for the truck to start. All these experiences became kind of samples and symbols forecasting the pattern of our lives in the years to come.

After that first long, hard and cold winter, spring finally arrived. Many burdens were lifted with the warmer weather. In June when twenty hours of sunlight blanketed our little world in warmth, it was possible to put our first difficult winter behind us.

Correspondence lessons were nearing completion, and we all looked forward to some time away from studying. It had been a trying time, always struggling to meet deadlines. It took a great deal of discipline and a rigid schedule to keep everyone focused, especially the younger children. Dad and Margaret were ready for a break, as were Mom and Annie from all their responsibilities. At the end of that school term, there was a feeling of satisfaction and accomplishment when everyone was promoted to the next grade.

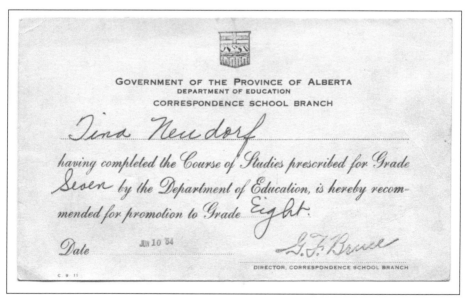

This is what a correspondence school report card looked like.

Twenty-Two

Community and Church

Starting this new chapter in life was a drastic change and more than an adventure. It came with many unforeseen difficulties and hardships and progress was slow at best. There were only a handful of people who drove vehicles and travel was slow and cumbersome on those narrow bush trails that were called roads. Means of travel was a novelty

Narrow bush trails like these were called "roads."

to all of us, as occasionally we still saw someone driving a dog team. Most people traveled with horses and wagon or buggy in the summer and with horses and sleigh in the winter and the church leaders wanted it to stay that way.

The Old Colony Church was the only denomination in this vast northern community. Since Mom and Dad had both been baptized and later married in the Old Colony Church at Hague in 1931, they were encouraged to conform. The Bishop came to our house and asked Dad

In front of Knelsons General Store in La Crete. People were still driving horse-drawn sleighs as late as the 1960s.

to consider selling his vehicles, buy horses and take up membership in the church. Dad didn't even consider this suggestion. Progress was slow enough without slowing it down more. The people who had moved from Saskatchewan had owned vehicles before their move north. Now the reasoning was that progress would pave the way for the "world" to come into the community and upset their peaceful way of life.

Life was slower in the 1950s. Travel was still mostly with horses.

When the Bishop visited our home, he asked us girls if we wouldn't like to wear dresses instead of pants. I suppose he didn't realize that we only had a few dresses to wear on Sunday or that it would be a big expense to change all our wardrobes. He also asked us if we didn't want to let our hair grow long and braid it. All the women and children in the Old Colony Church braided their hair and dressed in traditional clothing. I was familiar with this style of dress as both my grandmothers had dressed this way, but I had never seen children wearing dark, long-sleeved dresses that reached to their ankles covered by an apron and wearing white kerchiefs. At my young age I couldn't possibly understand any reasoning behind all this. My paternal grandparents had already left the Old Colony church in 1934 and had taken up membership in the Bergthaler Church, which was more lenient in dress code and other rules, although Grandma never changed her style of dress. Years later, when they retired in Osler, they occasionally attended the General Conference Church. I'm not certain when Mom and Dad left the Old Colony Church, but they had attended the Bergthaler Church for some time, although our family was also attending the General Conference Church in Osler at the time we moved north.

There were only a few families who dressed like we did and were able to read and write English. Some of the first generation who had moved from Hague, Saskatchewan were literate in English, but since there were no English schools in the community and the instruction of the children had been in the German language, this younger generation was illiterate in English. Looking back, the people who did not conform to the Old Colony Church must have been a threat to the community. Bringing in vehicles, a different style of dress, and being supportive of the public school system, which was associated with the English language and "the world," was contrary to their ideals. It is little wonder that our family, along with a few other families, were under the microscope and generally not well accepted into the community.

Mom and Dad believed in giving their family spiritual training. The Old Colony Church did not have any Sunday school for the children, and today, 55 years later, they still don't have a Sunday school or youth program in place inside or outside of the church setting. The first few years we lived up north, the church at Osler, where we had attended before the move, sent Sunday school lessons in the mail for us. Margaret and Annie taught the lessons and I remember how I enjoyed learning more about Jesus and heaven. While we were working on our lessons, Mom and Dad found a quiet spot and read from the Bible. Mom often sang a song from the *Je'sangBuak*, the German song book that has been passed down through the ages. When I allow my memory to take me back, I can still hear Mother sing #20 from that book.

Auf, Zion! Auf Tochter! Saume
Nicht, dien Konig kommt, dich
Freundlich zu umarmen; er brent
von Lieb,' von Mitleid und Erbarmen.
Halt' dich bereit, damit nicht Oel
gebricht: lass allezeit die Glaubens–
lampe brennen, dein Auge muss jetzt
Keine Schlafsucht kennen.

Arise, daughter of Zion
Do not delay.
The King is coming to lovingly embrace you
He burns with love and compassion.
Be ready with oil in your lamps
To keep your faith burning.
Stay alert, always be ready
Do not doze off, slumber or sleep.

Dad never sang and couldn't have carried a tune in a basket if he tried. There's a genetic flaw flowing in his bloodline and somehow a mono-tone gene had been passed down to him and his siblings, to me and my siblings, and is still being passed down in the generations that follow, although quite a number of his grandchildren sing beautifully. When I hear angelic voices united in song, I always wish it would never stop. I only sing when I'm all by myself and only God hears me, but I'm thank-ful He hears my heart and is not concerned about my voice. I rest assured that someday, way up yonder, I will join in that heavenly choir.

Since the Old Colony Church did not meet the needs of our large family, Mom and Dad sought other means for spiritual training. Together with other families who had chosen not to become a part of the Old Colony congregation, they decided to gather on Sunday mornings, alter-nating the meetings in each other's homes, sharing from God's word, singing and reading Bible stories to the children. Occasionally this turned out to be a social event as well. When the roads were very bad, or most everyone had a long distance to drive, food was brought along and a common meal was shared. It took much effort and determination to meet spiritual needs considering the tedious travel and often dismal conditions in those early years.

The John Gibb family, who lived three miles away, was affiliated with the Anglican Church in Fort Vermilion and invited us to come to Vacation Bible School. We were acquainted with them, as we had spent some time with their family socially. I was thrilled when Mom and Dad allowed us to go. The students that lived in Fort Vermilion went home for the night but the rest of us stayed in Fort Vermilion for the duration of the Bible school. We slept in out-buildings; the boys in one building and the girls in another.

We did many interesting things besides studying the Bible. Reverend Blackstock and his wife, Audrey, hosted the VBS Program. Mrs. Green-field, an elderly lady from England, and another lady, headed up the program affiliated with the Anglican Church Sunday School Mission under the Diocese of Athabasca. The teachers taught us many crafts and took us on nature walks along the river to study various trees, plants, weeds and wild flowers. I was surprised when I was awarded first prize for the best nature study notebook in the junior girls class; a book called, *The Apple Doogan Family and the Strange Shipwreck* by Ken Anderson.

Enjoying a craft session at St. Luke's Anglican Bible Camp. Standing on the right are me, Betty and Hazel Gibb. Sitting in front is Pauline Flett. In the foreground on the left is our teacher, Mrs. Greenfield.

This was the second book in my library collection and finds a place on a special shelf.

In the evenings we sat around a campfire playing games, singing songs like "Kookaburra Sits in an Old Gum Tree" and drinking hot chocolate. What a surprise we had one day when Mrs. Denise Eek, who owned a restaurant, baked a bunch of Saskatoon pies from the berries she had picked that day and brought them over for all the students to enjoy. For two summers my sisters and I enjoyed attending St. Luke's Vacation Bible School in Fort Vermilion, where we were introduced to the Native community. I did not know what racism meant, but the community in general was very cautious of mingling with the Native population. Mom and Dad had no reservations and allowed us to attend. We accepted them and they accepted us, and together we had a great time studying from God's word and doing other fun activities.

Twenty-Three

Birth, Marriage and Death

After much back-breaking work that first summer, 60 acres of newly broken land was ready for seeding in the spring, although it was still in very rough shape. The biggest roots had been picked and the land needed more work. However, for this first time seeding, it would have to do. Dad rented 100 acres from Mr. Pete Peters in West La Crete, about five miles west of our homestead, making the prospects for producing a crop favourable. Mom planted a large garden on this rented land, as there was still no garden plot on the homestead. Distance complicated matters, but weather conditions were ideal – receiving enough sun and rain at the right time resulted in a bountiful garden and good crops.

Spring thaw and the frost coming out of the ground caused the narrow dirt roads to sink out of sight when an attempt was made to travel on them, but, unfortunately, some things couldn't wait until the mud holes were dried up. This was the case in early spring of 1954 when Mom and Dad had to get to Fort Vermilion – about twenty five miles away – where my youngest brother, Leonard, was born on May 6. Mom had to stay in the hospital for a whole month. Dad went to visit her as often as possible, although it was no easy undertaking when the tractor was the only means of navigating the road, which at times, was one long mud hole stretching for twenty-five miles. This took many hours, and often, an entire day. On one trip when Dad came back from visiting Mom, the tractor got stuck several miles from home with the back wheels half-way buried in what seemed to be bottomless bog. Dad had to walk home to get help, and then came the difficult job of pulling the tractor out. These were trying times, but they were circumstances that simply couldn't be changed, so the next best thing was to accept them. There was no choice in the matter and life went on.

In the summer the house was insulated and a ceiling was put in. No one wanted to spend another winter like the previous one. Later that summer a *Somma'tjäatj*, "summer kitchen," was built just a few yards from the house, and most of the cooking was done in there to keep the house cool for sleeping. In later years we found other good uses for that summer kitchen. The floors in the house were raw wood and scrubbing them most often fell to Annie and me. Mom usually had us wipe the floors down with linseed oil after they were washed to help keep the dust down. Dad brought jugs of cod liver oil home for the pigs, and it came in the same type of jug as the linseed oil. When Mom asked Babe to give the floors the linseed oil treatment, she accidentally took the cod liver oil jug and WOW! Something smelled fishy in that house for a long time after.

Later that summer Uncle Frank and Aunt Margaret Neudorf, from Saskatchewan, arrived at our door with their nine children. They were moving to La Crete, although they had no land or place to live. Mom and Dad took the entire family in for over a month until they had a place of their own. Uncle Frank squatted on crown land at West La Crete and built a structure on it that served as a house. He was later able to lease the land. Mom had a bountiful garden, which helped in providing the meals for two large families. Finding a place for everyone to sleep sent Mom on a tailspin. Two granaries had been built near the house and they ended up serving as bedrooms. Aunt Margaret brought out all their blankets, Mom contributed a few and everyone had a warm – even if not the most comfortable place to sleep. In the following summers, whenever Mom and Dad had overnight guests, these granaries continued to serve as a bedroom – but not for the guests!

We planted extra potatoes in spring. In the fall, when the back-breaking job of digging and gathering all the potatoes was done, Dad loaded them onto the big truck and peddled them in the Manning and Grimshaw areas. In these early years Dad butchered hogs and steers and sold them in the Northwest Territories. On his return trip he purchased large quantities of fish at Hay River and again tried to earn extra dollars by peddling them in the community and beyond.

Occasionally, in the midst of the business of everyday life, trials came our way. One afternoon when Jake was coming home from the field, going through the ditch with the tractor and plough, the hitch buckled and the plow came forward. The depth control lever came down and tore his leg open. He had a very deep cut about six inches long and it needed immediate attention. Dad said to Jake, "We're going to have to take you to the hospital to get it taken care of." Jake's reply was, "Are they going to give me a needle?" Jake detested needles all his life and got pale and weak-kneed at the sight of one.

Except for needles, Jake was never afraid of anything, always ready to accept a challenge. The tire from the 44 Massey Harris tractor had come off the rim. Dad looked the situation over and thought perhaps they could get the tire back on by going in circles at a good speed. Jake, of course, was more than willing to give it a try. We were all standing and watching as he was having the time of his life doing something like this with permission, when suddenly the tractor flipped on its side and Jake bailed off. He wasn't even hurt. In those days it was not uncommon to come up with creative solutions to problems before going for help.

On another occasion, some years later, Leonard was the victim of a near tragedy. A wagon was loaded with oats, and we were pushing this wagon by hand to move it ahead just a short distance when Leonard tripped and fell. The loaded wagon ran right over him. Dad made another trip to the Doctor in Fort Vermilion, but Leonard suffered no lasting effects from this accident.

In September it was back to studying again. All our correspondence courses had arrived, and I was actually looking forward to routine. I missed school at Altona, especially the music classes. We had a guitar, but no organ. I missed playing the organ and I had a desire to learn to play it better. Dad brought home cases of corn flakes that came in very large cardboard boxes. I turned an empty box upside down, and cut a hole in it, big enough to fit a chair. I drew all the black and white keys on the box and pretended I was playing the organ. With time, many things that meant so much to me faded into the distance.

John had lived away from home for several winters, working in lumber camps in BC. Therefore, we hadn't seen much of him. I vividly recall the day when he left home for the first time. Mom was pre-washing clothes with a scrub board in a big galvanized tub when he came to talk to her. When he kissed her good-bye she started to weep. After John left, Mom continued scrubbing the clothes, and I watched as tears blinded her eyes and fell into the water. I couldn't understand a mother's heart then but I'm sure God heard her heart's cry to keep her son safe. Lack of communication proved to be very difficult. We had telephone service in Saskatchewan but there were no phones in the bush camps. Mom and Dad had many children but each one was special.

During these times, a lovely girl by the name of Margaret Petkau had captured John's heart and they were planning a wedding. John had a studio picture taken before we moved to Alberta that Mom was very fond of. One day she asked John about this picture and he told her he had lost it in BC. Mom was shocked and said, "John, you have lost that picture? Where could you possibly have lost it?" John grinned and Mom caught on that he had given it to his special friend. They decided to get married at Cheslatta, BC, in Marge's parents' home.

John was the first one in our family to be married, and Mom and Dad certainly wanted to be a part of it, so they undertook the long journey. Margaret, Annie and Jake went along with Mom and Dad; they also took Martha, and Leonard who was then six months old. Pete stayed back to look after all the outside chores; splitting wood, milking cows, feeding the animals and cleaning the barn, while I was the oldest girl left at home to take on the responsibility of the whole household as well as looking after the children.

It was complicated then, with no modern conveniences in our home. All the meals were cooked from scratch on a wood cook stove; we couldn't even buy bread in the store. These were the days before electricity, so kerosene lamps were our source of light. They had to be filled with oil on a regular basis, and daily before the lamps were lit, we cleaned the lamp chimneys with crumpled newspaper and trimmed the lamp wicks so they would burn with even flames. Our water supply came from melting snow, and the used water was carried back out. The firewood boxes needed continual replenishing and the ash boxes emptying. My younger siblings helped a lot with some of these menial chores, but there was still much involved in keeping the household running.

Harry, who was almost three years old and slightly handicapped, was not yet toilet trained, adding another responsibility. We were all studying by correspondence, although I don't recall that much studying got done during this time. As a young teenager, I felt this was a tough assignment for me. John and Marge were married on November 7, 1954. It was my 14th birthday.

When Mom and Dad came home, they had some good news. While driving, they were fiddling with the radio dial and discovered that Peace River had just launched a radio station, CKYL – 610 on the dial. Now we had one radio station in the region that came through fairly clear, especially in the winter. Reception was much poorer in the summer, but we didn't have much time to listen anyway. We got better reception with an aerial hooked to the top of a high pole outside the house. The radio was powered by a 12 volt battery; when it ran low, Dad took it out to the vehicle to get it recharged.

Despite resistance from the community, another school was built. When it appeared that the one-room school was the end of an era in the rest of Canada, it started up again in northern Alberta. In 1955 the West La Crete School opened its doors and Mr. Cornie Boldt, with his wife Maria, who had been our neighbours in Saskatchewan, came to teach at this school. Mr. and Mrs. Boldt also had to move into the school, as their house wasn't ready. They partitioned off a room for themselves at the back

The students at the West La Crete school, 1955. I attended 120 days during my grade eight year. From the left, I'm the first one in the doorway. My brother Jake is standing far right.

MONTH	Days Present	Days Absent	Times Late	Report No.	PARENT'S COMMENTS	PARENT'S SIGNATURE
September				1		
October						
November						
December				2		
January						
February						
March				3		
April						
May				4		
June						

Total 120 days

1. At the end of June this report card will be kept by the pupil. It will be handed to the teacher at the opening of school in the fall.
2. In case a pupil moves to another school during the school year he should get this card from his teacher and hand it to the teacher of the school to which he has moved.

CERTIFICATE OF PROGRESS

(To be signed at the end of the school year)

I hereby certify that the progress of _Tena Neudorf_

during the year warrants his or her assignment to GRADE _Nine_

(Write in Words)

Comments: _____

DATE: _June 29_ , 19 _56_   _C. Boldt_   Teacher.

of the school and patiently waited for their house to be built.

We lived outside the boundaries of the school district, six miles from the school, but with some financial support from the school division to help cover travel expenses, we were able to attend there. Due to poor roads and often harsh weather conditions, we only made it to school for 120 days out of the 200 required to complete one school term. Jake, who was one year older than I, also attended school here this year – we were both enrolled in grade eight. It was very convenient with Jake as our chauffeur, resulting in one trip a day instead of two. On one occasion when we were en route to school, a thump and a jolt left us sitting on the trail like lame ducks. Somehow the wagon got detached from the tractor while moving. Jake kept right on driving full speed ahead, until eventually, he looked back, discovered he had lost his load, and came back for us.

Mr. Boldt was a very strict teacher in every area and we didn't fool around in his presence. He had many of his own ideas although we didn't care much for some of them. He created an imaginary line in the middle of the room separating the girls from the boys and we weren't allowed to cross over. At noon hour he waited as long as he possibly could, keeping

REPORT ON PUPIL'S PROGRESS—PROGRAM OF STUDIES FOR THE ELEMENTARY SCHOOL

NAME Tessa Neiderf   DIVISION II.   GRADE VIII

PERSONAL GROWTH

The following scale is used to rate Personal Growth:

1 – Outstanding progress for this child
2 – Satisfactory progress for this child
3 – Unsatisfactory progress for this child

PERSONAL GROWTH, as observed at school:

	Report No.	1	2	3	4
Self-Respect: Controls his emotions; appears happy and at ease; takes a balanced view of his own work, ability, progress, and conduct; is attentive to sound health habits and personal appearance					
Creativeness: Exhibits some originality in discussions; expresses his own ideas well; shows some individuality in handiwork					
Reasoning: Recognizes problems; observes and listens carefully; thinks before speaking					
Co-operation: Works and plays well with others; respects authority; respects the rights of others					
Responsibility: Takes care of materials and property; is trustworthy and honest; carries out plans well; exhibits independence and initiative in daily work					
Social Concern: Shares freely with others; is courteous to all; is concerned for the welfare of others					
Work Habits: Works with purpose and dispatch; is neat and orderly; uses time profitably					

SCHOOL SUBJECTS

The following scale is used to grade progress in school subjects:

H—Excellent   A—Above Average   B—Average
                     C—Below Average   D—Unsatisfactory

SUBJECT PROGRESS	Report No.	1	2	3	4
Reading: (a) Oral and silent reading					A
(b) Free reading and literature appreciation				B	H
Language: (a) Oral expression: discussing and reporting				H	A
(b) Written assignments				H	H
Spelling: Word lists and written work					
Arithmetic: (a) Fundamental skills				A	C+
(b) Problem solving					
Writing: Legibility and speed					H
Music: Including enjoyment and appreciation as well as skill and ability					A
Art: Including enjoyment, appreciation and imagination as well as skill and ability					
Physical Education: Including class activities and participation		A			
Enterprise Activities: Including the gathering and organizing of facts and materials, understanding of problems in Social Studies, Health, and Science, participation in group activities, and construction skills				A	B

Social studies   *Science*   *Health*

NOTE TO TEACHERS AND PARENTS

The following matters will be made the subject of a personal letter to the parents, or of a personal interview with the parents, as circumstances may suggest or require.   (a) Special abilities.   (b) Physical health.   (c) Conduct.   (d) Immaturity of the child, making the grading of his progress difficult.

TEACHER'S COMMENTS:

First Report

TEACHER'S COMMENTS:

Second Report

TEACHER'S COMMENTS:

Third Report

---

close tabs on us, before leaving to eat his lunch. Eventually he did go home and the minute he was out of sight we all spent more time on the opposite side of the fence than we otherwise would have. Students were always on the look out and when someone announced his return we all bounced back into our stalls as though we had never left.

There were times when not everything went according to plan, and one winter day, for whatever reason, we got stranded at school. All we could do was sit in the semi-darkness, look out the windows, and wait for our ride home. The Boldt's had their mantle lamp burning, but it gave off very little light over top of the makeshift walls of their domain. We were getting hungrier by the minute and could smell Mrs. Boldt cooking supper. The aroma of her food permeated the whole building, as it often did during the day. We were surprised when she came out through the blanket walls of her little kitchen and brought us some food. We hadn't realized that she was in the process of making a pot of soup and some biscuits for us. We appreciated her effort to take care of our rumbling stomachs. Later that year and for several years to come, Mr. Boldt taught Sunday school in the school on Sunday mornings. We attended, as did quite a number of other families from the West La Crete district.

Harry, a few months before he passed away.

My little brother Harry was born a sickly child and seemed to catch every bug and communicable disease that made the rounds. He came down with smallpox when he was about a year old. I didn't think it was possible that a child could suffer that much. He broke out in large blisters that were filled with fluid and pus. These blisters broke open, not leaving a dry spot on his small body. Harry was in awful pain whenever he had to be handled. Later, when the skin dried up, scabs formed and eventually fell off. No one else in the family got the dreaded disease, and Mom and Dad made sure we all got immunized for it. That was no picnic either! The vaccine left our arms hard, flushed and swollen – and so painful that we couldn't use them for weeks. I still bear the big scars as a reminder.

November 3 of 1955 was a day when all our daily cares were laid aside as sorrow overshadowed our home. Harry, who was almost four years old, passed away late at night after being very sick with convulsions for over two days. Someone was by his bedside continually, and it was very difficult to see him suffer so much. He had experienced convulsions numerous times before but had always been strong enough to come back. This time, however, the Lord saw fit to take him home. Harry was a sweet, lovable child and his passing caused us all much grief and pain.

In those days everyone took care of their own when there was a death in the family. Mom prepared the little back bedroom for Harry, closed off all the areas where heat could enter, and kept him there until the funeral. Blankets were used for doors, allowing some heat to get in, but Mom and Dad made sure that we didn't go in too often, although, occasionally several of us went in at the same time. I recall one incident when Mom entered the room and discovered Martha, who was five years old, sitting beside Harry quietly spending time with him all by herself. This was heartbreaking. It was winter and when Mom dressed him for the funeral, she dressed him in warm, flannel underclothes and socks – then covered him with a soft, flannel blanket.

The Mennonite tradition is to dress the body in white with only the hands and face visible. The white shroud that is used to dress the body is extended to cover the whole casket and overlaps the coffin about six inches all around. It's pleated and lightly tacked around the edge of the coffin, then trimmed with black ribbon. A black ribbon is also used to decorate the sleeve cuffs. Harry had no more pain, and he looked so peaceful and angelic dressed in pure white.

Pete was working for the John Gibb family who had moved to the High Level district the year before. Without telephones there was no way for Mom and Dad to get the message out to him. The ferry had been

Harry, the day of the funeral. In the background is the garage in which the funeral service was held and the pick-up truck with the coffin lid in the back.

pulled for the season and the ice bridge wasn't ready. Pete however, had a premonition that he should come home for the weekend. He and another fellow crossed the ice on foot, which was risky business, but they made it without incident. The other fellow had a vehicle on our side of the river, and Pete caught a ride home with him. Mom and Dad had to tell Pete the sad news but were ever so thankful that he had come home. Margaret was on a trip with some friends to Manitoba, and John and Marge were living in BC, so they weren't able to attend the funeral. Ironically, Dad was able to get the message out to them via telegram, but not to Pete, who was only a few miles from home.

Since Mom and Dad had not become members of the Old Colony Church, they were not allowed to have Harry's funeral in the church. It was the only denomination in this isolated community, therefore, they had no choice but to find another solution. Our 24' x 34' garage would have to do. This meant much extra work in getting the building ready. Dad had a carbuncle on his neck and couldn't move his head, leaving Jake, who was only 16 years old, to take the lead in doing all the heavy work. There was no heat in the garage. Dad had converted a forty-five gallon oil drum into a heater and it needed to be set up. Chairs, tables and dishes were borrowed from the neighbours and had to be hauled home. Much stuff needed to be moved out of the garage to make room for the chairs. The dirt floor was uninviting, the greasy work benches loaded with tools and all the other paraphernalia strung up on the walls completed the dismal atmosphere. How could it be that Harry, a sweet innocent child, did not deserve to have his farewell in a church setting?

It was well past the time for the funeral to start but the pastors and the song leaders just sat there. Dad went to inquire what the hold up was. An old stringless guitar hanging on the garage wall was the culprit and had to be removed before the service could begin. None of this made any sense to me, and the rules of religion began to take on a negative connotation. The Bishop did, however, agree to conduct the funeral service, and allowed Harry to be buried in their graveyard.

The day of the funeral was very difficult for me. I was weeping as we stood around the coffin when Mrs. Boldt came up to me, put her arms around me and whispered in my ear, "He's safe in the arms of Jesus." Somehow, then, a peace came over me, and I began to realize that I must look beyond the grave. I knew it didn't end there, but I found it extremely difficult to have Harry put into that cold, deep, dark hole.

After the service Harry was taken to his final resting place – the procession to the grave yard, a six mile drive at ten miles an hour, seemed endless. The coffin was placed on two pieces of wood that were laid across the open grave. It was opened one more time for our final goodbye and then came the dreaded moment. The coffin was slowly lowered on ropes – the creaking noise breaking the deafening silence – into a wooden box waiting at the bottom for it. Someone lowered Dad down to close the box lid, and when he came back up, the rumbling of falling earth began as the men passed spades one to the other, the frozen clods pounding the hollow box. The noise lessened as the hole was filled and the mound shaped – a silent prayer followed.

Several families stayed back and brought in and set the tables and rearranged the chairs. After the graveside service the people came back for the traditional funeral *Vaspa*, which consisted of buns, sugar cubes and coffee. The sugar cubes were dipped into the coffee and then eaten with the buns. The Mennonite tradition is that all the families that come to the funeral bring several dozen buns, sparing the bereaved family the work of all the baking. The simple *Vaspa* was a symbol of a solemn occasion rather than a celebration. Annie penned a poem shortly after Harry passed away.

HARRY WAS CALLED AWAY

On November the third, the year fifty five
There was a little boy who was sick and who died.
Harry was called to glory that day
I know it was God that called him away.

When Harry was happy we were all having fun
When we called his name he started to run.
When we call his name now he isn't here
It's so good to know that God has him near.

He had a loving home, a mother and dad
Five brothers and eight sisters is all that he had.
This sickness was with him right from the start
And at three years and ten months from us had to part.

We felt sorry for him while on his sick bed he lay
Too sick to walk and not a word could he say.
For over two days he suffered that way
We didn't know God would call him away.

After suffering so much both day and night
Harry had no sleep and we came into sight.
Little Harry he died his life it is gone
Now in West La Crete, there's a heartbroken home.

I know he's an angel in God's peaceful home
Playing with children in a mansion of gold.
When we laid him to rest in tears we all bowed
We know Harry's happy up there with God now.

Harry's tombstone reads, "*Budded on earth to bloom in heaven.*" He truly was a rose bud, and I believe he has blossomed ever since he went to be with Jesus.

Twenty-Four

Sunday Social Life

Visiting in each other's homes continued to be the heart of our social life. Sunday mornings we had our worship meetings, but the afternoons and evenings were set aside for visiting and, as everyone was free of work duties, except for chores, we always looked forward to our day off. The Andrew Knelsen family from southern Alberta moved into the community a year after we did and settled in the West La Crete area. Their daughter Annie, who was my age, also enrolled in correspondence school for grade 9, and was quickly accepted into our circle. The Knelsen family joined us in our Sunday morning worship meetings, so we all bonded rather quickly. The Jacob Peters family who lived at Wilson Prairie (Mr. Peters was Mom's cousin) had moved north from southern Alberta as well, and were also enrolled in correspondence school. Sarah was my age, and Eva and Henry were a bit younger. We spent quite a lot of time with their family socially. A low lying area behind their farm buildings filled up with water in spring and summer and in the winter when it was frozen over, we spent many Sunday afternoons skating on that pond.

One afternoon when we were visiting at the Wieler home, Betty, their daughter, who had become my good friend, asked me to join her in her room. She got herself a book and without asking any questions, handed one to me, and we both spent the afternoon reading. The Wieler's had moved from Edmonton where they had lived for quite a number of years and had more access to books than we had in Saskatchewan. They had brought books, comics and other reading material with them, so it was always a pleasure to go visit them.

After a while we started to mix with the young people and discovered many beautiful individuals among them. They could accept us more readily than the older folks, but not without incident. After some time we joined them in their Sunday evening gatherings and eventually we became part of the social fabric of this community. It was the norm for the young people to gather at someone's home – they called it "the crowd." Someone with a mode of transportation, whether a big ton truck, two-ton truck, or a wagon pulled by a tractor or horses, offered rides to anyone along the way and then headed for the crowd. The parents usually went visiting in the evening, allowing the youth to have the house to themselves. It was decided from one gathering to the next where the crowd would be the following week.

We enjoyed different types of entertainment. Since some of the young people had learned to play musical instruments, dancing, especially square dancing, became the popular activity and we all got our share of exercise. On Sunday evenings some of us girls wore skirts kept in place with a wide black elastic cinch belt. Crinolines made with layers of stiff netted material were the fad, and we wore them under our wide circle skirts, which was great for all that 'swingin'. I don't recall that there was any drinking at the time. The nearest liquor store was in Peace River and I doubt that the truck driver would have brought it had anyone ordered it.

For the most part we felt socially accepted, but one incident stands out in my mind. Not all the young people were convinced that a new style of dress was acceptable. One Sunday evening a young fellow came up to Annie and told her to go home and get changed, as they didn't allow girls to wear petticoats at the gathering. Annie was wearing a dress with cap sleeves. The evenings usually ended at about eleven o'clock when the parents came home. Mom and Dad trusted us and never set a curfew, although we knew they wanted us home before midnight.

It was an unwritten rule in our home, and, I believe, in the community at large, that the young people were to be home by midnight. When we did come home very late, Mom and Dad knew there must have been trouble, either getting stuck in a mud hole or two, a flat tire, or something else beyond our control. One evening when the crowd was at our house it was getting rather late when Dad suggested that it was perhaps time to go home. My cousin remarked, "But Uncle Jake, I was going to stay for the evening." My Dad was a respected friend of the youth, therefore they felt comfortable to joke around with him.

We often played ball on Sunday afternoons or evenings and occasionally went on a wiener roast. We, the young people who lived in the West La Crete area, were referred to as "The West La Crete Gang." We could come up with some pretty wild ideas about having fun, and one particular Sunday afternoon was no exception. We decided to go down to the river at West La Crete where garter snakes made their home in the sandy river bank. In very hot temperatures, the snakes in the snake pit were crawling by the hundreds, many intertwined in knots, basking in the sun. We had brought large pop bottles from home and decided to have a contest to see who would be the first to fill their bottle with snakes. We were having our fun when suddenly, a loud panicky scream, accompanied by some smoky words that weren't found in the Bible or dictionary, filled the air. My cousin, who was wearing cowboy boots and tight legged jeans over his boots found himself in a predicament. Somehow, a snake got into his pant leg and was slithering up yonder. There was no way he could get that snake out from the bottom, so, quick as a flash, down came his pants. It never registered with him what exactly he had done, until he had freed the snake. Then, with a sheepish look on his face, he quickly pulled up his pants. We were a mixed crowd, but sometimes you just react instinctively, forget about protocol and let the pants fall where they may. These were the times when you remembered moments rather than days.

Often on Sunday afternoons we found ourselves at Wieler's Creek in West La Crete where my friends Betty, Lena and Annie lived. Accompanied by our younger siblings, we headed to the bottom of the creek, which had a very steep embankment about half a mile down. Usually we went down and up that creek bank several times a day. On mild winter days we went skating on the frozen creek if there wasn't too much snow. In the summertime we spent hours exploring the woods, and in autumn, after a heavy frost when all the creek banks blazed in a rich riot of colour, we took in the breathtaking beauty. It didn't take a lot of money then to have a lot of fun.

When the Buffalo Head Prairie Forestry Tower Road was passable, my siblings and I, together with some friends, packed a picnic lunch or supplies for a wiener roast and headed to the tower for something to do. The tower man was lonely, living by himself all season, and was always glad to see someone. He allowed us to climb up the tower and into the little house on top to view the majestic scenery below; the beautiful hills and valleys with farmland stretching for miles. The vast fields of flax, a soft blue when in bloom, the green hay fields, and acres of golden grain

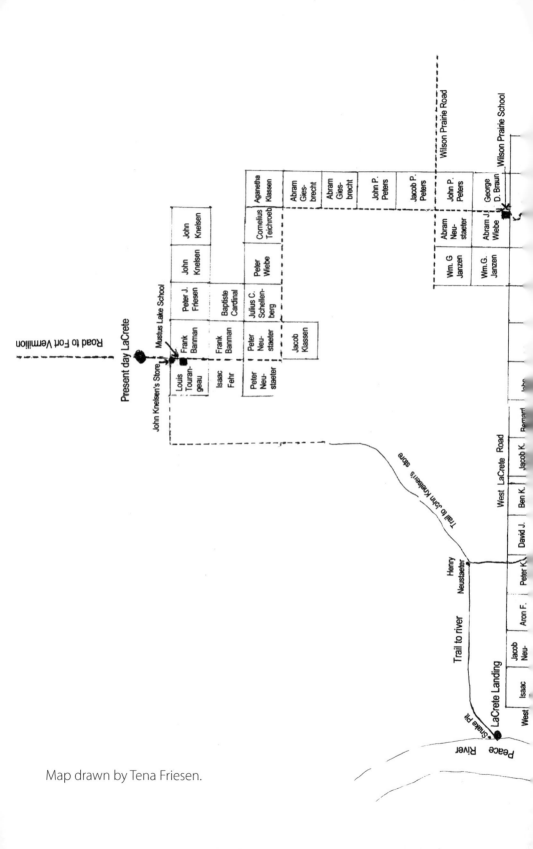

Map drawn by Tena Friesen.

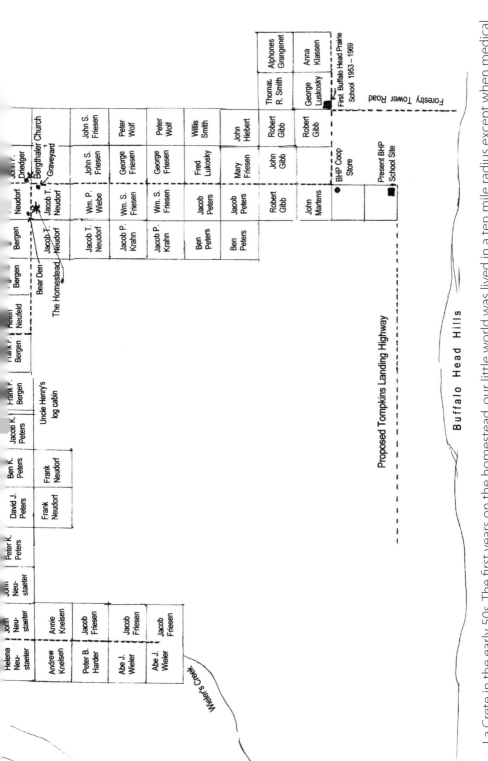

La Crete in the early 50s. The first years on the homestead, our little world was lived in a ten mile radius except when medical emergencies warranted a trip to the doctor in Fort Vermilion or for other needs that couldn't be met in the community.

mixed with fields of black summer fallow boasted a symbol of progress. The tower man explained to us the map that he worked from; how he communicated when there was a fire and how, during lightening storms, he was expected to stay up there as many fires started during these storms. When we came down from the tower, we went exploring in the woods for awhile, ate our picnic lunch and then enjoyed the scenic drive home.

Twenty-Five

Ups and Downs of Homestead Life

Progress in the community continued and two more schools were built in 1956. The Mustus Lake School, the name later changed to La Crete Public School, was situated in what is now the town of La Crete. The Wilson Prairie School was located only two miles from our homestead, marking the end of correspondence lessons for my siblings. Since the teacher, Mr. Martin D. Goertzen, was hired to teach grades one to eight, I was back to studying by correspondence for grade nine.

This was another difficult year. In the fall Dad went to work for Smith Sawmills in Chinook Valley to help supplement the farm income, and Annie was hired to cook for the workers. Margaret was working at the hospital in Fort Vermilion, and Pete had gone to join John and Marge working in the lumber camps in BC. Everyone older than Jake was working away from home which left me without any help in my studies. Mom leaned heavily on me to help keep the household running, and I scrambled daily for time to get my lessons done.

Often I could only get to my studies in the evening, which created problems all its own. The big mantle lamp wasn't working. That left us with one coal oil lamp and a kerosene lantern with a cracked globe, all taped up and covered with soot. We didn't dare try to clean it for fear it would fall apart. When anyone walked swiftly or the children ran in the kitchen, the flame flickered and added more smoke to the lamp chimneys. The kitchen was only dimly-lit after dark and the two small bedrooms were shrouded in unfriendly darkness, but a little light was better than no light.

If we needed anything from the bedrooms, we took the lamp with us which left the kitchen with no light. Studying became very difficult when the pages began to blur and I tried to concentrate in the meager glow of light. Mom put a large syrup bucket or other large container up-side-down on the kitchen table to elevate the lamp, allowing the light to spread to a larger area; casting shadows on the walls whichever way we moved. When the wood stoves were loaded up with firewood, the dancing flames and crackling sound of burning wood were comforting however, and provided a secure feeling during the long winter evenings.

The lantern also had to be used for outside chores after dark. This taped up treasure served as a guide when the animals in the barn were merely dark shadowy forms blending into the night. We had no vehicle at home, and I don't recall the exact circumstances surrounding this dilemma, but whatever the reason, it made for some long winter evenings when the sun set at three in the afternoon and didn't rise again until ten the next morning, before the days of Daylight Savings Time. In our densely wooded surroundings we were even denied the comfort of being able to see the dimly lit homes of our isolated neighbours. Pioneer life made many harsh demands on our family and life became very difficult.

Since there was no vehicle at home, my sisters and Bill walked the two miles to school every day. They didn't miss many days due to cold weather, as determination was a key factor to getting an education. There were no telephones to relay a message. One morning, when the children had walked to school, they came right back home. Mom questioned their unexpected return, and they told her there was a note on the blackboard that read, "School closed, Mr. Goertzen is the proud father of a new baby girl," signed, "Doctor Martin D. Goertzen." Later that day, he came to ask Mom if she would come over to make sure everything was alright, which she gladly did. She had enough experience to know if there was any sign of complications. When Mr. Goertzen brought Mom back home, I went with him to help out for a few days. The Goertzens also experienced first hand the trials that came with living in this remote northern community.

Working and studying took up most of my day, but I still needed some time away from these duties. Some evenings Jake and I, or one of my sisters, played crokinole until our fingers were sore. It was a tough competition, as we sank all 12 blocks in the 20 point hole in the center, round after round. We had an atlas, which gave us many hours of enter-tainment as well. Sitting by the light of that coal oil lamp, Jake and I memorized all the states and their capitals. I still remember most of them today. The correspondence school sent a thin monthly newspaper, called *World Affairs*, which I needed for grade nine social studies. Finding the locations of the different countries and cities mentioned was a challenging exercise. I believe my interest in geography today goes back to those days when learning was part of entertainment.

Winter was one time when the densely wooded forests were a blessing. The wind could not pick up enough speed to cause the roads to get drifted in. The farmers who opened up land left bush standing along the road sides, a condition set by the government.

Mom found Sundays lonely with Dad gone. The Peter I. Friesen's, our neighbours, dropped by one Sunday afternoon and asked Mom if she would like to go with them to visit some friends. Mom gladly accepted the invitation. After Mom had left, Betty and I decided to go visit our friends; walking of course, was our only means of transportation. We had a good visit, but by the time we left for home, the sun had set and darkness veiled the landscape. The temperature had dropped considerably and we were cold. We hadn't walked very far when we noticed a light coming and hoped it would be the Friesen's and Mom. It was, but what a disappointment we experienced when they motored right past us. Mom, of course, wasn't aware that Betty and I had ventured out to visit friends.

I detested the dark, and we were still about two miles from home. It was a calm, crisp, clear night, with millions of stars gleaming across the heavens, the constellations easily visible. Shortly, a half-moon appeared, filtering its light through the tall trees, and the flickering aurora borealis gave us some light, but I was scared spit-less. Wild animals roamed freely, and I was afraid we would meet up with one or two. As we were walking, trees were snapping in the forest from the extreme cold, and at times it felt like my heart would stop. When we got safely home Mom was very relieved, but I'm sure her relief couldn't possibly have matched mine. I purposed in my heart that never again would I get lonely enough to be tempted to go visit friends, walking after dark. It was the first and the last time.

That winter we again experienced very cold temperatures, which was an added hardship. When the short northern days drew to a close and the twilight faded into darkness, a more intense cold crept in. As the sun disappeared and the grey light filtered through the clouds it revealed a landscape caught in the hard, uncrackable grip of winter. Mom felt sorry for the young pigs on those very cold days; so much so, that she brought them warm water from the house to drink. Spring weather took it's time

Mom and Dad during the early years on the homestead.

coming, but with it came changes in our routine. Dad and Annie came home from their winter work, lifting the heavy load from Mom and giving me the extra time I needed to finish all my grade nine courses.

The date for writing exams was set for the last week in June. We wrote the exams in the West La Crete School under the supervision of Mr. Cornie Boldt. The roads were atrocious, so there was always the fear of not making it to school on time. The schedule for writing was dictated by the government, with no flexibility. Since we lived six miles from the school with many mud holes to navigate, I did not want to risk losing a whole year's work. Mom and Dad made arrangements for me to stay at

We had just finished writing grade nine provincial examinations,
June 30, 1957. From left to right are Annie Knelson, me, Betty Wieler and
Lena Friesen. We were the first students in the community to reach grade nine.

the Wielers as their daughter, Betty, was also writing grade nine finals.
Mr. Wieler drove us the two miles to school each morning, and Betty and
I walked back afterwards. On June 30 I was finished writing grade nine
departmental examinations. Four of us girls had completed grade nine by
correspondence and we were the first students in the community to have
a grade nine education.

My education in Saskatchewan had not been of the highest quality. As
I continued to study on my own, many things started catching up with
me. I had not learned to use the dictionary for proper pronunciation of
words, and due to the fact that I was mostly reading and not hearing the
proper pronunciation, some words that were not in my everyday vocabulary came out sounding more like John Chretien when he tries to speak
English. For Italian I would say "It a lin" and for political I would say "pol
a tickle." Bill still teases me about this, and I really don't mind. If a prime
minister of Canada can get away with this, was I that far out?

All the Mennonite people shared one mail box in Fort Vermilion.
Anyone who went to town on business picked up all the mail in Box 156
and when he returned, it was put in the labeled cubicles that were nailed
to the wall in the store. I witnessed the arrival of mail one afternoon and

oh what a commotion! Many people had gathered waiting for mail, and when the bags were emptied onto the floor everyone tried to find their letters, heads down, bumping into each other. It was quite an experience to say the least.

La Crete didn't get a post office until June of 1956. It appears ironic that a French name was assigned to a post office in a community that is predominately Low German Mennonite. Even today, the Mennonite community stretching from the river crossing at Tompkins Landing to the river crossing at Fort Vermilion is almost 100 per cent Mennonite.

The name La Crete originated in 1914 when World War I broke out. Since Canada was going to war on behalf of Great Britain, the French in Canada were reluctant to participate due to bad feelings between the French and the English. In order to avoid being drafted into the Armed Forces, three broth-ers from Quebec sought refuge by fleeing to the north and landed five and one-half miles south-west of La Crete on the SW-23-105-16-W5. Etienne (Etna) Rivard laid claim that he and his brothers, Conrad (Con) and Anistoch (Cook) named La Crete Landing: "We first arrived in the country in 1914 and built a small shack at the mouth of a small creek that flows into the Peace River. On the north bank of this small creek is a hogs back or hill that resembles a rooster's comb. It was along this hogs back that we had a footpath to the top of the riverbank. The French word for rooster comb is la crete so we referred to the place as La Crete." [10] The name stuck and when the post office was named the Government decided to call it La Crete.

All through the summer I patiently waited for my exam results. It was in late August when Dad went to John Knelsen's store for some business and the mail. Since it was an effort to go to the store, especially in the summer when you could count on staying stuck in a mud hole or two, it could take up the better part of the day. I had already gone to bed and Dad still hadn't come home. I was so anxious for mail that I didn't want to fall asleep. Finally I heard the tractor in the distance revving up as it struggled to get through a mud hole and then back to normal until it hit the next one. I had this overwhelming feeling that my exam results would be there. Good or bad, diploma or no diploma, I couldn't wait for Dad to get home. Sure enough, he handed me a big brown envelope containing my diploma from the Department of Education. I was more than relieved when I discovered I had passed all the courses with good marks and was able to go on to grade ten.

---

10 *La Crete and Area Then and Now Society, A Heritage of Homesteads, Hardships and Hope: 1914–1989: La Crete, 1989.* Page 3.

Entertainment was all homemade. Mom was grateful for the sheep buck that provided wool for all the *Socke*, mittens and blankets needed for the family. Mary, Bill, Babe and Martha rode that sheep buck every chance they got, and gave the younger children rides, three-deep, until it dropped dead. One day Martha overheard Mom asking Dad if he thought the sheep buck had died because the girls had been riding it. He told Mom that he didn't think so. This may have spared them from getting a spanking, but they all knew the truth and I don't know that it relieved any guilty feelings they may have had. I'm certain that Mom wasn't totally convinced when she made them pick all the wool off that dead sheep when it was already bloated and stinky.

Leonard was always the quiet one in our family, but mischievous none the less. Growing up, he often untied Mom's apron strings or else tied many knots in them when she was working in the kitchen. Mom would comment that he was like a mosquito that she couldn't get rid of. One evening, when Jake was reading quietly, Leonard, just a youngster, had been busy making paper bags out of catalogue pages. He filled a bag with air, walked up behind Jake, and with a bang broke the bag beside his ear. Jake was just taking a sip of coffee, so he put the cup down on the table and then jumped up and faked surprise. Leonard was so upset that he slapped his face. This time Jake was genuinely surprised and didn't waste any time in responding.

As a young girl, Martha challenged anyone who crossed her path. Martha and Leonard were always playing together, and when Jake bought a BB gun for Leonard and not one for her, she was very upset. This was evident when she took that BB gun and shot Jake in the behind. Annie and I were busy washing the floor when Martha came dashing for cover with Jake in close pursuit. We had a hard and fast rule that nobody came in until we were done washing the floor. Martha managed to sneak through. Jake didn't! We stopped him in his tracks which didn't make us very popular with him either. He always found a way to get even, and I'm certain payday came later.

Making our own entertainment could be painful at times and have lasting effects. Betty and I were having a wrestling match on the summer kitchen floor, as we often did. This time she flipped me and I went flying, knocking the breath out of me. Dad and John were observing our wrestling session and quickly came to my aid. They worked on me for quite some time before I was breathing normally again. Though I was in a lot of pain for several months, it appeared that I would be okay without a visit to the doctor. Unfortunately that was not the case. My whole rib cage had

I'm feeding one of the bear cubs, Mom writing a letter, May 1957.

shifted although that wasn't discovered until years later. It's been my thorn in the flesh ever since.

Pete had filed on a homestead that bordered Mom and Dad's property, and the land was in the process of being cleared. As the brush-cutter was cutting down trees and uprooting them, the operator was shocked when he opened a bear den. The mother bear was still in the depths of her hibernation and did not wake up with all the noise of the big machine and all the commotion going on. It was the 17th of March and the mother bear had already given birth to two baby cubs that were busy nursing. Pete quickly went home to get a gun. They had no choice but to allow the mother bear to continue sleeping but they brought the cubs home and they became real pets. Their behaviour was so much like a baby's, sleeping for hours when warm and fed. Often times the feeding fell to Jake and me, and we really didn't mind. One Sunday night when Jake and I had come home from "the crowd," the bears were sleeping peacefully, so we decided to go to sleep as well, not realizing the bears had not been fed before bedtime. When we had nicely fallen asleep, the cubs began to whimper, and then cry, and after a short while they meant business. It wasn't as simple as just getting up and giving them a bottle. We had to build a fire in the wood cook stove which took a long time to heat up, then warm up the milk and feed them, so we lost a lot of precious sleep.

When the bears went to sleep after being fed, it was difficult to wake them up. Mr. Pete Peters, Mom's cousin, was very interested in the bears and frequently came over to watch them. He mentioned that instinctively the smell of smoke would always wake the bears. Mr. Peters, being a smoker, held his cigarette close to the bears' noses and immediately they were awake.

Near the end of June, Mr. Nafziger asked if he could bring all the students from the Buffalo Head Prairie School to our house to see the bears. He asked if we would consider feeding them while they were there, which of course we did. They stayed around for quite some time watching the bears, and I believe every student enjoyed this particular field trip.

As the bears grew, there was more work involved in looking after them and there was also a cost involved. Dad brought home 25 pound bags of rolled oats, which we cooked up for them. They were getting more difficult to handle as they started to roam

Buffalo Head Prairie School students watching me feed the bear cubs.

the yard freely; forever chasing the chickens, following them into the hen house. There was a big tree right beside the summer kitchen that Mom was very protective of, and the bears would continually climb up the tree, often breaking branches in the process as they made their way onto the roof of the summer kitchen. The bears were starting to play rougher every day, and the younger children were often crying because the bears had hurt them, leaving black and blue marks as evidence. The time had come to search for a solution.

The Western Producer was still making its way in to our home. I checked out their Animal and Zoo section and found the names and addresses of three zoos listed. I wrote letters to each one and told them we had two bear cubs that needed a home. The zoo in Calgary, Alberta was not interested. The other two, one in Yorkton, Saskatchewan, and another one in Kenora, Ontario, were interested and open to accepting the bear cubs. In their reply they advised us to check with Alberta regulations for shipment of the bears out of the province. I checked it out and was informed that we were not allowed to ship them across the border. We knew we could not release them into the wild, as they had not learned to fear man and their chance for survival would be very limited.

In July, when the bear cubs were four months old, Mom and Dad took us back to Saskatchewan for a holiday, and without Dad letting any one of us know, he had made arrangements for Pete and Jake, who stayed back, to take care of the bears while we were away. One night on this vacation I had a vivid dream that the bears had died, and I knew within my spirit that the bears would not be there when we returned home. And they weren't. Pete and Jake had been unable to carry through with their assignment and asked their cousin to do the job. They chose the cow pasture behind the barn for the burial ground. My sisters and I frequently went to visit their graves. I suppose I hadn't realized how closely I had bonded with these beautiful animals and couldn't help feeling that their trust in us had been betrayed. But under the circumstances, it was the kindest thing to do.

Mom and Dad's social life consisted mainly of visiting friends, and Mom frequently invited friends over for a meal, usually for Sunday dinner. She was busy preparing food one Saturday to have people over the next day, and she was making a special desert. She baked pie shells and cooked an apple pie filling which, when cold, she put into the pie shells, and then topped them with whipped cream. Mom put the cooked pie filling outside, beside the house, to cool. There was still some snow on the ground – a good place when there was no fridge. We had piglets running loose that hadn't ventured near the house before, but when Mom heard a commotion, she went outside to check and discovered the pigs were thoroughly enjoying her apple pie filling. How utterly disappointed she was; all that hard work and nothing to show for it. Since there wasn't the means to have dessert often, we had all looked forward to this special treat, although her guests were none the wiser.

The boys got the chance to learn how to drive the pick-up truck, but I guess Dad didn't think it was all that important for the rest of us. That didn't stop me from wanting to drive. It didn't look all that difficult and it didn't stop me from trying – without permission! Wow! I drove that new truck right into the tree that stood just in front of the summer kitchen. That tree was a real blessing! If it hadn't been there I would have driven right into the summer kitchen, and someone could have been hurt. Dad wasn't very happy. He gave me a look that could have killed me, and that's all he did. But I knew what that look meant. I would never try that again! In those years no one had to go for a driver's test. We just went to Fort Vermilion and Mrs. Campbell, the Notary Public, issued a license allowing us to drive legally, but only for a 100 mile radius. Unfortunately, accidents could and did happen within those 100 miles!

Our clothes were all wearing thin, as we had only a few. Annie and I had allowed our desires to get the better of us when we dug out the Eaton's catalog and each ordered a dress. We knew we had no business doing this without permission. Dad bailed out the C.O.D. order and wondered what Mom had ordered that was so expensive. Mom, of course, knew nothing about it. We thought for sure we would get a good reaming-out, but Dad came and gently informed us that we would have to send the dresses back. There wasn't enough money now, was his explanation; maybe later, he told us, we would be able to get some new dresses. He wasn't even angry, as he knew how much we needed and wanted some

My sisters and me in our new dresses. From left to right are Martha, Babe, Mary, Helen, Betty and me, and Esther is in front with her doll.

new clothes. I knew I would never try something like that again. A year or so later, a little while before Christmas, Dad brought home enough material for all of us girls to have a new dress for the holidays. We didn't question his choice of material, colour or design – we just gladly sewed them (all the same style – we likely had only one pattern and adjusted it to fit each one of us) and proudly wore them and even had a picture taken in front of our spindly Christmas tree. In those days people quit spending when they ran out of money!

Mom was always thankful when we had a cow that produced enough milk for the family. Dad had purchased a cow named Nancy, and she provided a good supply of milk, cream, butter and cottage cheese. Annie and I hated to milk this cow, as it took everything we had to squeeze the milk out of her. Her teats were as hard as a broomstick, and I'm sure we had built up enough muscles in our arms to compete with body builders. At milking time one morning, when we got to the barn yard, we found Nancy lying on her back having turned her hooves up for good. Mom was devastated, and it was one of the few times I saw my mother cry. Annie and I felt relieved and guilty at the same time. We reasoned there had to be an easier way of getting milk. It wasn't until 50 years later that Bill told us at a family gathering what had actually happened to that cow. Mom had asked him to take her into the barn for the night, and he had not been obedient. Nancy slipped and fell on a patch of ice, landed on her back, couldn't get up, and thereby met her fate.

Churning the butter held a sense of satisfaction for Mom, as she was always thankful when she had saved up enough cream to make butter. Mom and Dad had commitments one afternoon, leaving Annie and me in charge of the big job. Mom had taught us to take care of the butter once it was made, how to knead the buttermilk out, giving it many rinses, salting it, shaping it into pounds and then wrapping it up in special butter paper. Sometimes Mom added yellow butter colouring, and it looked like store bought butter (and, of course, that made it taste better, as we seldom had anything store bought). Our butter churn was a big crock with a wooden lid that had a hole in the center. Some kind of wooden contraption was attached to a long handle which fit the hole in the lid, and we had to pound that plunger up and down, taking turns, until we had butter. Annie and I began the tedious task by pouring all the cream into the crock and then we started pounding away. We were relieved when we heard the buttermilk splashing, indicating that the butter was done. We proceeded to take it out of the crock, and, to our horror, we discovered a mouse in the butter; it must have drowned in the cream, although we hadn't noticed anything when we poured it into the crock. How that mouse came out in one piece after all that pounding still remains a mystery. There were some bad experiences like these on the homestead, as well as good ones. Laughter and tears were common place in those early years, leaving us no choice other than to accept whatever was dealt to us.

I don't recall Mom singing very often in those days. Life was too difficult. I do remember, however, one beautiful summer afternoon she came from the barnyard carrying eggs in her apron, singing a familiar tune. Containers were scarce before the days of plastic. We had only glass canning jars, lard and syrup pails in various sizes, and galvanized buckets. She often made a container out of her apron and used it to carry eggs, produce from the garden or wood chips to start a fire. She was creative in so many ways.

A mouse in the butter!

Twenty-Six

This Cruel and Lonely Land

Life in this vast northern wilderness was often cruel, and it seemed like there was always an obstacle to face; when you conquered one, another one seemed to be looming in the distance. We had experienced all too quickly, that the magnificent beauty of this Peace River country was marred by the inconveniences and discomforts of everyday living. In spring and summer there was always an endless battle with mosquitoes, black flies, no-see-ums and other insect pests. Smudge buckets were ever close at hand both day and night, smoking out the house to help us obtain some peace, but, despite our efforts, our rest lasted only for a little while.

The ever-cumbersome means of travel, especially from spring thaw until winter freeze-up, created many hardships. Mud holes during wet summers seldom dried up from spring until the frost stiffened the mud in the fall. Many times people were able to pull the vehicles through by building corduroy bridges – cutting down poplar trees from along the side of the road, and laying them across the mud holes. This northern community was situated in the heart of a vast boreal forest, and only enough trees had been taken down to make room for narrow dirt roads. Tall trees stood along the sides of the road; the mighty spruce, poplar, birch and pine all giving off enough shade so the sun couldn't find its way in to dry up the roads. When they did dry up, traveling was a little easier. Many times there was no wind to move and settle the dust that was kicked

213

up by the wheels of the vehicles. It hung in the air reducing visibility to almost nil. We automatically got a natural application of lip liner and a new shade of hair colour. Our noses and ears practically got plugged with the air-borne dirt, and with grit in our teeth, we would remark that there was enough dirt in them to plant potatoes.

In addition to the day-to-day problems, there was always the struggle trying to make a living off the land – hoping and trusting the weather would cooperate. We all learned early that there were no guarantees in farming. Would there be enough moisture in the ground for the seed to germinate? Would the frost stay away and would the rains come on time to produce a crop, and, if so, would the rain and snow stay away during harvest time?

An excellent flax crop boosted Dad's morale one summer, making the future look more promising than it had for several years. On the eighth of August he went to Peace River and bought a car, planning on the flax crop to make the payments. That very night a killer frost took care of all his hopes and dreams of better times ahead. He kept saying, "If only I would have waited another day." I couldn't understand the depth of his pain, but it was etched very clearly when he silently hung his head in disappointment, which he rarely did. Several years September was the wettest month of the year, and occasionally an early snow fall resulted in crops staying out over winter. But despite all the hardships and disappointments, this land still echoed upon my parents' heartstrings, a melody, vibrant with hope and with promise of achievement. Hope is a survival tool for all mankind, and without it I don't know how our family or the other people around us could have survived. We experienced several consecutive cool summers, and one day, in July, my cousin Ben remarked, "Last year we had summer on a Wednesday but this year we don't know yet."

Communication was extremely poor. We did have newspapers and the radio but often the reception was sporadic. There was no post office. When we did get a letter, it could be from ten days to two weeks old depending on if and when we would be able to pick up the mail at the store. In those early years when someone went to the store, people who passed by other homes would stop and ask if they needed anything. These were the days when neighbours needed each other and these hard, simple times stripped away the superficial wrappings of men and women and let their souls shine through.

Lack of communication occasionally happened at home as well and could bring tears of laughter – a much needed antidote to help us survive. Mr. Pete Peters from West La Crete stopped by our house one day and asked Dad if he needed anything from the store. Dad asked him to bring two rolls of toilet paper – likely a treat for Sunday! Dad, with his slight accent, asked him to bring "tie-let" paper. Mr. Peters had understood tar paper and that's exactly what he brought. Two, three foot rolls of heavy black tar paper! We were thankful we didn't have to settle for a substitute that time. Dad returned the tar paper on the next trip to the store. When emergencies arose with no communication, the pangs of isolation were a constant reminder of the better times we had left behind.

The only store we had was owned and operated by Mr. John Knelsen. It was a relatively small building, and he stocked mainly staples that were essential for survival: flour, sugar, yeast, matches, coffee and a few other items. All the groceries were hauled on big trucks together with barrels of gasoline and kerosene from Peace River. I remember the time when all the flour got contaminated with gas. There would be no more flour until the next load arrived, which could be a week or more. Mom spread the flour on cookie sheets to allow the gas to evaporate, hoping we would be able to eat the bread. It didn't make much difference – the bread still tasted like gasoline. Some time later, the Isaac Knelsen family, Mr. John Knelsen's brother, moved to La Crete from BC and started up another store close to the first one, and a better selection of groceries became available.

Education was a constant struggle; it was often difficult to get all those lessons in on time. My siblings usually walked the two miles to school. When the roads permitted Dad would drive them to school in the morning and pick them up in the evening.

There was a lot of hard work and few rewards. We continued to live in a dwelling that was much too small for a large family, although another room had been added to the east side of the house, which served as Mom and Dad's bedroom and living room combined. A small porch had also been added to the front of the house. There was never extra money to make life easier. The floors, walls and the ceiling remained raw wood, which we had to scrub with a scrub brush, often getting splinters under our fingernails. We often moved around on our behinds while scrubbing the floors, getting splinters in places where we didn't deserve to have them.

Loneliness was an ever present companion. I had made some friends, and, although we were a close family, I missed my friends, cousins and relatives in Saskatchewan. I especially missed my cousins, John, Benny and Harold Klassen, whom we had spent much time with. I had left behind the only life I had ever known. One day while we were picking roots on Pete's land close to our yard, we heard a horse and buggy coming, clippity, clip, clop. Trees were hiding the view, so I quickly ran through the trees to see who it was. I thought to myself, maybe, just maybe it might be our cousins. Deep down inside I knew it couldn't possibly be them, but that was one time when loneliness overwhelmed me. It was Mr. and Mrs. Peter Harder coming for a short visit to have *Vaspa* with Mom and Dad. *Vaspa* is an afternoon coffee time when cakes, cookies or cinnamon rolls are served.

River freeze-up in the fall and river break-up in the spring were times of testing. Everyone knew it was coming, but oh it was so difficult! All transportation and communication to the outside world came to a virtual stand still. There was a small emergency cable car suspended high above the river on large pulleys. In emergencies it was possible to cross the river when the ferry wasn't running. Whoever needed to cross the river would sit in this little seat and pull the cable car, hand-over-hand to the other side. People risked their lives when crossing the river this way, but there were times when there was no choice. Often, people crossed the ice when it wasn't safe, and many vehicles ended up taking a bath in the frigid waters.

The river crossing at Fort Vermilion was the only gateway in to the community, and, the ice bridge, depending on cold temperatures and snowfall, could take quite a few weeks to be safe enough for any vehicle to cross. The big trucks hauling supplies had a much longer wait until the ice was strong enough to haul the big loads, therefore, no groceries or any other supplies came in until the ice bridge was crossable. If you had failed to stock up before river freeze up, you just did without until everything was back to what we called 'normal'. There was no water on the homestead, which created the never ending job of hauling water home for the household and the animals, or else melting snow.

With all the many hurdles to deal with, there was also the concern about medical issues. Physically, we were a strong family, and Mom and Dad had taken precautions by immunizing us for communicable diseases and small pox before the move. Not too far down the road, though, we discovered that we were not immune to any flu bugs or viruses that would sweep the community.

When the Asian flu swept the land and found its way into our home, it hit hard and no one in our household was spared. This flu bug was unforgiving and had to run its course, which lasted well over a week. I was the oldest one at home at the time, taking on the responsibility to help as much as possible. When Mom and I were the only ones still upright and both of us quite sick already, Mom felt the need to make some chicken noodle soup. No one felt like eating, but she reasoned that if she made some soup, maybe the children would start to eat and then start to improve. It wasn't like opening a package of Lipton's chicken noodle soup, adding contents to boiling water and serving. We had never heard of packaged soup. Mom had to boil the chicken, make the noodle dough, then cut all the noodles by hand. I helped her as much as I could, and when the soup was done, I asked her if I could lie down for just a little while, then I would help her again. It was more than a week until I was upright, and needless to say, Mom went down shortly after I did. Dad, who was also sick in bed, knew that once Mom wasn't able to take care of us, we were all in serious trouble. She was the strong one, and every one depended on her in times like these.

Margaret was working away from home and didn't know about our sad household until she came home for the weekend. I doubt if Mom and Dad had ever been more thankful to see one of their children's faces. Margaret dug right in and did what had to be done to get all of us through this and back on our feet. The first thing she did was fire up the *Mie'a'grope*, and shovel snow into it to replenish the water supply. I don't recall that going to see a doctor was even mentioned. The nearest medical help was about twenty five miles away. It was winter time with only a pick-up truck and no one in any condition to drive it. We were ten people all down at the same time, making for a very difficult experience. It took a long time for everyone to fully recover, but thankfully Margaret didn't succumb to it.

When Helen came down with abdominal pains one afternoon, Mom and Dad thought it was likely a stomach flu, which in time would go away. Her pain didn't let up, justifying another trip to the doctor in Fort Vermilion. The doctor diagnosed appendicitis and proceeded to perform the surgery, only to discover her appendix had already ruptured. The hospital and the doctor were not equipped to deal with this emergency. Therefore, he stitched her back up and then ordered a mercy flight from Edmonton. Mom was terrified of flying but she didn't hesitate to accompany Helen on the flight. When the plane landed in Edmonton it caught on fire, which did nothing to ease her fears, but every thing turned out alright.

There was no stability for our spiritual training considering there was no pastor or central meeting place. Mom and Dad, together with the few other families that were in the same situation, banded together and strengthened and encouraged each other in the faith. Mom and Dad's faith never wavered. It was faith that proved to be enough, time and again when the going was so difficult and there was no other place to turn but to the Lord. It was by their example that I learned to be strong.

The pain of all the hardships and disappointments of life in this cruel and lonely land have faded with time, but the memories have never vanished.

Twenty-Seven

A Time of Testing

It was a beautiful morning for September; the changing leaves had already heralded the coming of autumn. An early frost had changed the colour of the landscape; all the birch and poplar trees and small brush surrounding the yard had turned from various shades of green to the brilliant autumn colours of yellows, gold and crimson. Here and there, dark green clumps of spruce and pine contrasted with the summer-browned grass and the golden grain fields rippling in the breeze. The warm sunshine, a soft gentle wind tapping the leaves, and the sighs through the birches created an atmosphere of peace and tranquility and the promise of a good day ahead.

As the years went by it appeared that life was getting a little easier. Either that, or we were slowly adapting to this way of life. For the most part, our family had learned to accept the things we could not change, and this beautiful September day would be a test of that, especially for Mom. Jake had gone up the road with the tractor and wagon to fetch several barrels of water from the ditch. Mom needed water in the house, and after Jake got back she went to get a bucket of water and somehow, misstepping when she climbed down from the wagon, fell and broke her foot. Dad took her to the doctor in Fort Vermilion, who examined the injury and assured them there were no broken bones. He ordered her to use ice packs and then sent her home. The next day Mom's foot and part of her leg were black and blue and her pain was almost unbearable. She couldn't possibly bear any weight on that leg, and, many weeks later, when her pain subsided somewhat, she started using a chair to get around, resting her knee on the chair, then dragging it around the house to do her work.

This accident affected me very much. I was taking grade ten by correspondence, and being the oldest one at home, much of the responsibility fell on me. My siblings were all attending school except for Leonard, who was a preschooler, and Betty, who had finished grade eight. With this added burden in the home, it had all the makings of another difficult year ahead. It was definitely going to be a test for my time, as I was determined to finish grade ten in one year. It would be a test of my availability, endurance, and strength. Would I have the ability to master the grade ten program on my own with so little time?

In early January, Dad took Mom to the hospital in Fairview. Dr. Julius and Dr. Hannah Kratz, a team of doctors who had practiced medicine in Fort Vermilion for quite a number of years, had left to continue their work in Fairview. Since Mom had put her trust in them when Leonard was born, Dad decided to take her to Fairview, where baby Esther arrived on January 7, 1958. The doctors took care of Mom's foot immediately and discovered that numerous bones had been broken and had healed without being set. He put a cast on her foot, and, after about a month she was able to come home. Before Mom left for home, the Kratz's presented her with a beautiful dress, which she loved and wore until it was threadbare. She appreciated their kindness.

At this time, Margaret quit her job at the post office and came home to help out. With a new baby and needing a chair to get around, this was definitely a time of testing for Mom's endurance and patience. It was a full year before she was able to bear any weight on that foot, and it bothered her all the rest of her life.

With Margaret coming home to help out, I was able to spend more time studying, and I was able to finish all my courses in time to write the exams. When my results came in, I was pleased that I had passed in every subject and was promoted to grade eleven. Difficult circumstances at home with Mom being physically limited, a heavy workload, a new baby and all the younger children to care for as well, made me decide to take a year off from my studies. Although I had thought it through very carefully, I found it very difficult to make this decision. Chances were Mom would never need my help more, and I felt I had some time on my side. I must have been stressed but didn't recognize it at the time – in times of need we all did what needed to be done.

As teenagers my friends and I were longing to reach outside our shells but I had made a conscious decision to wait another year. Betty Wieler and Annie Knelsen applied for work at the hospital in Fort Vermilion and were fortunate enough to get hired. Lena Friesen went to work at the hospital in Peace River. She died tragically a few years later, and I lost a good friend. We had spent many hours sharing our woes and dreaming of a brighter future. We were tender roots – transplanted onto foreign soil – and there were times when we didn't know if we could survive. Life was very trying for young teens who had tasted of another world.

I would have liked to get a job for the summer as well, but I was committed to help out at home, and it gave me time to re-evaluate my situation. I knew I wanted to continue studying, but there were no guarantees at this point. Jake felt sorry for me when I stayed back. He knew how much I wanted to learn how to type, so he spent $50.00 of his hard-earned cash and ordered a typewriter for me from the mail order catalogue. That typewriter meant so much to me that I have never parted with it.

Although I was under a lot less stress, the gears in my mind were at full speed ahead. I knew I needed to finish high school to reach the goal I had set for myself. I had my sights set high – at least under the circumstances, I thought they were high. I wanted to be a teacher. I didn't think that I could tackle grade eleven on my own, which led me to pursue other options. I applied to

As a 16 year old, I wondered what the future would hold.

Rosthern Junior College in Rosthern, Saskatchewan, to finish my high school. Some of my cousins and school friends from Altona had chosen this college to finish their education, making me believe it would be a good choice. I wrote a letter to the college inquiring about requirements and conditions, and they sent me their information package. When I finished going through it, I knew it wasn't even an option. There was room and board to pay as well as tuition, the cost of the trip to Saskatchewan and numerous other expenses. These costs were much too high for Mom and Dad's income, as they were still struggling financially. After thinking it over, I laid that idea to rest. I would not give up my dream, although I didn't know how I was going to accomplish it, or when, or where.

A federal election was coming up on March 31, 1958. Dad was interested in politics and paid close attention to up-coming events. Election campaigns were under way in our community, and he attended most of the meetings. One night, Mr. Gerald "Ged" Baldwin who was running for the Progressive Conservative Party in the Peace River Riding, came to deliver his campaign speech. Dad, being a staunch conservative, couldn't possibly miss this meeting. I had also taken a keen interest in politics; perhaps Dad influenced me, but I was also studying world and current affairs in my social studies courses and found them extremely interesting. Margaret and I decided to accompany Dad to this meeting. There were only a handful of people in attendance, as the majority of people in the community did not support voting due to religious convictions and, therefore, did not take part in any political activity. Their reasoning was that they wanted to keep church and state separate. Since the few people that attended the meeting were mainly conservative supporters, there was no long question period. Mr. Baldwin revealed his platform, how he intended to implement it, and that basically took care of the business meeting.

We sat around and visited for awhile as it was still early in the evening. During the course of our conversation, I told Mr. Baldwin about my dream of finishing high school and becoming a teacher, but at the present time I could not see my way through financially. He must have been sensitive to the desires of my heart for, before the evening was over, he had struck me a deal. He told me they had a two-year-old son and due to their busy schedule in public life, they very often needed a baby sitter. He offered me room and board in exchange for baby-sitting and light housekeeping after school and on Saturdays. I felt confident that I was highly qualified for both. I knew that this assignment would take up much of my time, but I was very efficient, which led me to believe I would be able to handle the workload on top of any homework I would have. I was willing to give it a try.

Dad got in touch with the Fort Vermilion School Division regarding me leaving the community to finish school. They informed him that the Division would pay $1.00 per day for any student leaving the School Division to continue their education. This was an added blessing, and I think I was the happiest girl around. In later years, Helen and Mary chose to go to Manning to finish their schooling, and Babe was in the first high school graduating class in La Crete in 1966, with six students graduating.

It was during these years when I was struggling so much to get an education that a group of people in the community were struggling just as hard to avoid it. School attendance had become compulsory in the Fort Vermilion School Division. Many parents still refused to send their children to school, resulting in the government cutting off their Family Allowance cheques. It was time for change. Some people felt the government was controlling their lives, which in turn would change their way of life. It was time to move on. Once again history was repeating itself. Whenever Mennonites felt their way of life, their traditions and culture were threatened, they sought to move to remote areas far removed from civilization.

In the mid 1950s, land shortage in the Chihuahua colonies of Mexico, where the Mennonites had settled in the early 1920s, was becoming a problem. In a private conversation, Peter H. W. Wiebe, an Old Colony Mennonite from Mexico had with the U.S. Vice-Consul, C. Juarez, he discovered that land might be available in British Honduras. In 1957 a number of delegations discovered that the British were willing to guarantee satisfactory conditions and that large blocks of land were available. By the spring of 1958 migration via truck and train was underway. Over 130,000 acres of land were purchased by Old Colony Mennonites and, in time, over 200 families settled to found the Shipyard and Blue Creek Colonies. [11]

It was during this time period that more than 30 families from the La Crete area, who were troubled with the new wave of progress, targeted British Honduras in Central America as a refuge. Other Mennonites had paved the way, and with British Honduras being a British colony, they felt a measure of protection under that political umbrella. Over the years, other migrations took place, and by 1987 the Mennonite population in this tiny country had increased to 5000. Currently it is estimated that

11 Excerpt from: *Mennonite Historical Atlas.* William Schroeder and Helmut T. Huebert, Winnipeg, MB, Springfield Publishers, 1996.

Mennonites total approximately 11,000, or 3.6 per cent of the total population of 300,000. They are still able to have their own private German schools and churches, and their own financial institutions in the various communities.

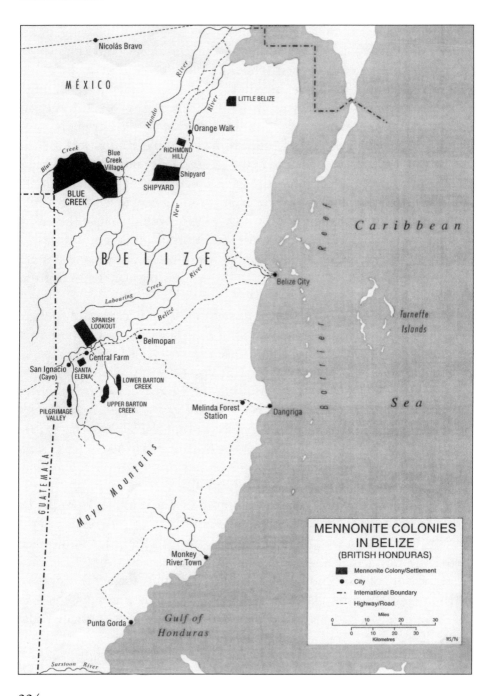

MENNONITE COLONIES
IN BELIZE
(BRITISH HONDURAS)

▓ Mennonite Colony/Settlement
● City
—·— International Boundary
---- Highway/Road

On September 21, 1981, British Honduras achieved independence from Britain and was re-named Belize. The Mennonites have retained their cultural privileges in Belize by displaying their Christian characteristics. They are generally well-liked and respected in their adopted homeland, although there are petty local jealousies because of their economic success. Another Mennonite colony, named Spanish Lookout, is used by the government to demonstrate what can be accomplished in Belize.

In this same time period, another group of about 30 families also had serious concerns about the public schools at La Crete being forced on them. They decided to try out another remote region some 300 kilometers to the southwest near the British Columbia border, at Cleardale in the Worsley area, which is near Grande Prairie, Alberta. There were no public schools in the area at the time, but their isolation didn't last too long. When school attendance became compulsory in their community the school division there was very lenient with the Mennonite families. Since the majority of the students came from Mennonite homes, many of their requests were granted. The school week and programs were modified so their school week consisted of four days to allow the people one school day at home to teach the children German and Religion. The Jacob Peters family, who had been the support to our family since before our move north, also decided to sell and move to Worsley.

Twenty-Eight

Could it be Love?

It was in early March of that same year, 1958, that I met a handsome fellow by the name of Carl Friesen. His family had moved to the High Level area from Lethbridge several years earlier, and they were looking to relocate in the La Crete area. Mom and Dad had heard about the Friesen family living near High Level and were interested in meeting them. When passing by that way one day they stopped in to introduce themselves and had a short visit. When Carl and his Dad came to look for a place to live, they dropped in at our house. It was getting late when they discovered some trouble with their car. Since it was a long trip back to High Level, Mom invited them to stay for supper and spend the night, which they did.

I don't remember too much about their visit. I do recall, however, asking Carl who he was going to vote for in the upcoming federal election. He told me he wasn't old enough to vote, and before he finished answering me, the expression on his face told me he had given himself away. He was under 21 years of age. When the March 31 election results were in, the Progressive Conservatives had won 208 seats in Parliament, a stunning victory for Prime Minister John Diefenbaker. The once great Liberal Party had been reduced to fewer than 50 seats.

One beautiful evening in June, shortly after Carl's family had moved into the community, Carl and his sister Sarah stopped in at our house. They asked Jake and me if we would show them the way to a local farmer where a dentist had set up a clinic for a while. Since Carl and Sarah had not lived in the community, they did not know where people lived. Sarah had a tooth that needed attention and we were willing to help them out. This was the dentist's last clinic day and he closed at 8:00 p.m. The roads were bad, causing concern to meet the deadline. Of course we got stuck in a mud hole about one half-mile from our destination. The minutes were going by fast, which gave us no other option but to start walking. It would simply take too long to free the car from that mud hole. When we got there the dentist had already started to pack up his tools, but he did take care of Sarah's tooth. On our walk back to the car, the mosquitoes were thick and heavy, prompting Carl and Jake to cut willow branches and we swatted mosquitoes all the way back.

When we got home, Carl asked me if he could take me to the *Falafnis* on Saturday night. A *Falafnis* is a Mennonite wedding tradition where the wedding celebration is held one week before the wedding, always on a Saturday. The wedding invitation is a letter listing all the names of the people who are invited to the wedding celebration. It is the responsibility of the people on the list to take the invitation letter to the next family listed. The week following the *Falafnis,* the young couple makes the rounds to visit all the people who had received an invitation, at which time they are presented with a wedding gift. After a week of visiting, the couple is married right after the regular Sunday morning church service. They usually have lunch at the bride's parents' home, and that's it. Wedding's over! Anytime there was a *Falafnis,* the 'crowd' would gather at the bride's home in the evening. The young people didn't necessarily have to be invited – it was expected that they would gather there. I agreed to go with him.

When I realized Carl was taking an interest in me, I was ecstatic. Since there were no telephones, I could only guess when he would come the next time, although Sunday's were a given. It was customary that couples who were 'dating' usually had a date, or would at least see each other, on Wednesday evenings. I couldn't be sure if Carl, being relatively new to the community, was aware of the norm. In any case, I started polishing my shoes religiously, and I made sure that my best pair of jeans and shirt would be washed, ironed and ready to wear in case he popped in unexpectedly.

Pete and Carl's sister, Sarah, were seeing a fair bit of each other, and we usually spent the evenings together. One beautiful summer evening when we were driving around the county side enjoying nature at its best, Carl gave me that first kiss! Somehow, after that, nature got to be more beautiful. The grass got greener, the skies bluer, and the warmth of the sun penetrated more deeply!

On Sunday's I occasionally dressed up, but what a painful experience! These were the days before we were introduced to panty hose. We had to wear a tight girdle to hold up our nylon stockings, which had dark seams running up the backs, and I was forever conscious, making sure the seams were straight. The tight girdle was extremely uncomfortable and I felt bloated all day. I didn't dare let my slip show, as it was a disgrace for a boyfriend to see one's slip. Oh! The measures we took to look pretty and

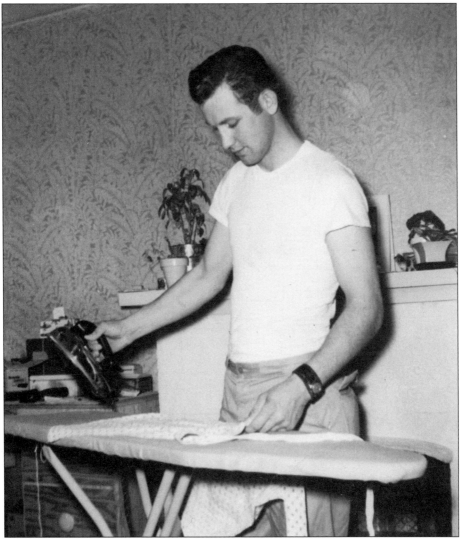

Carl, the handsome young man I fell in love with.

make a favourable impression! It was a different era. I saved my precious "Evening in Paris" perfume for these special times. Billowing smudge buckets were the only form of mosquito control and smoking out our houses gave each one of us that unique aroma. I sometimes wondered if my perfume was noticeable above the haze of smoke that had settled on me. This new scent could more aptly have been named, "Evening in Paris – *Special Smoke Edition.*"

We did see a fair bit of each other during that summer, and we both enjoyed being in each other's company. We had become good friends. When Carl came calling on Sundays, he often had to wait until my sisters and I had finished milking the cows and slopping the hogs, before he got any attention from me. When Pete and Jake were away working or had other commitments, doing the chores automatically fell to us girls. Coming home after an evening out, that summer kitchen served us well. We built a fire in the wood cook stove and made some coffee. It was okay if it took a while for the coffee to get done! In the summer, Mom often had a bucket of half-pickled dills and some good buns, and we enjoyed a delicious night lunch. The summer passed too quickly. In the fall Carl went back to work in Lethbridge. We couldn't have guessed at this time that our courtship was heading for a "post office romance."

Twenty-Nine

Newness of Life

As time went by, more people from different areas who were not affiliated with the Old Colony Church moved into the community, and the need for their own church arose. Reverend Abraham Buhler from Aberdeen, Saskatchewan, who was the head of the Bergthaler Church there, had made several trips to the La Crete area to encourage the people in the faith. In the summer of 1957, Mr. Buhler, together with several other pastors, came again to conduct a series of meetings including baptismal and communion services. Eighteen different families attended meetings to address concerns. After several meetings the conclusion was that a building was warranted to accommodate all the families that were meeting in homes. John Driedger donated the land for the building site; Dad donated the land for the graveyard, and shortly thereafter, the construction of the church began.

Over the next few years Mr. Buhler made several more trips to La Crete, conducting pastor and deacon elections, and he served as their mentor until he felt they were able to stand on their own. Church rules were religiously put in place, although I couldn't understand them. One day my friend Betty said to me, "From now on all the young girls have to wear their hair up." I asked her, "Who told you that?" She said her Dad came home from a brotherhood meeting and that's where it was decided. Our conversation took place about a week after the meeting, and I was anxious to talk to Dad, as he had also attended the meeting. When I asked

The first Bergthaler church was built in the community in 1957.

him if that was true, he gave me a very wise answer, one which I was to learn and glean insight from in the years to come. He said, "It has nothing to do with your salvation." If I hadn't asked him about it, he would never have mentioned it. Dad read a lot in the Bible, and I can only guess that he had received a glimpse of God's grace and that he possibly understood Ephesians 2: 8 and 9. *"For it is by grace that you been saved, through faith – and this not from yourselves, it is the gift of God – not by works so that no one can boast."*

In early July of 1958, Mr. Buhler, together with several other pastors, again made a trip to La Crete, this time to conduct a special service dedicating this church building to the Lord. Pastor Buhler, as well as the other visiting ministers, conducted quite a few church services during the week, and they often addressed us, the young people, encouraging us to live lives that would be honouring to God. They spoke to us in such a loving way that we didn't feel threatened.

It was July 6, during one of Mr. Buhler's messages, that the love of Christ radiated from that pulpit as the spirit of God was moving and captivated me. Right there, in that new church building, I found newness of life. In my spirit I said, "Yes Lord, I want to live my life for You," and I purposed in my heart that I would live a life that would be pleasing to Him. It was always my desire to be obedient to my parents, so I experienced no difficulty taking this to a higher level. I didn't know the terminology then but, by the nudging of the Holy Spirit, I had been born again. I didn't tell anyone because I couldn't explain it; neither could I understand it, but I knew I had experienced something wonderful. Nothing much changed over the next few years. There was no follow-up teaching, and the teaching and materials needed for spiritual growth simply weren't available. That part of my life would have to be put on hold.

Thirty

Leaving Home

My year away from school had not quenched my desire for more learning. Mr. Baldwin's offer still stood, and the Fort Vermilion School Division was coming through with their $1.00 a day grant. I saw this as an open door and an answer to my prayers.

The summer leading up to my leaving, however, was most difficult. Mom had medical problems and spent all of June, July and August in the hospital in Edmonton. Annie had married the year before and was busy with her own household. Margaret had married in January, so we couldn't depend on her anymore to help lighten the load, which left me, the oldest girl at home, to take charge of the household. There was still a whole month of school left after Mom had gone. This meant I had to get the children ready for school; hair combed, breakfast cooked and lunches made. I was in charge of baking all the bread and cooking all the meals.

I had a full load with all the cooking and baking, and was surprised when Uncle Henry and Aunt Helen Neudorf drove into our yard one beautiful summer morning. Aunt Helen brought me a batch of bun dough and asked if I would bake it for her. I couldn't just set the temperature and wait for the oven to be hot enough. The wood cook stove needed to be the right temperature, and it was tricky to put the exact amount of wood in the stove to bake the buns evenly.

The Mennonite tradition is that the women, family or friends of the wedding couple, gather at the bride's home the day before the *Falafnis*

Pete is holding Esther, ready to take the children, Bill, Babe, Mary and Martha (Helen is missing), to school.

Esther and me, taken in July 1959, when Mom spent all summer in the hospital in Edmonton.

and mix all the bun dough. It is then distributed among the people who are invited to the wedding to shape and bake the buns. My cousin, Pete Neudorf, Uncle Henry and Aunt Helen's son, was getting married. Later, when Aunt Helen came to pick up the buns, she thanked me for the great job I had done. They turned out very good, she told me. As a teenager, I felt a sense of self-worth to think she trusted me to bake buns for a wedding. She encouraged my heart and it boosted my self confidence.

Esther was only eighteen months old when Mom was away for so long. It is little wonder that I became a mother figure to her and a special bond developed between us. Esther was plagued with stomach aches, and we, my siblings and I, often took turns carrying her day and night to help ease her pain. I was so thankful for my younger sisters, who helped so much with the housework and garden. Taking care of the children was not so much a problem, but everyone missed Mom so much. She had planted a big garden, which needed hoeing and later, harvesting. One morning in June I remember getting up at five o'clock to hoe in the garden. I recall it being a beautiful morning; the sun was shining and the birds were singing, but I was overwhelmed. I was so tired that I leaned my head on the hoe, broke out crying and went back to bed.

Pete took charge of the outside duties, as Jake was away working on the construction of the Dunvegan Bridge and Dad spent much time in Edmonton with Mom. Pete had as much work as he could handle as well, when he took the responsibility of building our barn that summer. When Mom came home, she was so thankful when she saw all the canned vegetables, pickles and jams. Margaret and Annie came home at different times to help me with the canning and pickling, thereby lifting my load and my spirits.

Since that day in March when Mr. Baldwin offered me the opportunity to continue my schooling, I had mentioned numerous times to Mom and Dad that I planned to go to Peace River to finish high school. Either Mom wasn't convinced or she had blocked it out of her mind. She came home at the end of August and school started the first week in September. When I told Mom I was serious about leaving, she was devastated. She told me she had been so thankful that I would be there to help when she came home. She was still weak and couldn't do any hard work, so obviously she couldn't see her way through. The biggest concern she had was harvesting the rest of the garden. All the potatoes and carrots, about fifty to sixty 100 lb. bags, had to be dug and carted into the dirt cellar. This was a family project and I promised Mom I would not leave until it was all done. I felt so guilty leaving, and in a sense felt like I was betraying her.

I reasoned that I was almost eighteen years old, and I needed to invest in my future. Mom cried when I left and that made it very difficult to carry through with my plans. I left for Peace River at the end of September, one month late for school.

Dad took me to Baldwin's who lived on the Shaftesbury Trail on the West Peace River road several miles from town. When we arrived there, the Baldwins were out for the evening and Anne Sheard was their baby sitter. Dad left for home and Anne and I got acquainted. After talking for awhile, I discovered I would be in her class at school. How fortunate I felt that I had met one of my classmates before I even got to school and there would be a familiar face when I entered the classroom. Anne lived about a mile farther up the road from the Baldwins. Her dad was the school bus driver who would pick me up every morning, and I felt I was off to a good start.

Entering that classroom was no easy feat for me. I felt so lost and was most thankful for Anne and for my home room teacher, Mrs. Mitchell. The dear soul sensed my lost condition and took me under her wing from day one. I found school quite difficult, as it was such a big change from studying by correspondence. Correspondence school was very struc-tured, and I had felt secure in what I was doing. The lessons were set up in a question and answer format, and in order to complete a lesson, every question had to be answered. Now it felt like I was left on my own.

The teachers explained the lessons; I had to pick it up from there and try to make some sense of it. I had to get used to this new way of learning. The teachers were very supportive and helped me catch up what I had missed in September, but at times it felt like I was drowning.

It didn't take me long to feel at home in the Baldwin residence. Babysitting and housekeeping were familiar territory for me. At differ-ent times when they were late coming home in the afternoon, I would get supper started. This was not part of my assignment, but I naturally stepped in and did what needed to be done. Not thinking, I could very easily have overstepped my boundaries, but that proved not to be the case. When I offered to bake bread and buns on Saturdays (I was hungry for home made bread), they were more than pleased. The Baldwins lived in the river hills and occasionally Mrs. Baldwin and I went for nature walks in the hills and valleys, taking in the majestic scenery.

During the course of that first school year, Mr. Baldwin informed me that he had been elected as a Member of Parliament, and they were being transferred to Ottawa. What devastating news for me, as I had nicely settled in. I was agonizing over my situation and wondered where I would go from here. One afternoon Mr. Baldwin asked if he could speak to me. We sat down and he asked me if I would consider moving to Ottawa with them. I suppose I had proved my worth, but this was too much for me to digest – I would need time to think about it. He offered to put me through school; they would pay all my expenses plus pay me a small wage. I really had nothing to lose financially, but I couldn't fathom moving three thousand miles away from home. How could I possibly cope? I was often so lonely for home and my family that I cried myself to sleep at night. Part of me wanted to go, but I knew deep inside my heart that I would decline. I couldn't begin to imagine entering a big high school in Ottawa. Small town high school had been difficult enough. When I declined, I was wondering if I would be left out in the cold, although Mr. Baldwin assured me they would help me find a place to live.

I confided in my new friend, Anne Sheard, and told her all about my dilemma. That same day she mentioned my situation to her parents. After several sleepless nights, I knew again that my prayers were answered when Anne's parents offered that I could stay with them for $1.00 a day, the exact amount the school division was paying. Through all this, I knew that God was truly looking after me. Later in his career, Mr. Baldwin was

Me and Anne Sheard, taken in her yard in February 1960.

sworn in as the Government House Leader in the House of Commons, and I felt honoured when they kept in touch with me.

I moved in with Anne's family and felt very privileged. Mrs. Sheard was an excellent cook. I was a farm girl used to much hard work and her wonderful meals were a great blessing, satisfying my hearty appetite. I had more time for studying; Anne and I often studied together, which helped me a lot. The Sheards treated me very well, and I felt like I was part of their family. Staying with them allowed me to take part in school functions as I could travel with Anne and I didn't have to worry about babysitting. Anne's dad drove the school bus, allowing me the convenience of stepping into a warm bus instead of walking to the road and worrying about catching it on time. There were many positive aspects to this move, and I felt rather fortunate. We still crossed the river on the old railroad bridge which was constructed in 1918. Originally intended only for rail traffic, it was modified to carry road traffic until a separate road bridge was built in 1968. It is still used as a railway bridge today.

When I left for school in Peace River, Carl went back to work in Lethbridge, and we decided to keep in touch by letter. I was always looking forward to letters from him, my family and friends. Carl's letters came very faithfully, and mail days became the most important day of the week. When he wrote and told me that he loved me and missed me, I didn't know if it was still relevant by the time I got the letter. I was especially thrilled when he wrote and told me that he was coming home for Christmas, and that he would pick me up in Peace River and bring me home.

Despite me being so busy with school work, I had been very lonely and couldn't wait to see everyone again. My friend, Betty Wieler, had married and she and her husband, Abe, had moved to Peace River. I spent quite a few evenings with them; any connection to home lessened the pain of loneliness. One day when Dad came to Peace River on business he dropped in to visit me. He brought me a new winter jacket, boots and a pair of blue jeans. I was ever so grateful, especially for the jeans, as I had only one pair. About every second evening I washed them by hand and hung them to dry over a chair, close to the wood stove. Now, I wouldn't have to do this quite as often.

After I had been home for Christmas I settled down more and, somehow, being away from home didn't affect me in quite the same way anymore. I still got very lonely and missed my family and Carl, but I had accepted the fact that this was the way life was going to be until I finished high school.

The winter seemed to pass by fairly quickly with most of my time being taken up with studying and letter writing. I had been looking forward to Easter break and was wondering if I'd be able to make it home. It was no longer safe to cross the ice bridge, and of course, the ferry was not yet operational. I had a ten-day break, and I desperately wanted to go home. Lloyd Northey, who owned a small aircraft, had the contract to fly the first class mail across the river during river freeze-up and river break-up. Dad got word out to me that he had made arrangements with Mr. Northey to fly me across the river once I got to the river crossing.

It was an effort for Dad to make the trip, although 19 miles of the old river road between La Crete and Fort Vermilion had been constructed in 1957. It was only a bush trail until then. I don't recall how I got to the crossing, but I can't ever forget that I was scared half to death of getting into that little airplane. This was a first for me and it wasn't pleasant. Air pockets caused the aircraft to drop suddenly, and I'm sure my knuckles turned white from hanging on. In my fright I had to concentrate on both ends but fortunately nothing came up and nothing got slippery! I vowed never to climb into an airplane again although that vow was broken right shortly when I again had to fly across the river a week later to continue school in Peace River.

Someone made it across the ice bridge when it was no longer safe to cross.

With spring came the last stretch of the school term and warmer weather. I joined the community baseball team, playing for Strong Creek. I was in great physical shape and had no problem hitting home runs. Mr. and Mrs. Sheard operated a market garden, and my love for gardening took me outdoors many evenings when, perhaps, I should have been studying. It started to feel more like home, and it was good to get some physical exercise again. This school year finally came to a close, and I was excited to go home for the summer. I had passed all my exams and was again able to enjoy the sweet smell of success.

Thirty-One

Summer Holidays

It was good to be home again, and I was relieved to be free from studying. A few days after I came home, I applied for a summer job at the convent in Fort Vermilion and was hired. The Sisters of Providence operated a residential school, and all the Native children from neighboring reservations were brought there for the ten-month school term. The first Indian Residential School opened in Fort Vermilion in July of 1900 when the Sisters of Providence arrived to provide educational and medical services to the Aboriginals and early settlers.

The hospital was adjacent to the convent and was also operated by the Sisters of Providence. The convent remained open after the children had gone home for the two month summer break. The Brothers planted a large garden, which had to be hoed and harvested; they also had cows to provide milk and butter for all the children and staff, creating a heavy workload. Cooking and laundry service for the Sisters, Fathers, Brothers and all the guests they would receive during the summer was mandatory. I felt fortunate when I was hired as kitchen staff.

The Sisters were always fussing when the Fathers or other Sisters came for a visit or retreat. We were instructed to prepare the food in the most attractive way possible. We were taught to make roses out of radishes, fans out of celery sticks and other decorative things.

One night when the Sisters were having special guests, we, the kitchen staff, thought we had done a super job of setting the tables. We were instructed to place a bottle of wine on every table. (The Sisters always served wine when they had special guests.) We made the vegetable platters as attractive as we knew how to make them. No sooner had they sat down at the dining room table and said table grace when one of the Sisters came marching into the kitchen with a vegetable tray, disgust written all over her face, and we were in for an earful. On top of the lettuce were two big, juicy green worms, thankful, I believe, to have been invited to the banquet table! They were camouflaged so well they were difficult to spot but the Sisters must have seen the movement. We had been very careful, washing every lettuce leaf separately, but the worms must have clung to the underside of a leaf and then made their way to the top. In any case, the pride we had in our work went down the drain in a hurry.

We all had a good laugh later, imagining one of the Fathers chewing on those juicy green worms. The next time the Sisters did a thorough inspection before they invited their guests to sit down for a meal. I rather enjoyed work there, and as an added bonus, I was able to go home for weekends.

When pay day came around, I noticed that holiday pay had not been calculated into my pay cheque. I knew that everyone was entitled to it, as did my friend Justine Goertzen, who was also working at the convent.

I spoke to the other girls who had worked there for some time and asked if they had received holiday pay on their cheques. They said they never had.

Justine and I discussed it, joined forces and decided to do something about it. We wrote a letter to the Labour Board so we could back up our claim. When we received their letter, we decided to take a trip to visit the Father who was in charge of writing out our cheques. I had the letter in my pocket, in case we ran into any resistance. When we knocked on the door, the Father answered and said, "Well, girls, what can I do for you?" We said we had come to collect our holiday pay. He didn't say another word – he sat down and wrote out our cheques.

Unfortunately, the other girls were illiterate in the English language and after Justine and I left, the girls were back to no holiday pay on their cheques.

Thirty-Two

Back to School

The summer passed by all too quickly. In September, I returned to Peace River to finish grade twelve and get back to routine. I continued to live with the Sheards, which created a sense of stability in my life. Carl was still working in southern Alberta, so it was more of the same – writing letters to him, and my family and friends at La Crete.

Studying took me to a level that I had not experienced before. This year would be a test of my strength, my determination, my potential and my very character itself. It was an assumption by my teachers that I knew what subjects I needed to take in order to graduate with matriculation standing if that's what I had in mind. However, no one had ever informed me. When Mrs. Mitchell discovered the goal I had set for myself, she took the time to set my feet on the right path. I was thankful that it was still the beginning of the school year. Mrs. Mitchell laid it all out for me, and I was in for the shock of my life. In order to enter any university, I needed 100 credits to graduate with two science courses, mathematics, social studies, English and a second language. All were grade twelve courses.

In grade eleven, I had taken all the subjects I was interested in: typing, bookkeeping, office practice and extra literature courses, which I took by correspondence. I was ill-prepared to attain the academic standing required to enter any university. Since I hadn't taken any courses in a second language, I was faced with taking grade ten, eleven, and twelve in whatever language I chose. At this point, I was truly grateful for all

This is an excerpt from the German letter I received from my grandmother, dated October 27, 1958. Beneath it is the translation.

The 27th of Oct. 1958

"Now Good-Evening beloved grand child, Tena Neudorf, far away from me.

Since I have just received a letter from you. I will answer it right away.

Wishing you, your Mother & dad, and all your sibblings good health and wellbeing.

I will close for now, and write back. From grandmother, by by write back.

the experience I had in studying by correspondence and more grateful for my German heritage. I was well versed in the German language. I spoke Low German, and our church services were in High German. I could read High German and was even able to write at an elementary level, so without a doubt German would be my second language. When I was taking grade eight at the West La Crete School under the instruction of Mr. Boldt, Friday afternoons were allowed for religion, at which time

244

he also taught us some German. He taught us to write in the German alphabet. I recall writing a letter to my grandma in Gothic script, likely, at a grade one level. But she appreciated it so much that she answered my letter, and I was thrilled.

I had already enrolled in another literature course by correspondence, which I felt obligated to finish. I was taking Biology 30, and I would need another grade twelve science course, which I couldn't fit into my timetable. This would prove to be a full schedule by anyone's standards.

Living away from home didn't affect me in quite the same way as it had the first year. I was slowly getting used to living on my own. This winter, my sister Betty came to work in Peace River and that helped me a lot. Ben Klassen, my cousin, who I had chummed with in Saskatchewan, was working for Spittles Meats in Peace River. In early spring, when he went home for a weekend to visit his parents in Doe River, BC, he asked me to go with him. What a great weekend that was! It was good to be together with family again. I had really missed Uncle John and Aunt Sara, and the weekend passed much too quickly.

Over time I had made several more good friends at school. Alice Yurkowski, who had grown up at Keg River in northern Alberta, had experienced life in this remote area in Canada's north just like I had. We shared some common ground which drew us together. Pauline Naturkach lived on a farm near Nampa and was also bussed to school every day.

Some time during the winter months I felt a need to move into town to be closer to school. I needed extra time for research – to have ready access to encyclopedias and other reference materials. Alice felt the same need so we began to explore the possibility of moving into town. We heard that Frank Kiseo, who was the postmaster in Peace River at the time, and his wife, Bernice, were looking for a live-in high school girl to be available to baby sit their three children whenever they went out. Alice and I went over and asked if they would consider taking both of us in. They were willing for $30.00 a month each. We both agreed to the deal and moved in, sharing a room. Babysitting took up more of my time than I had bargained for, and I soon realized this situation was not ideal for me. With my heavy school workload, I simply couldn't afford any more time for baby-sitting and neither could Alice. Soon we were on the lookout for another place.

Pauline had moved into town for the same reason Alice and I had, and she was rooming at Kaylans, who were her relatives. Pauline informed us that Kaylans had a room available, across from her room, and it was set up with a small kitchen. It had several feet of cupboards and the dishwater

This is a letter I wrote home notifying Mom and Dad of my living expenses for the month of April, 1961. We made do with very little in those days.

drained into a bucket underneath the sink. The room was upstairs so we would have to cart the full bucket down the stairs to empty it. Alice and I were both used to this type of sewage disposal, although we never had to

246

cart slop buckets down the stairs. We went to check it out. We talked to Mrs. Kaylan about our needs, and she was willing to take us in. We would now have to shop for our own groceries and do our own cooking, but it wasn't a big concern to either of us. This was only going to be for a few months. We decided to move in, again sharing a room.

In February, all the grade twelve students in Alberta were invited to attend the annual Varsity Guest weekend in Edmonton. I was thrilled to go on this trip. The purpose of the trip was to get students acquainted with the university. Registration booths had been set up, and whoever had plans to attend the university was asked to fill out an application form. Enthusiastically, I filled one out – giving me an even greater desire to accomplish my goal. We toured quite a number of places and I experienced a very educational weekend.

Studying now took up most of my time. I found myself staying up later and later, trying to get all my correspondence courses in plus complet-

Taken in the Legislative Building in Edmonton after a legislative session during the Varsity Guest weekend, February 24, 1961. From left to right are: Anne Sheard, Bonnie Plante, Pauline Naturkach, Alice Yurkowski, me and Marie Paluck.

ing assignments and studying for final exams. I had now finished grade ten and eleven German, and I was struggling away with grade twelve. I was totally on my own, as there was absolutely no one who could give me any help. Mom would have been able to help me a lot had she been available, as she was fluent in the German language; in speaking, reading and writing. She wrote in Gothic script as well as in cursive English. Mom spoke English although she never attended English school a day in her life and with great determination she had taught herself to read and write in the English language. She was very sensitive about spelling mistakes. In later years, when we both had the telephone, she would phone whenever she needed help in spelling a word. When the first phone call came, I knew I could expect many more calls that evening until her letter would be finished.

Thirty-Three

My Graduation

Graduation day and departmental exams were coming ever closer. Although there seemed to be no break from studying, there were times when I just had to get away for awhile. Mrs. Mitchell was sensitive to my needs and often helped me after school. She also sensed that I had another need. With graduation coming up, she knew that both Alice and I could use a few extra dollars. She asked us if we would consider doing a few hours of light housekeeping for her on Saturday mornings. We gladly accepted. Graduation Day was scheduled for Friday, May 12, and it was approaching fast. The grad class was responsible for decorating the gym. There were clothes to buy and other errands to run, which took up some of my precious time. I had ordered my graduation dress as well as a pair of white gloves from the catalogue – all the girls wore white gowns and gloves for the ceremony. I bought my shoes for $9.95 at Mann's Shoe Store in Peace River. I was grateful to Mr. Mann for allowing me to buy my shoes on payments for $3.30 a month.

On May 10, Dad came to Peace River to tell me that Esther was very sick and that he and Mom may not be able to come to my graduation. I couldn't understand why this was happening and at a time like this. I experienced a sleepless night. The next day there was a knock at my door. It was Jake and Carl coming to take me home, as Esther had taken a turn for the worse. Jake told me the doctor said that if anyone wanted to see her, it would have to be soon. I packed up a few clothes, jumped into that car and we headed for home.

When I walked into that hospital room, Esther managed to give me a smile, but she was so very sick. The doctor would not allow her to have any fluids, and she was begging for water. She was pleading with Mom to take her to the bathroom. Mom had just taken her there, so she asked her if she needed to use the bathroom again and Esther said no. Mom asked why she wanted to go to the bathroom again and she said, "There's water in the toilet." My heart broke in a million pieces to see her suffer like this, so I switched the focus of my circumstance onto hers. I stayed at Esther's bedside all night, together with Mom, and by morning her condition had improved somewhat. I was wondering what would come of all this, but I was getting too tired to think or even care. I had worked so long and hard towards this milestone in my life, and now I was going to miss my graduation.

As the morning progressed there were more signs of improvement, and by noon it looked like Esther would survive. Jake offered to take me back to Peace River if I wanted to go. I said yes, I wanted to go. Jake, Carl, Betty, Helen and I all climbed into the car and headed for Peace River.

Back row: Ken Broughton, Bill Hibbard, Ronald Sears, Douglas Rognvaldson, Nick Roshuk, George Gour.
Front row: Anne Sheard, Donna Hees, Pauline Naturkach, Trudy Rumbold, Marie Paluck, me, Bonnie Moro, Bonnie Plante, Lynda Macarthur, Alice Yurkowski.

Road signs didn't mean a whole lot on those two trips, and I made it back on time to get ready for the graduation banquet. It was a blessing that Jake and Carl were both working at the same job site – on road construction – and were rained out.

My chair had already been removed from the stage, but Mrs. Mitchell was pleased and thankful to put it back. I was so grateful that I was still able to attend my graduation, although it felt like I was only there in body. I had been awake for two days and a night – I could hardly stay upright. I didn't even consider going to the grad party, as my whole body felt numb. After the ceremonies, Jake and Carl took me back to my room and I collapsed on the bed. I was blessed to receive a letter of congratulation from Mr. Baldwin.

My high school graduation photo, May 12, 1961.

HOUSE OF COMMONS
CANADA

O T T A W A
May 24, 1961

Dear Tena:

     I am most happy to congratulate you on reaching the stage in your education where you are included in this year's graduation class ceremonies.

     I know very well how much hard work, struggle and effort have gone into this achievement, but I am confident that you will never regret what you have accomplished.

     Please accept my best wishes for your success in the coming examinations and I hope that in the years that lie ahead you will make good use of your education, to contribute not only to your advancement, but to the betterment of your community and society as a whole.

     Kindest regards,

     Yours sincerely,

     G. W. Baldwin
     Member for Peace River

Miss Tena Neudorf
PEACE RIVER, Alta.

I had promised Esther that I would come back the next day. I went back home with Jake and Carl and returned to Peace River again on Monday. Esther stayed in the hospital for two weeks, and my mind was constantly with her, which interfered with my studies. Many evenings I studied until midnight and when it was time to go to sleep, sleep would not come. I spent many hours praying to God, pleading with Him to spare Esther's life. Often I was more tired in the morning than I was when I went to bed. During this time my Grandma, Mom's mother, passed away. Mom couldn't even grieve her mother's passing let alone go to the funeral, with Esther's life hanging in the balance. Through this whole ordeal, my faith was stretched and I claimed Hebrews 13: 5 and 6 *"God has said, 'Never will I leave you; never will I forsake you.' So we say with confidence, 'The Lord is my helper; I will not be afraid … "*

I still had another grade twelve science course to pick up and I also discovered that I needed three credits in physical education in order to get my high school diploma. I had had more physical education in the last years than I could possibly have gotten in any gym, but of course that didn't count. There obviously wasn't any phys. ed. course available by correspondence. I was in a dilemma. I discussed my situation with Mrs. Mitchell, who got in touch with the Department of Education; they informed her that in my circumstance they would grant me the three credits. I was at a total loss, however, as to how I could possibly get the extra science course I needed. I didn't know what I was going to do. I had run out of options, and I was fast running out of time.

Mrs. Mitchell often made an announcement to the class, and this particular afternoon, when she needed to get the attention of the whole class for a very important message, I really couldn't have cared less what the announcement was. As far as I was concerned, there was nothing left for me. I'm not a pessimist by nature, but I had explored every avenue and I couldn't possibly see anything positive happening that would benefit me. When she started to deliver her message, my ears perked up. I couldn't believe what I was hearing. She told us that anyone who wanted to re-take a course to raise their marks, or anyone who needed to pick up a course, would be able to do so. A summer school had been set up in Red Deer for this purpose.

Classes would be held in the Lindsey Thurber Composite High School with high school teachers and professors coming to teach. The offer was open to all students in Alberta. The old army barracks would serve as dormitories; it would be a six week stay, the girls staying in one dormitory and the boys in another. I was elated, but of course, I would have to

One of our pyjama parties, waiting for Hannigan's to deliver our orders. I am third from left. From left to right are: Sheila Carter, ?, me, Shirley Erikson, Pauline Naturkach, Carol Preece, Hallia Romanchuck and Sandra Hilton.
Red Deer Summer School, August 1961.

run this by Mom and Dad for their approval. Money was always an issue and they were the only source I had. There was room and board to pay, tuition fees, bus fare to Red Deer and some other minor expenses. They managed to let me go. How thankful I was for my parents that they were always there for me when I needed them.

There was no time to go home after school let out. I had decided to take chemistry as my second science course, while Pauline had decided to retake several courses to raise her average. We had no time to spare. When the last day of school was finished, we packed up our clothes and boarded the bus for Red Deer.

I rather enjoyed taking Chemistry 30 and got a good passing mark, likely due to the fact that I was able to concentrate on one subject for six weeks straight. Summer school was lots of fun. Pauline and I roomed together, and we made many new friends. Quite a number of the girls felt a new freedom. They snuck out at night, and headed down to Penhold to meet the guys at the military training base. Our dormitory mother was very strict with enforcing our 11:00 p.m. curfew with no exceptions. Some of the girls who went out persuaded us to let them in through our bedroom window when they returned. Even though we were expecting them, we were still startled when this gentle knock on our window in the wee hours of the morning woke us up. The girls didn't get caught, keeping Pauline and me out of serious trouble.

We played softball, tennis, and other outdoor sports, and we enjoyed our late night dorm parties and Hannigan's midnight snacks. Hannigan's, a fast food joint, provided delivery service, and occasionally we took advantage of it. It was here, in Red Deer, that I first tasted potato chips when I bought a package that cost ten cents. When summer school was finished, Carl came to Red Deer to pick me up. How glad I was to see him again. We were able to spend uninterrupted time together while traveling home.

When my grade twelve school year was over, I had earned 58 credits. When my test results came in, I fell short of the overall percentage required for university entrance for the education program. I still felt I had another chance. Anyone who was interested in rewriting grade twelve departmental exams to raise their average was given that opportunity and quite a number of students took advantage of it. Mrs. Mitchell encouraged me to rewrite. She had written me a letter inviting me to come and stay with her during that time. She offered that I could come several days early, and she would help me as much as she could. I accepted her offer and decided to rewrite the two subjects where I thought I could gain some ground.

The night before my first exam she asked me what time I wanted to get up to study. I told her I would have to get up at least by five o'clock. At five thirty there was a knock at my door, and she brought me a cup of hot chocolate. The dear soul! How could I have managed the two years at T.A. Norris High School without her? I don't think I was ever able to convey my gratitude in words that did her justice, for she touched my life in such a profound way that I couldn't possibly ever forget her.

When I finished writing the exams, Dad came to take me home. I waited patiently for the results with little confidence that I would have raised my average to where it needed to be. When the final marks came back I fell one per cent short of the requirements for university entrance. I contacted Mrs. Mitchell and informed her of my near success. She contacted the university and interceded on my behalf. She pleaded my case; much potential and great determination - but to no avail. She encouraged me to go into nursing school but my interest did not lie there.

The word 'disappointment' took on a new meaning. I came to the realization that the human mind can only comprehend so much in any given period of time. I had earned almost twice as many credits as any of the other grade twelve students. A quote from journalist Les Brown reads, *"Shoot for the moon. Even if you miss it you will land among the stars."* I had shot for the moon and missed. My future would determine if there was any truth in the last part of the quote. Was there a remote possibility that I may have landed among the stars? It wasn't possible in those days to just pick up a course, as there was no semester system in place. It would be another whole year in school and also another whole year before I would be able to enter the university. I was ever conscious of the saying, *"Today's mighty oak is just yesterday's nut that held its ground,"* but I was tired and I needed a break.

On August 30, Esther took sick again and Mom and Dad took her to the hospital in Fort Vermilion where they kept her for five days while she was getting sicker every day. After five days the doctor ordered a plane from Edmonton and airlifted her to the Edmonton University hospital where they performed exploratory surgery. Mom accompanied Esther on the flight, although she had vowed never to fly again. With Esther so sick, Mom said she hadn't thought much about it until they landed in Edmonton. The surgery revealed a knot in her small intestine allowing no food to pass through, which resulted in the doctor having to remove a large part of her intestine. Esther came home on September 12. At the age of three years, she had already suffered more than many people do in a lifetime. We were all thankful that this was over and her medical problem was solved.

Thirty-Four

Wedding Bells

There wasn't much left of the summer, and I simply didn't know what direction I was going to take. Disappointment was my constant companion. I didn't feel compelled to study any more at this point. I had given it my all and it hadn't been enough, so, after some serious consideration, I decided to look for a job. During these years there was occasionally a shortage of teachers in the Fort Vermilion School Division, as teachers were not drawn to this remote northern region. When they were unable to hire a teacher for every school, they hired supervisors. Students would be in a regular classroom setting working from correspondence lessons, and the supervisor would oversee the operation, making sure the students completed their lessons and helping them with their work. I was very familiar with correspondence school, and I was certain I would be able to handle the job, as it was in my field of interest. Dad took me to Fort Vermilion and I applied for a position, should one come up. They filed my application and assured me they would contact me if the need arose. I also applied for positions in other remote school districts but, unfortunately for me, they were able to hire a teacher for every school that year.

A few weeks later, Dad took me to Peace River to look for a job. We inquired at practically every business in town but no one was looking to fill a position so I returned home disappointed. In a sense I felt relieved to be free of commitments. Mom was pleased to have me spend some time at home, and, perhaps I needed some time away from a rigid schedule.

Carl came north for the summer months working for Moulson Construction building roads at Stein River, Northwest Territories. He was able to come home whenever he was rained out or had days off. His visits lifted my spirits a lot. On one occasion when he was rained out, he came home for several days and we spent some time together. No one traveled more than necessary in those poor road conditions and short cuts were taken whenever possible. We were on our way to Knelsen's store when we met the man who was delivering mail to the Buffalo Head Prairie store. John Knelsen's brother, Abe, had built a small store in the Buffalo Head Prairie area several years earlier, and he had also built some cubicles in his store to sort the mail. This way, the people in this area were spared a trip to La Crete to pick up groceries or mail. Some years later Buffalo Head Prairie got a post office and it's still housed in the store. Carl flagged the mailman down and told him he was desperately looking for some mail, but we were heading in opposite directions. The mail man took the bag of first class mail, dumped it on the side of the road, and Carl got his cheque.

Despite the fact that we had seen so little of each other, our relationship had continued to blossom and had developed into a love relationship. We had kept in touch mainly by letter, as there was still no telephone service available. During my high school years in Peace River, I had been too busy to think seriously about a lasting relationship. The same had not held true for him. He was ready to settle down.

We started talking more seriously about building a home and a life together. I had unanswered questions. Would I leave my lifelong dream of becoming a teacher unfulfilled? How would my future unfold? When Carl asked me to marry him, I knew that my decision would determine my destiny. I understood that if I married Carl, it would be a commitment, not only between Carl and me, but it was also a commitment we would make to God to be united "until death do us part." I had no difficulty submitting to the conditions, as I had spent enough time with him to know he was a good man. He met the requirements I considered essential to build a marriage, a home and a life. He was gentle, kind, considerate and he always respected me. Above all, he was fun-loving, and I was always happiest when I was in his presence. Carl recognized my strengths, my commitment to decisions, and my determination to make things work. Love was the main ingredient that would make it all work, and we had both fallen deeply in love.

Carl gave me a beautiful engagement ring and the stage was set.

St. Theresa Hospital
Fort Vermilion, Alberta
April 23, 1962.

Dearest Carl

Despite the fact that I knew how difficult it was for you to come to town, I waited patiently. I knew you couldn't come but still I waited ---- don't ask me why!

Did your road get any worse, or was it as bad as it could get? I'm not being sarcastic, I was just thinking maybe you couldn't get through with the tractor.

Remember the times when we were only able to see each other every four or five months, and then were priviledged to seeing each other every two months or so - Now it seems like murder not to share our company at least once a week - Times have changed! When we part I always remember the saying - "Parting is sweet sorrow." I better watch myself or I'll end up in the "missing mess" you were in. - At least I've got my pjama's on (right) shoes off, duster off, although I'm only half finished pin-curling my hair! No, not bad at all!

I must go, Carl, and please if you have a few extra moments, do drop me a few lines. It always helps to pass the day.

Please remember I love you and miss you more every day, and if we both work together surely thing will turn out to our benefit, don't you think? I don't want to get carried away so I'll run along and hit the soft spot I start work at seven in the morning. Don't work too hard, Poncho and rest your eyes. Loads of love Tena + o+ +o+ + o o+ +x

Together we set a wedding date. Although this was not a decision I took lightly, I knew in my spirit that if we allowed God to guide us, He would prove faithful. Scripture teaches *"A three-stranded cord is not easily broken,"* (Ecclesiastes 4:12) and this would prove true time and time again.

We decided on a summer wedding and set our date for August 26,

April 25 - 1962
Box 100
La Crete Alta.

Dearest Tena

Just a few lines to let you know
that I made it home alright.
I am sorry that I had to leave
so early, but I just couldn't help it.
I can still see your hair-do as I saw
it when you got into the truck
last night. You were very pretty.
That is something I'll never forget.

Every time I stop to take a little
rest or have a smoke I see you
just like as if you were right
there in front of me.
I hope you get this letter before
Sunday.
The worst part of going home last
night was leaving you, and then
to top it all off it was cold going
home on the tractor, and blacker then
the ace of spades.
I don't know of much more to
write except that we're 50 miles apart
and I love you more then I can
put into words
Well I must go now Dear.
So don't work too hard and
keep your chin up

Your's for always
With all my Love
Carl xxxxx

1962. By the time our wedding date rolled around it would be four and
one-half years since we had first met. Extra money would be needed for a
wedding. Again, I applied for work at the convent in Fort Vermilion and
was hired. I received 60 cents an hour plus room and board. All the girls

260

ate at the convent and slept in the nurses' residence on the top floor of the hospital. Carl continued to work on road construction in the summer and stayed home to work on the farm for the winter. In the spring he went back to work on road construction, this time for Piggot Construction at Keg River, working for $1.80 an hour. In July of 1962, a month before we were married, he had worked fourteen and one-half hours in one pay period and received a pay cheque of $18.20. It was a meager income for both of us, but we had both learned to get by with little, so our expectations weren't high. When Carl left for work again we were back to communicating through the mail. These had been trying and challenging years – a test of our love and commitment to one another. We were both looking forward to our wedding day, when letter writing would be laid to rest for good.

One of the rules of the church was that no pastor would marry anyone unless they were baptized and had become a member of the church. Another rule was that the female baptismal candidates had to be dressed in black in order to get baptized. This meant that I had to get busy and start sewing my dress. I was thankful I had learned to sew at home and that I had taken a home economics course in high school where I improved my sewing skills.

One of the requirements for baptism was to memorize all 212 questions and answers from the Catechism in High German. This was a real challenge for me but I managed to memorize the whole Catechism and

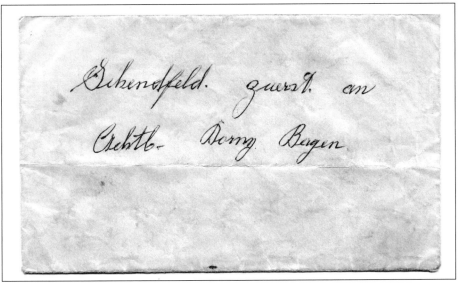

The envelope that carried our wedding invitation to local families

Families from the community were invited the old traditional way.

recite it without error. The Catechism dates back to 18th century Prussia, and all the topics are taken from the Bible, with Bible references for each set of questions and answers. Key subjects are Creation, the Fall of Man, Redemption, Faith in Christ, Justification, Sanctification, Baptism, The Holy Spirit and Grace. It is the foundation of the Christian faith.

In June both Carl and I were baptized upon our confession of faith in the Lord Jesus Christ. Since I had been in a relationship with Jesus Christ since my July 6, 1958 experience, I was prepared to take this step. I was only a baby Christian, but I understood that baptism was an outward symbol of what had already taken place in my heart four years earlier.

Wedding preparations required more time than I had bargained for. I ordered wedding invitations for our friends and out-of-town guests. The

The list of families from the West La Crete area that were invited to our wedding.

local families from the community were invited with a letter in the old traditional way – family names listed in the order where they lived and each family responsible for taking the invitation to the next family listed. The letter above was an invitation to families who lived in the West La Crete area. Two more letters were circulating – one in the Buffalo Head Prairie area and another one in the La Crete (town) area.

I needed two outfits; one for the wedding ceremony and one that I would wear later in the day. I ordered the material from the catalogue and got busy sewing as soon as it arrived. I sewed both suits, using the same pattern, but different colours. One suit was beige, the other black, as the church rule was that the bride had to be married in black. I chose a pretty white blouse to complete the outfits, and they looked quite elegant when complimented by the beautiful Alaskan black-diamond necklace and earring set Carl gave me as a wedding gift.

What a shock I had when the Bishop, Mr. Jacob Dyck, who was going to marry us, popped in at our house the evening before the wedding and asked to speak to me. He asked me what I was going to wear for the wedding ceremony. When I told him, he asked me very sympathetically if I would consider wearing the dress that I had been baptized in. I asked him why I was not allowed to wear a white blouse, although it was alright for Carl to wear a white shirt. When two and two don't make four, I will never rest until I find the missing number. I had a few questions that needed clarification. When I asked Pastor Dyck if there was any Biblical backing, he told me there was none. He clarified that whenever the Bible talks about the bride, the bride is described in white. He needed to protect himself from allowing something that was against the rules of the church. He understood my situation and I understood his. I did wear the outfit I had sewn for the ceremony and, to my knowledge nothing came of it, at least not at the time.

After months of planning and preparing, our wedding day finally arrived. Mom and Dad, my siblings and I, had been very busy preparing everything at home where the reception was held. We prepared a big meal for all the guests, a big assignment considering there was no running water or electricity. Mom cooked a *Mea'grope* full of *Komst'borscht*, many gallons of fruit *Mooss*, buns, cold sliced meat, cakes and squares. I baked a three-tiered traditional fruit cake for the wedding and decorated it myself. I was quite proud of my accomplishment.

Our wedding day had arrived. I woke up early in the morning, and I remember it as being a morning filled with promise. I slipped out at dawn to watch the day awaken. Part of my journal entry, which I penned the morning of our wedding reads, *"The sun rose nice and warm after a beautiful rain. The green grass, sparkling from the rain, received the sunshine with a smile. The earth smelled fresh and clean and all seemed new and wonderful. This was our wedding day ... a dream which we had dreamed for some time was about to come true."* A later entry, *"... The hour of our wedding arrived and we walked happily down the aisle. Our wedding bands, the symbol of our love, were slipped on our fingers, from now on to walk hand in hand down life's road no matter what life had to offer."*

Our wedding day would be the crowning day of our lives where the past, with its many impressions and influences, would blend the hopes and ideals of the future. The meeting of past and future would make the present an overwhelming, emotion-filled moment. We did not know

Our wedding day, August 26, 1962.

what the future would hold, but we knew the One who held the future. We were building our home on the Firm Foundation and trusted that the storms of life would not be able to tear it down.

L & C Income & Expenditures

1962

Date	Description	Debit	Credit.
Aug 26	Cash on hand:		
	Cheque from Jake	86 –	
	wedding gifts	146 –	
	advance cheque (Piggott)	45 –	
	loose cash	12 –	
	Total cash on hand	289 –	
	Expences on Honeymoon		
	Servicing on truck:		
	Barrel gas (Nampa)		10 69
	Barrel gas (Lethbridge)		10 49
	Barrel gas (Grimshaw)		10 58
	Oil Change		10 60
	Rear End		26 65
	Gear oil		5 60
	Total Servicing on truck		74 61
	Rooms:		
	Keg River		3 –
	Valley view		7 –
	Banff		8 –
	Innesfail		7 50
	Total Rooms		25 50
	Household Expenses:		
	Washing machine		20 –
	Silver ware		5 95
	Bread knife		3 65
	Frying Pan		3 65
	Two Sauce pans		3 73
	Carving Set		4 –
	Total Household Expenses:		40 98

A few dollars went along way in 1962

We honeymooned in Banff and Lake Louise, stopping in Edmonton on our way out to get our wedding portrait taken. During our stay in Banff, we rented a furnished suite for $8.00 a day. We bought groceries and did our own cooking. I couldn't impress Carl with my cooking, as he had often eaten a meal I had prepared. We spent a lot of time going for walks

Me and Carl feeding the deer along the trail at Banff.

in the park, feeding the deer alongside the trails and just spending time getting to know each other better. We were used to being separated so much of the time that I found it difficult to comprehend that from here on we would be able to spend all our time together, and we wouldn't have to go our separate ways once we got home. We went about a mile up the mountain on the gondola lift, where our honeymoon picture was taken.

On our way home we bought a second-hand washing machine and a few other things we would need to set up house. We had received almost everything we needed as wedding gifts. Nowadays, I'm sure the list of 'needs' would be much longer, but we had both learned to get by with little and our happiness would not lie in material possessions. We came back from our honeymoon ready to start a whole new life, and life the way I had known it would be forever changed. We were going to build our own home, and I would be independent from my parents. This would be a major change for me, as I had always depended on them when I had a need.

When Carl and I returned from our honeymoon trip, we arrived at Mom and Dad's fairly late in the evening. It was already past Esther's bedtime, and when she discovered the next morning that I was home, she came bouncing into our bedroom – stopped short, covered her mouth with her hands and said, "Oba, Tena, I'm going to tell Mom you're sleeping with Carl."

My life's journey had taken a turn, and as I began to travel this new road, I couldn't help but look back and view all the hills and valleys through which I had traveled. Many obstacles had lain in my path but had

On top of the world. The town of Banff is below on the left.

not had the power to block it. As the scenes of my youth flashed onto the screen of my mind, I began to evaluate my life, and I began to understand the meaning of it, unwritten and unspoken. Ever since I had moved to northern Alberta with my parents and life became so difficult, I had unknowingly pushed through invisible barriers – geographical, cultural, physical, financial, social, mental, emotional and spiritual. That season in my life had been a test of the human spirit … my spirit!

During my youth and early adulthood, life taught me so much more than I could ever have learned from books. I had learned to accept the things I could not change. I had learned to respect authority, accept responsibility and reach for my goal even though my sights were set too high – given the circumstances. Through all the experiences in my youth, I had learned to trust in God and I had developed a deep faith. These attributes were the foundation on which I would build all the rest of my life.

PART THREE

A New Beginning

1962 – 1990

Thirty-Five

Building a Home

The wedding and honeymoon trip were over. Carl and I were heading into uncharted waters, and we knew that the seas might be too rough and stormy without a guide and the lessons too difficult without a teacher. We would trust God to be our faithful Guide and Teacher, to see us through the good times and the bad.

Both Carl and I were raised in the same type of environment and the same faith. We had no cultural or language barriers to deal with. We spoke the same German language, so we really didn't have that many adjustments to make. Our mothers were both excellent cooks, cooking all the Mennonite dishes from the page-worn recipes that have passed the test through the ages. Carl didn't even have to adjust to a different style of cooking. We both felt confident that we could make our marriage work and build a home that would be a shelter from the storms of life, and a safe haven for children should God choose to bless us with some. Faith and love intertwined would hold it all together.

The Chinese philosopher, Confucius (c.551–c.478 BC), states, "*The strength of a Nation is derived from the integrity of its homes.*" What wisdom dating back over 2000 years! Family life has always been very important to me, and I truly believe it is the backbone of our nation. Now that we were building our own home, I felt a responsibility to put into practice and build on the values I believed in. Many years ago I read a poem that I thought was worth saving.

THE FAMILY

The family is like a book …
The children are the leaves …
The parents are the cover that …
Protective beauty gives.

At first the pages of the book …
Are blank and purely fair …
But time soon writes memories …
And paints pictures there.

Love is the little golden clasp …
That bindeth up the trust …
Oh, break it not, lest all the leaves …
Should scatter and be lost!

Our first home, at Keg River, with the washing machine we
bought on our honeymoon.

Carl continued to work on road construction at Keg River, having taken only a few weeks off for our wedding and honeymoon. Our first home was in a road construction camp at Keg River. We rented a small house trailer, moved it into the camp, and lived there until freeze-up when construction was shut down for the season. Carl was experiencing back pain due to running the heavy equipment. One evening he asked me if I would rub his back with liniment to help ease the pain. I did, and since his back was very sore, I gave him a good dose and a good rub. In no time his back was on fire and in less time he stood outside, scantily clad and in bare feet on the frosty ground, trying to cool off. I chuckled, but he didn't think it was funny, and after a short while I didn't either when I realized he was in a lot more pain. I had failed to read the instructions on the bottle just like Grandma. It said, "Use sparingly. Do Not Rub Into Skin."

During the winter, Carl worked at various jobs trying to earn a few dollars. In the spring Dad purchased the Imperial Esso Service Station and restaurant in La Crete and named it Jake's Esso Service. Along with

Carl and me in front of the Imperial Esso Service Station and Cafe, March 1963.

this purchase came the running of the bus depot and, a little later, Dad applied for and got the retail Cockshutt Dealership which he operated as Neudorf Farm Equipment. Dad needed help to run and oversee the business. When he asked Carl and me if we would be interested in going to work for him, we took him up on his offer.

Carl took charge of the garage part of the business, and I took charge of running the restaurant as well as the bus depot and keeping the books. There were living quarters in the back of the restaurant, where Carl and I moved into for the time being. Betty was working in High Prairie and came home to help out in the restaurant, as did Helen and Mary, who were living at home. We combined forces and did all the cooking, baking, cleaning, and served all the customers. Our menu was somewhat different from what you see in restaurants today. All the food; pastries, buns, bread and soups, was homemade. It was very time consuming as we served Mennonite dishes as well. One day a customer came in and asked for a fried egg sandwich which wasn't on the menu. I made it for him and charged him 25 cents for the sandwich and coffee.

Health inspections were mandatory, and it was our turn shortly after we started operating. Everything passed inspection except our water supply. The garage, which was attached to the restaurant, had a well in it and we hauled the water up with a bucket. The inspector asked if we added bleach to the water and we said no we hadn't. The requirements were that the well needed to be sealed off and the water led in through pipes.

He told us he would have to shut us down until requirements were met. Carl said, "Wait a minute," and explained to him how the restaurant in Fort Vermilion got their water supply and he had passed their health inspection. A resident of Fort Vermilion was supplying the town with water. He hauled water with horses hooked up to a wagon with open water barrels in the back. He backed the horses with the wagon down into the river, and then filled the barrels with a bucket. The horses in the meantime did their thing and it trickled down into the water. The inspector wasn't convinced that he should allow us to continue operating – Carl reminded him again that he had passed the inspection for the Fort Vermilion restaurant. He said, "Yes, but they add bleach to the water." Carl said, "You're going to allow them to continue operating and you're going to shut us down?" The inspector said, "O.K. add a little bleach to the water and we won't shut you down."

We had our ups and downs running that restaurant. It came with a juke box – a music box, which was coin fed. Twenty five cents gave the customer four songs. I tired very quickly of hearing the same songs

Carl was repairing the roof of the restaurant. We managed to sneak a little time for each other in our busy schedules. September 1963.

over and over. We had one customer, an old gentleman, who never got tired of one particular song "Poor, poor farmer, always on the go. Poor, poor farmer praying it won't snow … " He fed that machine with I don't remember how many quarters and punched this song in just as many times. Occasionally he brought his guitar with him and sang along with the record – "Poor, poor … " and I got annoyed beyond words. One day I thought I was going to lose it, and I knew I had to do something. Dad was at the front counter and he started talking to this gentleman, who was a bit hard of hearing, so he got up and went to talk to Dad. In the meantime, I busied myself with cleaning right around that juke box and somehow, accidentally, it got unplugged. This man was perturbed because he wanted his money's worth. Poor Dad tried everything to get that thing going and couldn't get it. Eventually he left and Dad continued to work on this machine. Finally he pulled it all the way out and discovered it was unplugged. He gave me that all-knowing look, and he knew I was the guilty party. He wasn't upset, but a little annoyed that I hadn't told him; him working on bended knee for a long time trying to solve the problem. I was hoping Dad wouldn't find out and we wouldn't have to put up with this gentleman any more.

The Con Dick family, who had moved from Saskatchewan to La Crete a few years earlier, decided to move to Bolivia, South America. They had built a new house, not completely finished yet, which they were trying to sell. Carl and I went to look at it, getting excited about the prospect of owning our own home. The Dicks could only take a few personal belongings and offered the furnished house with all contents for $1600.00. We scrambled; checked out a few possibilities and, thankfully, we were able to come up with the finances. Dad helped us out, so every dollar we earned was used to pay him back until it was all paid off.

The outside of the house was bare lumber and all the rooms in the house, the walls and ceilings, were also bare wood. The floors were masonite, painted a dark green, which showed every speck of dust. The house had three small doorless rooms besides the combined kitchen and dining area. I strung curtains, which gave us some privacy. This was a fairly small house – our very own – and we were excited to transform it into a cozy home.

We had purchased two acres of land right along what is Main Street in La Crete today, and we moved the house onto it. We heated it with an air-tight heater which didn't hold heat for very long. Many times in the winter the water in the wash basin was frozen solid in the morning, and our blankets occasionally froze to the wall. Small snow drifts formed underneath the single door if we forgot to seal it off with blankets or old jackets on stormy winter nights.

The single pane windows iced up so badly we had trouble looking through them. When it warmed up, the ice melted and dripped off the window sills, leaving puddles on the floor. We would think about improving things later; for now, we were happy to have our own place.

The Frank Enns family, together with their two married sons, Pete and Frank, and their families, moved to La Crete from Manitoba and were our next door neighbours. They were a very musical family, and many evenings our little house was filled with music. In the spring Mom and Dad sold the farm, moved the family into town and settled into the restaurant living quarters.

The walls in our new home were bare wood. Making music are, left to right, Carl, Mr. Frank Enns Sr. and his sons, Frank and Pete.

Thirty-Six

The Post Office

In August of 1963 a well dressed gentleman walked into the restaurant. We had a few of these city folk pass through now and then, wearing suits and ties on week days, but this particular man asked to speak to me. He made small talk for a short while, but he soon disclosed his mission. The postmaster position had unexpectedly become available and he was looking for a replacement. He had inquired around town and was informed that I had a grade twelve education. He came to ask me if I would be interested in filling the position. I didn't want to leave him stuck, so I promised I would take it until he could find a replacement. Thinking back, I doubt that he ever looked for one. I was the only person in the community with a high school diploma. My starting wage was $86.00 every two weeks, working from 9 a.m. until 5 p.m. Monday through Friday and until 1:00 p.m. on Saturdays. No outsider would ever have considered the job at such a low wage. I started work at the post office the next day and occasionally helped out at the restaurant in the evenings and on weekends, as well as doing the books.

Carl continued to work at the service station for awhile after I left. In the spring he went back to work on road construction until the fall, leaving me home alone most of the time. Neither Carl nor I were particularly fond of this arrangement and when Northland Utilities was looking for someone to run a mobile power plant to service the town with power, Carl took advantage of the opportunity when it was offered to him. He

This was La Crete's first post office, where I started work in August 1963.

oversaw the operation of the power plant for one year, being on stand-by twenty four hours a day, seven days a week for $60.00 a month – or two dollars a day. Every job has its moments, and Carl's trial came unexpectedly. While he was working inside the plant an oil line broke and sprayed everything with oil, including him. He came in looking like he belonged in the heart of Africa, and he spent many hours getting himself and the plant cleaned up. Needless to say, the clothes he was wearing were ruined. The positive aspect of Carl accepting the job was that La Crete had power, and we both had a steady income.

Thirty-Seven

Now We Are Three

April 26, 1964 was a beautiful day and the whole countryside was springing with new life. Much of the snow had melted and new blades of grass were peeking through. The pussy willows, adorned in their silvery silky catkins, were a sure promise of spring, as were the poplar and birch trees budding and swaying in the warm breeze. The robins had returned and were hopping in the front yard preparing to build their nests.

Carl and I had been preparing for this day for quite some time, making room in our hearts and our home for an addition to our family. Money was a word in our vocabulary, but that was it. We had no money to buy all the nice things for a new baby. I had managed to get a large basket and I lined it with a padded material. I sewed some blankets for it and Mom sewed a mattress which she made with sheep wool so the bed for the baby was ready. When LaDawn Lynn arrived, family life the way Carl and I had known it for almost two years was forever changed.

LaDawn was an absolutely beautiful baby. I counted her fingers and toes and checked her lips, nose and ears. I chuckled when she automatically burped or hiccupped. I marveled at this miraculous gift, so perfect, and I felt unworthy of the huge task that lay before me. I had much experience in looking after babies at home, but now the sole responsibility fell on Carl and me to care for her; to instill in her our values and beliefs and trust God for the outcome. Sometimes I find it ironic that, for practically

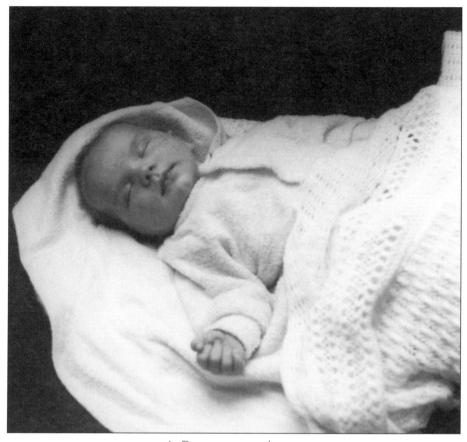
LaDawn as a newborn.

every job, some type of certificate or a grade twelve education is required. There is, however, no requirement needed for parenting, the most important job anyone will ever undertake. We were the happiest family around – at least that's how we felt.

LaDawn's arrival created many changes in our home. I still needed to go to work and since she was such a good baby, I often took her to work with me. I was thankful when Mom and Dad moved into town, only a few yards away from where we lived. My younger sisters were more than willing to baby sit LaDawn and give her ample attention.

When LaDawn outgrew her basket bed, we made another one for her. We pulled our bed away from the wall and placed two chairs together next to the wall. I put several blankets down to form a mattress, and that became her new bed. One summer day when LaDawn was sleeping in her hand-crafted bed, I went to work in the garden, which was right beside the house. The bedroom window was open, and I was certain I would hear her when she needed me. When I realized she had been sleeping for quite a long time I decided to check up on her. Her bed was empty! I panicked for a minute, until I figured out what probably happened. My sisters often came for her and took her home. I trusted that was the case. I couldn't be positively sure, and, since there was no telephone, I ran over to Mom and Dad's as fast I could and found her safe with many baby-sitters. I made sure that next time they notify me of their good-hearted intentions before they took LaDawn. Life was good with a new baby, and we enjoyed her every waking minute.

Thirty-Eight

Experiences in the Post Office

Some of the courses I had taken in high school were now serving me well. I had taken bookkeeping, typing and office practice, so I experienced no difficulty in managing the post office. Most everything was fairly straight forward, except that the post office account had to balance at the end of every month. This could be a challenge. No matter if it was short by $1.00 or $100.00 I had to put the money in. If it was over, I had to send the money in to head office in Edmonton. The account had to balance.

After I had managed the post office for about five months, Edmonton officials informed me of an upcoming audit. They volunteered no information as to the date of the audit or who they would hire to do it. At eight o'clock one Sunday evening, a knock at the door startled me. When I opened the door, a gentleman introduced himself as the postmaster from a neighbouring town and informed me that he had come to audit the post office. As I was talking to him, he lost his balance, tumbled into the snow and broke his glasses. This man came with many years of experience, but something didn't seem right. I clued in almost immediately that something was amiss, as audits aren't normally done on a Sunday evening. He had hired a chauffeur to bring him out, and I soon realized he was inebriated to the point where he couldn't walk straight, but he insisted we head for the work place.

Sunday was my only day off, so this didn't sit too well with me. He was my authority and so I complied. Carl came with me, as we had to build a fire to get the place warmed up enough to work. It was just past the end of the month, and I had already balanced the account for that month. He attempted to do the audit but simply couldn't do it, although, after a minor repair job, his glasses were still functional. He needed to add five digit numbers in columns of thirty without an adding machine. It was a tough assignment for him for that particular evening.

He gave the audit his best shot, but after a short while he said, "Tena, I know you are honest and I trust the work you are doing." So, with much difficulty, he copied all my figures onto his forms and sent them in to Edmonton. I kept looking over his shoulder to make sure he copied the figures correctly, as it was my reputation that was at stake here. Later I received a letter from the Edmonton office informing me they were pleased that the audit had gone so well.

The post office building was crowded for the volume of mail we were receiving, but for the most part it was still manageable. Most everything, other than groceries, was ordered from the mail order catalog – even machinery parts came in the mail, making for a large volume of parcels. This became a real problem in the fall, from the time the ferry was taken out until the ice bridge was built, and again during river break-up in the spring.

In late fall, or early winter, depending on the weather, it could take a long time for the ice bridge to be crossable. The first class mail was flown across the river but the parcels were left to accumulate on the other side until the ice bridge was strong enough for the big trucks to cross. I believe it was the winter of 1965 when the first vehicles crossed the river on December 24, the day before Christmas, and 65 bags of mail were delivered along with many parcels that were too big to fit into a mail bag. The mail couldn't possibly all fit into the building – much of it was left outside until we could get to it.

I was already off duty when the mail arrived. Word spread very quickly and I knew in my heart what I needed to do. Most families did their Christmas shopping by mail, and I knew that it would depend on me whether or not many children would have a smile on their face on Christmas morning. I didn't think twice about this one. Whatever preparations I had left to do would wait until next Christmas, and we would celebrate Christmas on December 25 just like everyone else.

Carl was so good and always willing to help me in times like these. We took LaDawn over to Mom and Dad's, and together we went to work and handed out parcels until almost midnight. That little post office lobby was crowded with people, as some of them had to wait until the last bags were emptied. We distributed the prepaid parcels as quickly as we could; the C.O.D.'s took longer due to the money transaction involved.

When the last person left, Carl and I went home. Although we were very tired, we sensed a feeling of satisfaction that so many children would have a good Christmas. We had arranged for Mom and Dad to keep LaDawn for the night and we picked her up in the morning.

Often during the summer, and in the fall, quite a number of Native people from Fort Vermilion camped on crown land in the sand hills on the way to the river several miles from town. They loved to be close to nature, especially during hunting season. It was early fall when one of these Native men came into the post office and asked me if a parcel had come for Mr. Ozay. I checked for a parcel and informed him that there wasn't one. For about a week he came walking into town almost every day to see if his parcel had arrived. He told me it was hunting season and he had ordered a new rifle and was anxious to have it. One day he asked me, "Whose parcel is that?" pointing to a parcel shaped like it could contain a rifle. "Is that my parcel?" I checked and told him that it was not for Mr. Ozay. "Whose parcel is that?" he asked. I told him that the parcel was for Mr. Auger and I spelled it out for him, A-U-G-E-R. "That's my parcel" he said, "and that's how you say my name, Ozay!" Poor man, he looked a little put out, walking to town every day, staring that parcel in the face and not being able to take it home. I apologized and felt sorry for him, but I wasn't about to give him someone else's parcel!

The end of the month had come around again and it was time to balance the account. I went to work and intended to quickly get it out of the way. I soon realized however, that I was short $100.00. It was the weekend, which gave me a few days grace. I was confident and determined I would discover the error. I woke up at night going over figures in my head until I felt dizzy. When I went over the 30 column, five digit lines I quickly learned to add, subtract and multiply all in one operation. I knew if I submitted the money it would be returned if the error was found. The problem was I didn't have the $100.00 to send in. I didn't know how I was going to handle it. On Monday morning, almost a week after Mr. John M. Schellenberg had come to buy money orders, he was back with a slight grin on his face asking me if I was short any money. I told him I was short $100.00, and I knew by the look on his face that he was responsible.

He had paid me, but with all the papers from his money orders on the counter, somehow he had taken the cheque back home. There were still no telephones so he couldn't phone me to let me know – this error just had to wait until there was a reason for him to come to town again. I was thankful for his honesty, but also thankful to serve a community where the majority of the people would have done the same thing.

One of my patrons had impaired vision, and he always brought his own pencil and paper with him and double-checked to make sure I had not made a mistake. He was a very honest man and did not want a single penny that did not belong to him. At the same time he wanted every penny that was his! One particular day he had a long list of money orders and it took quite a while before his figures matched mine. Patience was a virtue then, as it is now, and I learned to exercise it on occasions like these.

When he was convinced that all was right with his figures, he proceeded to pay me. He laid out his money, and he needed two more dollars to complete the transaction. In those days, two dollar bills and fifty dollar bills were the same colour. When he handed me a fifty dollar bill, I knew that his eye sight was failing him because he did have a two dollar bill in his hand together with the other bills. When I went ahead with returning his change he interrupted me and said, "You're giving me too much money. This isn't right, you're short changing yourself." I showed him the $50 bill he had given me and he remarked, "This could have been VERY bad."

Catalogue shopping was the norm for La Crete in the 1960s. This type of shopping automatically translated into the return of many parcels. I had one customer who was a chronic complainer, and I came to the conclusion that eventually he got tired of his own complaining. One memorable day he came stomping into the post office with a parcel, slammed it on the counter and said, "Beck to de Eatons," turned around and stomped out. End of conversation! I assumed that something hadn't fit right, so I sent it "Beck to de Eatons."

Thirty-Nine

More Improvements

M r. Isaac Knelsen, who owned and operated a business in town, installed a mobile phone in his store, giving the community a direct link to the outside world. Many people came to La Crete to make their long distance calls, and when calls came in, Mr. Knelsen tried his best to deliver the messages. It was during this time that my sister Helen was getting married in Edmonton, and Carl had been away working for six weeks straight. We were able to communicate, but it was complicated at best. Carl had access to a mobile phone in camp, so he would call Mr. Knelsen and ask him to deliver a message for me to call him back. I ran across the road and caught him while he was still in camp. We were able to make the arrangements for when he needed to be home in order to make it to the wedding on time. LaDawn would frequently ask me, "Daddy come home?" and it broke my heart. Sometime later Alberta Government Telephones provided telephone service to the hamlet of La Crete, but it wasn't until 1970 that telephone services were made available to our rural community.

During the mid 1960s Carl was still away working in the winters; being away from home long stretches at a time. We had become good friends with Joe and Anne Bergen, who lived in town. Their daughter, Irene, who had finished school and was still living at home, came to stay with me much of the time. There were many household chores to do aside from baby-sitting. We still had no running water so snow had to be melted for our water supply in the winter, wood had to be chopped and carried in, and ashes carried out. I was very thankful for all the help and company Irene gave me.

Carl and I realized all too quickly that this set up wasn't ideal for our family life. We were very much in love, and we found it extremely difficult to be separated for so much of the winter. LaDawn also missed and needed her daddy! Caring for LaDawn, running the household with all that it entailed and working eight hour shifts in the post office occupied my every waking minute. I didn't know that I was prepared, or wanted to continue this heavy workload by myself. At that time, jobs were scarce as hen's teeth, but in the fall of 1967, the Fort Vermilion School Division had an opening for a school bus driver's position. Carl filled out an application form and was hired. This was wonderful for our family life!

That summer Carl was pleased to inform me that we were the first people in La Crete to have running water. He mounted a big stock tank on a platform above the kitchen window, led the rain water from the roof into the tank, and then led a hose down through the window at the kitchen sink. It was a big improvement – providing it rained.

It was becoming obvious that a larger building would be needed to house the post office. Carl and I discussed our situation and started to throw some ideas around. We had a good friend who was the bank manager in Fort Vermilion, and we decided to meet with him to see if he could give us some advice. We needed $1200.00 to put up a 20' x 30' building. After some discussion he loaned us the money strictly on our merits. We started the building project immediately and moved in as soon as it was finished. The Post Office Department rented the building from us for $50.00 a month, allowing us to get rid of the debt in two years. We built the new post office next to our house, and Carl built a porch between the two buildings, sparing me the inconvenience of going outside to go to work. After he started his new job he was home during the day and often gave me a break from my postal duties. It wasn't difficult for him to learn the simple tasks, like selling money orders or stamps and handing out parcels, and I was always available if he needed me. This freed me up to do my housework and spend more time with LaDawn.

The community continued to grow, and the workload was getting too much for me even with Carl's help in sorting mail and other tasks. When I applied for some part time help, I was asked to submit a report on my workload. When the Post Office Department discovered all the favours I was doing for the people, they were reluctant to give me any extra help. Many people were illiterate in the English language, so I filled out their money orders for them, as well as their Family Allowance and Old Age Security application forms and many other forms. I had also been appointed a Commissioner for Oaths for the province of Alberta, not to mention filling out income tax forms for the people. These were the days when an income tax form consisted only of two pages, but it was time consuming none the less.

People couldn't always come to town during office hours so occasionally, when they were in need of some mail, they came to our house after hours. Shortly after I had submitted my report I had a reply from the Edmonton branch telling me to refrain from helping people with any paperwork, giving me strict orders not to fill out money orders for the people anymore. I wanted to be obedient to my authorities, but this didn't

I'm standing in front of the post office we built in 1965.

make any sense to me or to the public. Perhaps, I had failed to mention to my superiors that so many people in our community couldn't read or write English.

I refrained from helping for a while, but I couldn't stand to see my patrons in such need. They needed this service. This "new change" meant customers bought their money orders, and then they had to go and find someone to fill them out, and come back to the post office to mail them. This "new way" ended one day when an older gentleman came in to buy his money orders. I had always filled them out for him in the past, and he couldn't understand why I wouldn't help him anymore. This experience made me feel like I was a bad person, and right then and there I decided I would continue to help the people even if I had to work overtime. I was thankful when Mr. George D. Braun started to fill out income tax forms for the people. In later years Carl and I also asked Mr. Braun to file our income tax papers when my load at the post office got too heavy.

Forty

Changes in Family Life

As all parents know, family life is always changing. LaDawn was now almost four years old and had become very independent. She spent so much time with adults – grandma and grandpa, all her aunts, uncles and, of course, with us – that she started to speak and think like an adult. I had her sitting on the post office counter one day when a gentleman, whom we knew well, gave her a treat. He said, "Today I will give you lots of money," and he gave her five pennies. She looked at this man but didn't say anything. She took the five pennies, opened the cash box, put the pennies in and took out a nickel. This gentleman was very surprised, and so was I. On another occasion it was time for her afternoon nap. She had lost her *goygee*, "her soother," and couldn't go to sleep without it. The store was situated just across the road from us, so I gave her 25 cents, she ran across the street to buy her *goygee*, came home and went for a nap. I think she enjoyed being an only child getting all that attention, but that was about to change when a bouncing baby boy joined our family.

We named him Allen Craig, and he was a beautiful, happy and contented baby. LaDawn was thrilled to have a baby brother and her four-year-old motherly instincts took over. We were so thankful for a healthy baby boy, who weighed in at almost ten pounds. He was such a sweet, cuddly baby and a very good sleeper. There was extra work, of course, with bottles and diapers, but he was such a blessing that it didn't seem like

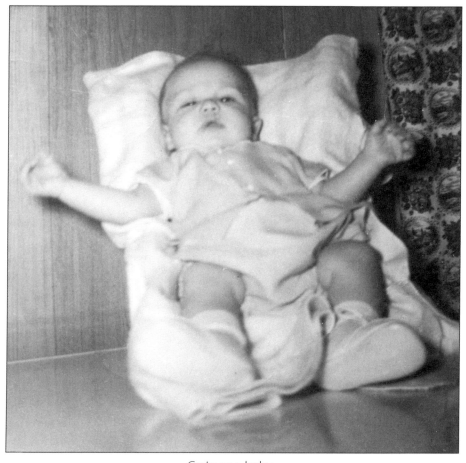

Craig as a baby.

much extra work. He was off to a good start, learning to walk and talk at a very early age, probably copying LaDawn.

When Craig was ten months old, Carl and I took LaDawn and went for a two week holiday. We left Craig with Joe and Anne Bergen, as they were no strangers to him. Irene bonded with him, and when we came back from our holiday she felt special when he shied away from us and reached for her. When we got home we put the children to bed, and after Craig was sleeping I stood beside his crib and silently regretted that I had left him behind. I had missed out on spending two precious weeks with him that I could never get back. I didn't realize how much I had missed him, and I vowed to never leave any of my children behind again, especially if it wasn't necessary.

Irene, who was our good friend and faithful baby-sitters, got married to Clarence Janzen on October 26. On November 7, she called me to wish me a happy birthday. She died tragically the next day after only two weeks of marriage. This was a terrible tragedy, and it took me a long time to get over it. Irene had been by my side for weeks on end over several years when Carl was away working, and we had developed a close friendship. I simply couldn't understand why this had to happen. Some of Irene's aunts and uncles from BC were coming to the funeral, but when they reached the river crossing there was too much ice on the river and the ferry had just been pulled for the season, so they turned around and went back home. This was just another example of the hardships people endured due to poor, or lack of, communication. What a disappointment that was having arrived only a few miles from their destination, but that's what life was like in the north at that time.

The workload at the post office continued to get heavier, and I kept lobbying the government for extra time. After a while they consented for me to hire someone for several hours a day. We had become well acquainted with a young teenager, Edward Froese, who was attending high school. Ed's parents were milking several cows and were selling milk and cream to the residents of La Crete. Their cows were pastured on the land where the Sandhills and Ridgeview schools now stand. Ed often delivered the milk and spent extra time with us. We had become very fond of him. He qualified for the job and knowing he could benefit from a few extra dollars I hired him. He proved to be a good choice and worked for me for quite a number of years, lessening my workload.

When you get to know Ed, you know that he is a person who always wears his heart on his shirt sleeve! He has always been there for us, just like a son and he'll always have a special place in our heart. Ed runs a sewer pump-out business and, in the fall, when he serviced our area, he usually dropped in for supper. One evening he had not notified us that he was coming, so Carl and I had gone out for supper and a visit. When we came home we decided to have a snack before we went to bed. I went to the cupboard to get a loaf of bread and discovered that the crusts were cut off on every side of the loaf. I showed it to Carl and asked him to guess who had been to our house. There was no guessing, as we both knew how much Ed liked the crust. It was great to know he would help himself even if we weren't home. Ed married Helena, a wonderful young lady, and we have remained good friends to this day.

Our family wasn't complete until another daughter arrived, and it was with great anticipation that we waited for her arrival. We named her Louise Lynette. She was beautiful, radiant, and she blessed us beyond measure by bringing rays of sunshine into our home every day. Many

Louise as a baby.

Our family in October 1970. Me holding Louise, LaDawn and Carl holding Craig.

times when a gloomy atmosphere prevailed, her sweet angelic smile and her good natured temperament would lift our spirits. She was one of those children that most everybody was attracted to, which remains an appealing part of her personality today.

Louise was a messy eater and, frequently, when she was finished eating and there was food left in her bowl, she turned that bowl upside down on top of her head and loved to watch the food dribble onto her high chair. She gave us that sheepish grin, letting us know she was having a good time. Occasionally when there was food left on her plate and she asked for desert, we asked her, "What about this?" pointing to the food on her plate, and she'd say, "Dat's for de pigs." She also let us know that her dessert compartment was still empty.

Louise loved mud puddles, too! On one occasion, when she and Craig both got new boots, they went to play outside after a rain. Craig didn't want to get his new boots dirty, but Louise waddled in the mud and sat down in the middle of the mud puddle, having the time of her life.

After Louise joined our family we had three children, and we needed someone to be with them five days a week. We hired Sarah Schmidt as our next housekeeper and nanny. She did all the laundry, cleaning, baking and cooking. She was an excellent cook and always had supper ready when I got home from work. She was a fun-loving person, always happy and smiling, and it reflected on the children. She was very good with them, and they loved to be around her. We were blessed to have her.

Forty-One

Mennonites on the Move Again

Progress in our northern community had been continuous, with many more families moving in and encouraging change. The land was ideal for farming considering the long, warm summer nights, which boosted the growing season. It is estimated that the growing season in northern Alberta is approximately nine days longer than in other parts of Alberta due to about twenty hours of sunlight during the longest days of the year. Bumper crops were produced when weather conditions were right. There was great potential here to make a living off the land, which had been the Mennonite way of life for centuries. Land has always been important to the people of the Mennonite faith, and access to land not only gave them the ability to make a living and raise their own food, but to live out a faith that they felt was connected to the land.

The people that moved into this Mennonite heartland came to pursue farming rather than to escape the pressures from the outside world, so change was inevitable. The Alberta government had built enough schools and had provided bussing for students so that every child of school age in the community was expected to be in school. Roads had been improved, and the community was serviced with electricity and telephone. All this progress did not sit well with the people who still wanted to live their lives without any government interference. Again it was time for the people who were unhappy about change to pull up their roots and find another underdeveloped country where they could raise their families without

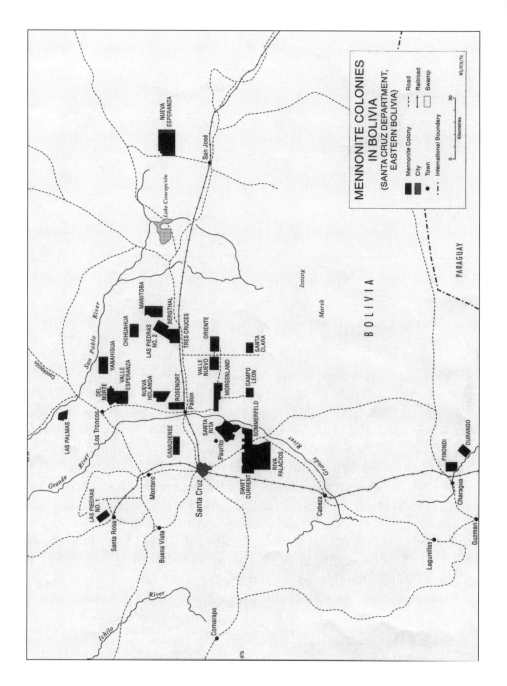

MENNONITE COLONIES
IN BOLIVIA
(SANTA CRUZ DEPARTMENT,
EASTERN BOLIVIA)

government intervention.

This disgruntled group of people targeted land-locked Bolivia in South America where a large group of Mennonites from Paraguay had already started a colony in 1954. *Land was still scarce in the Chihuahua colonies of Mexico, so by the mid 1960s, about 2000 Mennonites from Mexico had arrived in Bolivia and established a series of colonies.* [12]

In the late 1960s, delegates from La Crete were sent to Bolivia to check out the land to see if a move there would be feasible. The people who had moved to Worsley from La Crete were also interested in relocating, as school attendance had become compulsory there, resulting in the people from Worsley and La Crete working together for a possible migration. The delegates brought back a favourable report, encouraging a move to Bolivia. In the late 1960s and early 1970s, a large group of people from the La Crete area sold all their belongings by public auction and boarded planes for the jungles of South America.

There were additional Mennonite migrations from Mexico, Belize, Paraguay and Canada, and by 2006 there were 54 Mennonite colonies in Bolivia. We were affected when our relatives decided to join this migration. Mom's aunt and three uncles – with their families, who had moved to northern Alberta in 1937, and who had inspired Mom and Dad to move north – all decided to migrate together with most of their married children and their families. I was disappointed when Uncle Henry and Aunt Helen Neudorf decided to move together with all their family except their son Henry. Uncle Frank and Aunt Margaret Neudorf and their whole family also moved. The Jacob Peters family, who had moved to Worsley, uprooted again and joined the migration to Bolivia.

Prior to the migration, I got very busy at the post office and at home. Every adult over the age of sixteen needed a passport to fly to Bolivia. I'm certain there were others who helped people fill out their passport forms, but I got my fair share of the load. I was often too busy at work to help the people, and not every one was free to come in during the day, therefore, my work day was often extended to include evenings when I filled out their forms at home. Sometimes I wondered if people took for granted that filling out forms was part of my job and that it also included working evenings. The people may very well have been thankful for my services, I really don't know, but one kind old gentleman, Mr. Isaac D. Fehr, came to the post office one day and told me how much he appreciated all the help I had given him and his wife. He asked me to come to their house and pick a house plant from their large collection as a token of thanks. That plant meant so much to me that I thought it was the prettiest plant I had ever seen.

For those who moved to Bolivia, taming the jungle was quite a different operation from clearing land in northern Alberta. The jungle grew

---

12 Short excerpt from: *Mennonite Historical Atlas*, p144. William Schroeder.

back rather quickly in the hot tropical climate. After a few years, many of Uncle Henry and Aunt Helen's family moved back, although they themselves chose to stay. The Frank Neudorf family also chose to return. Many families were separated while moving back and forth causing much heartache and pain. I am so thankful that Mom and Dad never got caught up in this mentality, so our family has stayed united.

Several decades later when crops failed due to drought conditions, life in Bolivia became very difficult for many families, and a wave of Mennonites made the return to Canada – mostly to La Crete, Alberta, while others went to points beyond.

Forty-Two

Mennonite Refugees after World War II

In the years prior to the migration from Ukraine to Canada, and in the years after, the Mennonite people established a positive name for themselves. This served them well many times when they sought to relocate from one country to another.

The Mennonite Central Committee (MCC) was formed in the United States in 1920. Its initial task was to provide relief to Mennonites in the Soviet Union. After the Second World War it expanded its role worldwide to alleviate needs caused by droughts, earthquakes and other disasters. Their aid also included setting up refugee camps for victims of war. Today Mennonites are well known for their Mennonite Disaster Services (MDS) program. MDS is a service agency designed to provide help when disaster strikes anywhere on the North American continent. Help is provided wherever there is a need, whether within or outside the Mennonite community. Volunteer work crews are organized and sent out to help rebuild homes and lives.

Peter and Elfrieda Dyck, a young married couple, were serving with Mennonite Central Committee doing relief work in Holland and other parts of Europe during and after the Second World War. After the war, the victorious allies – the British, French, Russian and Americans – divided Germany into four zones, each occupying one zone. The city of Berlin, which was in the Russian zone, was divided into four sectors with each of the victorious allies occupying one quarter of the city.

After the war a large number of Mennonites (who were Russian citizens of Dutch-German decent) had escaped the Russian sector and were hiding in the British and American zones. Of course, the Russians wanted them back! They were loaded up like criminals and taken back to the Russian zone. From there, many were shipped, in box cars, to Siberia and were never heard from again.

There were about 1200 Mennonite refugees who had not been caught and were hiding out in the American sector of Berlin. When Peter and Elfrieda discovered Mennonites taking refuge in bombed out shelters in the American sector, they interceded and proceeded to find host countries for the refugees. They worked with government officials of various countries, trying to find a home for them. Canada and the United States had closed their borders to more immigrants, and Mexico didn't work out either. Finally they had a positive response from the government of Paraguay, South America. A large group of Mennonites had migrated to Paraguay in the 1920s and 1930s to escape the unwanted external influences in Canada, so the Paraguayan government was already familiar with the Mennonite people. They had tamed the Chaco, which was known as "the green hell which no man can tame." They conquered it, brought it under cultivation and made the land productive, transforming it into a beautiful, fertile region. The Paraguayan government stated one condition for the immigration of the refugees: "We will take everyone – the old, the lame, the deaf and the blind – providing they are Mennonites." Eventually, many of these homeless European Mennonites, through their endless sacrifice and toil, also eked out a living alongside those who had arrived earlier. Today the Mennonites are the leading milk producers in Paraguay controlling 70 per cent of the milk industry. [13]

13 SOURCES:
Mennonite Central Committee Production. *New Beginnings: Mennonite Refugees to South America (1947-1948) Part 1.* 1988.
Friesen, John. *Mennonites through the Centuries: From the Netherlands to Canada.* Steinbach, MB: Mennonite Heritage Village, 1985.
Global Anabaptist Mennonite Encyclopedia Online, www.gamea.org, 1996–2011.

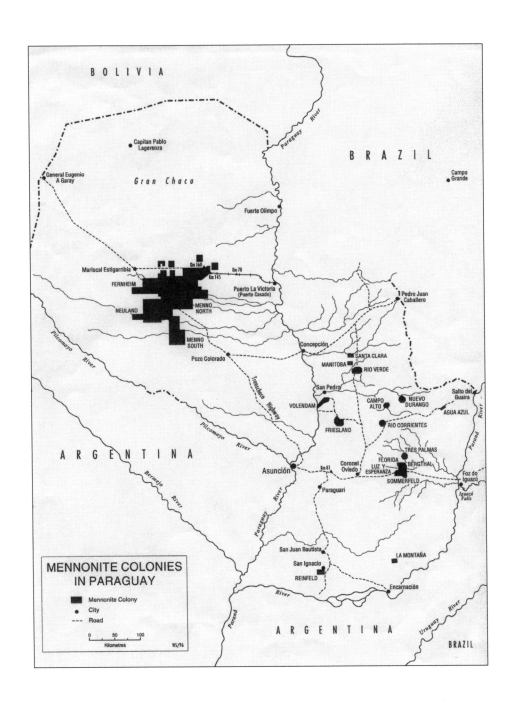

MENNONITE COLONIES
IN PARAGUAY

■ Mennonite Colony
● City
--- Road

0   50   100
Kilometres   WS/96

307

Forty-Three

New Developments

In the La Crete area, farming and trying to make a living from the land continued to be a struggle for most families, although food on the table was usually plentiful. Most families grew big gardens; the vegetables were canned and root vegetables were stored in earth cellars under the house. Meat – chicken, pork and beef – was readily available from the farm as well as eggs, milk, cream and butter, but there was seldom a steady income. Many families who were milking quite a number of cows shipped cream to bring in a little cash. They took the cream cans to the store where they were picked up by a freight truck and hauled to Peace River. The cream cans often stood in the hot sun while waiting for the truck, causing the cream to expand in the heat and bubble over, making a big mess in front of the store, which was often a free meal for a roaming cat or dog.

Not having a steady income created hardships for many families, especially for families who were experiencing medical problems. Many times people simply didn't have the means to pay the doctors for their services. This all changed when the Alberta Health Care System came into effect in 1969, relieving the pressure to pay when there wasn't the means.

Mom was diagnosed with Type 2 Diabetes in 1969, and she was devastated. She knew, and we all knew, that something was bothering her. With all her many visits to doctors no one clued in to her problem. Finally, one day, Dad took her to Manning to see if the doctor there would be able to help her. He examined her and told her he couldn't find anything wrong. On the way out of the clinic, Mom was getting very lethargic and had to sit down. Dad called the doctor and he took her back into the examining room. Mom was still conscious enough to ask him if he thought it could possibly be diabetes. He tested her blood sugar and discovered the level was so high she was in a comatose condition. Upon further testing, the doctor concluded that she must have had the disease for at least ten years.

With her sugar unbalanced, she often got frustrated and upset about little things. She spent much of one summer in the hospital in Edmonton due to her illness. Her diet was very controlled and needed monitoring. The doctor asked Dad to take a whole week of special training at the University of Alberta, where he learned how to cook for her, administer the needles and adjust her insulin. Everything Mom ate was either weighed or measured and, after awhile, it was so overwhelming for Dad that he asked if some of us girls would consider taking the course as well so we could relieve him when it was needed. Babe and I both decided to go. It was a real eye opener for me to understand the importance of proper diet. I'm sure, though, that we ate healthier then than most people do today. We grew all our own organic vegetables, organic meat, and baked our own whole grain bread. We had few desserts and no processed or fast food. These courses were also covered by the health care system, making the venture affordable. We had our own busy schedule that summer, but Carl encouraged me to go and Dad was thankful to have us share the load.

Our family doctor for quite a number of years, and until she retired, was Dr. Mary Percy Jackson, who practiced medicine from her farmhouse at Keg River Post. Dr. Jackson had come to northern Alberta from England in 1929 – her plan was to stay for a twelve month period. Circumstances led her to stay, as there was a great need here for her services. She fell in love with this vast northland and its people, serving two distinct cultures – the Natives and the Mennonites – and she loved them both. Her patients in turn grew to love, trust and respect her. She had treated the Mennonite people who settled at Carcajou, about 40 miles east across the river from Keg River Post in the 1930s. Later, all the Mennonites left Carcajou and most of them settled at La Crete. Years later when road conditions improved, many of the families went to Keg River Post from La Crete, about 100 miles away, for Dr. Jackson's medical services.

Dr. Jackson received the Centennial Medal of Canada in 1967 in recognition of valuable service to the nation. She writes in her book, *The Homemade Brass Plate* page 119: "*I highly respected the Mennonites.*

I respected their moral life. I never saw a case of venereal disease among them. Their ethical standards were so high and they were so hard-working that it seemed a shame to me that all that ethical strength was locked up in northern Alberta instead of benefiting all of Canada." Likely, Dr. Jackson was only familiar with the Mennonites she worked with and possibly didn't realize that this moral strength was a strong characteristic in this particular ethnic group all across Canada.

Sadly, over the years, living alongside mainstream society, moral standards have shifted and the Mennonite people have not been exempt from conforming to destructive lifestyles. Many parents take comfort in claiming Proverbs 22: 6 *"Train a child in the way he should go, and when he is old he will not turn from it."* For the most part, the youth who have strayed from the straight and narrow will at some point denounce their immoral and destructive lifestyle and come back to living a respected life.

Before the health care system came into effect, many of Dr. Jackson's patients were not able to pay for her services in cash, so they often paid her in goods. The Natives would bring her moose meat, moccasins and berries while the Mennonites brought garden produce, wool comforters, wool mittens and *Socke.*

One afternoon when I went for a doctor visit, Dr. Jackson discovered during the course of our conversation that I was the postmistress at La Crete. She was experiencing great difficulty keeping her records straight, as so many people had the same names. She was concerned about giving her patients the wrong medication, as medicine was most often sent in the mail. She also needed to keep her records straight for health care billing. For instance, there were seven Peter Friesens and many other duplicate names as well, causing her much confusion. Second names were not common among the Mennonite people, therefore, identifying them, especially when she didn't know them or didn't see them, could create a real problem. When the young men left home, most took the first initial of their mother's maiden name for identification. Peter Neudorf would become Peter K. Neudorf because his mother's last name was Klassen. Even if the people had an initial, they didn't always use it.

Dr. Jackson was particularly concerned about two families. The fathers and the mothers both had the same names as did their youngest two children who were also about the same age. In the post office I dealt with every family and could identify people by either box number, initial, or name. Seniors, either male or female, received their Old Age Security cheque in their own names, family allowance cheques came in the mother's name and post office boxes were in the father's name.

When my doctor visit was over, Dr. Jackson asked me if I would consider staying until her office hours were over and help her straighten out her records, which I readily agreed to. After clinic hours, she made a pot of tea and we sat in her living room for quite some time until she was satisfied that her files were correct. We did this numerous times afterward when she had questions. Carl thoroughly enjoyed visiting with Frank Jackson, Dr. Jackson's husband, listening to his stories from the early years in the 1920s and '30s, while we were busy with medical files. Frank Jackson was a great storyteller, which was evident by the books he wrote.

Our family life continued at much the same pace, and I was so thankful that I didn't have to leave a warm building to get to work. Either Carl or I were with the children all the time. After some time though, Carl took a job at the school bus garage doing mechanical work between bus runs for $3.00 an hour. We managed financially, but the time came when the bed sheets and towels wore so thin we could spit through them, and we never had enough chairs to sit on. We frequently had much company making it difficult to seat everyone. We brought in five gallon buckets, turned them upside down and used them as chairs. We never bought anything unless we needed it!

After work one day I went to the Marshall Wells store to check out prices for chairs. We also needed a new dining room table, although we could still manage with the one we had. When I got home I asked Carl to come to the store with me, and I showed him a nice dining room set that would fit perfectly into our dining area. The first thing he did was turn those chairs upside down to see how well they were built. He wasn't impressed! I told him I wanted to buy the set. He never said a word, and I was frustrated and let him know about it. I really didn't have that much to talk about the next morning, and I silently left for work. I was sure the sun would continue to rise and set even if we didn't have a new table and chairs. When I came home from work, Carl was very busy building a padded L-shaped bench into the corner of the dining room that would seat five or six people. I had to admit it was much better than chairs.

There were no thrift stores or yard sales in those days, as everyone needed what they had. My sisters and I passed the children's clothes around, and when the children outgrew them, we passed them back if they were still usable. Within one year all nine of us that were married had a baby. Not many clothes were passed around that year.

Our social life in the summer was fun, especially on Sundays when we headed down to the river with Joe and Anne Bergen and their family to go fishing. Anne and I packed picnic lunches while the children gathered live bait – worms, grasshoppers, or bugs – as we did mostly angle fishing. When we got to the river, Carl and Joe pounded willow sticks into the soft sandy dirt near the water's edge, attached bait to the lines, and the children sat and patiently waited for any sign of movement.

There was always much excitement when the children caught a fish which also held true for Carl and Joe. On one occasion Carl had big-time movement on his line and had caught a good sized pickerel, a prize catch for sure. He took the hook from the fish's mouth and proceeded to wash the dirt off of it, and with a few swishes of the tail it headed for safer waters. Joe couldn't quit laughing and Carl's eyes were so big you could have knocked them off with a stick. He didn't say a word! In the years following this was always a good fish story – a true story about the fish that got away.

One spring evening Joe and Anne came over to spend time with us, and they informed us about an important decision they had made. They had moved to the homestead a number of years earlier, and now they had decided to take the whole family to Taber, Alberta for the summer to hoe

The fish that got away.

sugar beets to supplement the farm income. Carl and I couldn't believe what we were hearing, as this would change our social life – no more fishing trips to the river or spending time together otherwise. Many times we played games until two or three o'clock in the morning several nights a week, not to mention the suppers we shared at each other's homes. We were disappointed, but understood their situation. When the beet harvest was completed, they informed us that Joe had taken a job that would keep them there for the winter, and so it continued. They never did move back. We were thankful when we were able to spend time with them whenever they came to La Crete for a visit or when we traveled to southern Alberta. Time and distance did not dim our friendship. Joe and Anne passed away within a year of each other, and it felt like we had lost family.

Forty-Four

Another Move

With many more people moving into the community, the post office we had built was also getting crowded. The government decided to construct a new building to accommodate the ever growing population. The building project started in 1969, and we were able to occupy the new post office in the fall of 1970. It is still in use today and situated across the street, north of the La Crete Public School. Carl and I had purchased sixteen acres of land bordering the town limits in the winter of 1969. The Treasury Branch is now located on the southeast corner of that property. After we moved the post office into the new building we were free to sell the two acres we had occupied and relocate onto the sixteen acre property.

Our little house had become a bit crowded with three active youngsters running around. We had a basement made in the summer and moved the old post office building onto it. We added a living room and porch to the existing building which then became our new home. We had moved our little house onto this property and lived in it until our new house was livable, at which time we sold it.

Carl hired two Native men from Fort Vermilion to dig a well and sewer line by hand for $3.00 an hour, giving us the convenience of having running water and sewer. We also installed a forced air furnace, giving us the comfort of a warm house all the time. Carl built a fireplace in the living room which helped with heating bills. He laboured endlessly build-

The new government post office, built in 1969-1970.

ing his "masterpiece." He hauled rocks from the field, split them, than started the huge task of chipping them to fit right. We had rocks and rock chips in our living room for months. Many of the rocks were very colourful, and the fireplace was beautiful when it was finished. The crackling wood and the dancing flames created a cozy atmosphere on cold winter days. We also enjoyed the privacy of our new premises and it provided ample space for the children to run and play.

We started a mini farm on this property, giving the children something to do and thereby teaching them responsibility. Carl fenced a large portion of the land and purchased cows, horses, pigs and, in the spring, we bought baby chicks. He purchased and moved a small log barn to house the pigs and built a chicken coop with a fence around it, allowing the chickens to be either in or out. The cows provided us with milk, cream and butter and the horses were entertainment.

At two-thirty one summer morning, the sharp yipping sound of coyotes filled the night air sending shivers up my spine. Carl and I woke up at the same time, thinking they must be right underneath our bedroom window. We both had this strange feeling that something was

The back entrance of our new house, 1970.

wrong. When we looked out the window – it was already getting daylight – we noticed that something didn't look right. We got dressed and headed out to the barn yard. We discovered, to our horror, that most of our chickens were dead. The culprit, from the evidence that was left, led us to believe that it was a mink and her babies. Some of the chickens had large tooth marks while others had small ones. The coyotes likely knew what was going on and were ready for their share in the pie. Carl and I got the little red wagon and the wheel barrow and started gathering up what would have been our winter's supply of chicken. We loaded the carnage onto the pick-up truck and headed for the garbage dump. What a disappointment that was, as the chickens were about a week or two away from heading into the deep freeze. We lost about 80 out of the 100 chickens. In the winter Craig set weasel traps around the chicken coop and occasionally he caught some, thereby protecting my laying hens from the same fate.

Our family was very fond of our faithful dog and she was very good at staying around the yard. One evening we noticed she wasn't at home and we couldn't figure out what could have happened to her. We started

317

calling her often during the day and many times late at night in the days that followed. We heard dogs barking late at night but, unfortunately, we couldn't draw any conclusions from that.

One family in town was in the process of building a new house – they had dug the basement and were waiting for the brick layer to lay the bricks. When they realized they would have to wait for a while, they decided to go for a short holiday. Somehow, our dog had fallen into this basement and couldn't get out. They were gone for almost a week and discovered our dog's predicament when they returned home. The poor thing was so weak she could hardly walk or lick water. She must have heard us calling her, and she probably answered us, but we couldn't distinguish her bark from the other dogs. We nursed her back to health, but it was heartbreaking to think of how much she suffered so close to home, begging for help and not understanding why we wouldn't come.

We had our moments on this little farm. The children were very fond of our mother cat with her babies. The kittens were at an adorable stage when we noticed them behaving strangely. Carl identified it as distemper and, of course, they died. Carl dug a grave in the pasture and we had a funeral. The children picked wild flowers and placed them on top of the grave but it was a difficult day for them. We were thankful that we hadn't needed a funeral for the dog.

Forty-Five

More Progress

With the community growing, more extra help was needed in the post office. I usually hired high school students for part time work, which was mutually beneficial. Students graduating from high school soon found fulltime work, leaving their position vacant. This caused frequent changes in support staff over the years. When I hired Frank Goertzen, another high school student, I soon realized that he showed an interest in the work. He decided to keep working after he graduated from high school, creating stability in the work place. Several years after I resigned from the post office, Frank was hired as the postmaster and served until his retirement.

In the spring time it was not unusual to have from one to two thousand chicks dropped off at the post office when the mail arrived. The smell was enough to knock anyone over and the noise was deafening. It was another one of those times when you simply did what needed to be done. I accepted it as part of my job even though it wasn't really my responsibility. As long as the post office was housed in the building attached to the house, it really wasn't such a big deal if the people couldn't pick them up before five o'clock; they just picked them up after hours. Once we moved to the new building it was more of an inconvenience. Circumstances would occasionally arise when people didn't show up that day, so Carl usually helped me bring the chicks home. Since they had been in transit for a whole day, the poor little things were dying of thirst. We took them out of the crowded boxes, watered them, and after their needs were met, they settled right down and went to sleep. The children loved this little bit of excitement and enjoyed helping.

After we moved to the new location, we needed a fulltime nanny and housekeeper. We had heard that Nettie Unrau was a very good housekeeper and was looking for work. I hired her for $3.00 a day, the amount she was asking for. I soon realized she was very dependable, efficient and hard working, and she was very good with the children as well. In addition to looking after the children, reading to them and doing other fun things, she did all my cleaning, cooking, baking, sewing clothes for the children and always had supper ready when I came home from work. We asked her to make sure that Craig and Louise would have an afternoon nap, that way Carl and I could spend all our time with them in the evenings. Since they were not yet at school it wasn't important for them to be in bed at a certain time. I felt guilty paying Nettie such a minimum wage for the quantity and quality of work she was doing, so I upped her wage to $5.00 a day. By this time I had received a small increase in salary and by 1966 I earned $233.39 a month, but $100.00 a month was still a big chunk out of my measly pay cheque. Nettie ended up staying with us for quite a number of years and became like a member of our household.

Our family life was changing too much, too quickly. It seemed like only yesterday since we brought LaDawn home as a baby, and now it was time for her to start school. It wasn't a difficult transition for her as she had already waited for this day for quite some time. She was anxious to learn how to read and write and always pretended she knew how. We had always read to the children and instilled in them a love for books. I ordered the Learn How to Read series, Dr. Seuss series and others. We always read Bible stories to the children at bedtime, so she was well familiar with books. Looking back, I believe the transition was more difficult for us than for her.

Although we had a good nanny, I still kept busy with the children and the household, and was involved in community affairs. I was the news reporter for our local newspaper, *The Northern Pioneer* in the early years of its existence. In 1974, I served as the secretary on a committee to pursue the possibility of starting kindergarten classes in La Crete. We had several meetings with the Fort Vermilion School Division and ran into some dead ends. The division was definitely in favour of kindergarten classes but there was no room in the school to house another class. We needed to find another place. An old fire hall had been moved into town and was situated across the street from the school. We inquired about the possible use of the building and were told there was space available. We ran into a problem with that idea as the building was not serviced with water and sewer. We had another meeting with the FVSD and they gave us the green light, which meant, taking all the children to the school to use the bathroom and library, crossing a busy street. There were some trying times, but La Crete had kindergarten! It was here that Louise and Craig started kindergarten, the first kindergarten class in the community.

After several years we decided to develop our sixteen acre parcel of land into lots. It was mandatory for us to supply power, culverts and driveways for each lot. Since the town wasn't serviced with water or sewer, we were spared the cost of that but it was still a big overhead expense. When the people bought the lots and applied for power, Northland Utilities refunded the money we had paid to service them.

We had already sold several lots when an older gentleman came to inquire about the price. Carl told him we were selling the small ones for $750.00 dollars and the larger ones were more expensive. His reply was that he wasn't interested in purchasing sixteen acres – he only wanted to buy one lot. He told Carl he didn't plan to make a Garden of Eden; he was only going to live here for a little while. He ended up making a purchase.

More and more people were building new houses in and out of town. There was a need for mixed concrete to build the foundations for their houses as well as cementing their basement and garage floors. Carl had two small tractors; he mounted portable cement mixers to them and did custom cementing for quite a number of years.

Forty-Six

The Bridge

After years of lobbying the government, the decision was finally made to build a bridge to span the mighty Peace River near Fort Vermilion. This would give the La Crete and Fort Vermilion communities access to the outside world year round. As well, this would change life as the communities had known it since the first settlers arrived many years before. River freeze-up and river break-up would no longer affect the communities in such a profound way as it had in years prior.

I had experienced many difficulties with the river crossing; flying across the river at different times when the ferry wasn't operating or the ice

The ice bridge under water before river break-up.

bridge unsafe. The worst example I experienced when crossing the river in unsafe conditions came one Easter weekend. Carl and I had taken his parents for a visit to Pete and Olga's (Carl's brother and his wife) who lived at Bezanson. The ice bridge seemed fine when we left but by the time we came back the barricades were up and the river crossing was covered with water. What should we do? A common practice was to remove the fan belt to keep the motor dry when crossing in deep water. It

When the ice was unsafe to cross, the barricades went up.

was the only choice we had and after Carl and his dad finished discussing the matter they decided to risk it. Mom and I were sitting in the back seat and we both started to breathe very heavily when the water started running into the car. Mom Friesen was a woman of few words and when we arrived safely on the other side, she breathed a sigh of relief and with thanksgiving in her heart she sweetly hummed a soothing tune.

There was always the problem, spring and fall, when mail service was interrupted for weeks on end, and I had to deal with the mess later. Because of this, the new bridge was reason to celebrate, and I wanted to be a part of it.

The bridge was several years in building and the date for the official opening was set for September 19, 1974. Numerous dignitaries were coming to participate in this historic event. The announcement had been made that the businesses in town were shutting their doors for the day and that schools would also close down to give everyone a chance to take part in the celebrations. I wrote a letter to the Post Office Department in Edmonton explaining the event and told them that the whole town would be shutting down. I asked permission to close the post office for the day so I could attend as well. There was no consideration whatsoever; the answer was a flat "No." I felt like I had been slapped in the face, and it took me a long time to chew and swallow that one. I sat in that post

The new ferry at Tompkins Landing, 1987.

office all day with not one single soul darkening that door. I can't find any words to express how I felt, but I knew it was the beginning of the end working for Canada Post.

The small cable ferry we had crossed when we moved north in 1953 had been replaced with a bigger one some years earlier. When the bridge opened to traffic this ferry was moved to the Tomkins Landing river crossing. A secondary road to Tompkins Landing had been built in 1961. During the months between river break-up and river freeze-up most of the people living south of La Crete traveled this shorter route to the main highway leading to Manning and beyond. In 1987 Tompkins' Landing got a big new ferry, the road was paved, and the people have enjoyed fairly smooth sailing from spring to fall ever since. In the winter, the ice bridge is still the only means to cross the river.

Mrs. E. Ward Revard, a long time resident of Fort Vermilion, penned this poem especially for the bridge opening that so many people could identify with.

THE FORT VERMILION BRIDGE

Thru the long years we waited
Tho it seemed an idle dream
To see a bridge near the Old Fort
Right across this mighty stream.

Where the Peace flowed unchallenged
Since the dawn of time began

Now we see this giant structure
Built by skill and power of man.

Great chiefs with their warriors
Fought their battles here
And all our famed explorers
Passed below these giant piers.

River craft from time forgotten
Made a highway of this stream
Birch canoe, raft and dug-out
Boats powered by gas and steam.

Men came to seek adventure
Priest and Parson seeking souls
Rival traders fought their battles
Miners came in search of gold.

Men faced its cruel hardships
Starved along its frozen shore
Faced its solitude and silence
Followed those who passed before.

Now no more stop or waiting
You can travel north or east
There's a bridge across the river
Near the Old Fort on the Peace.

No more waiting for the breakup
Never mind the winter freeze
No more waiting for the ferry
You can cross just when you please.

Will someone in the years to come
Check the traffic that will pass
The bounty rich beyond one's dreams
From all this land so vast?

May we all join in humble thanks
May its service never cease
May it join in trust and friendship
This great land beside the Peace.

Printed with permission from Mr. Edwin Ward

Forty-Seven

The End of a Career

The postmaster's position had never been fulfilling for me; it was a job and that was it. There was no challenge for me and there was never any consideration or any word of encouragement from my superiors, although I knew they weren't looking for anyone else when my annual reports came back. Although there were many days when the folks in the community would cheer me up and make me feel needed, I often felt discouraged. I had unexpectedly stepped into this position, but the time was approaching when they would have to find a replacement. In March of 1975 I wrote my letter of resignation after twelve and one half years of service. I was required to give three months notice in order for them to find someone to fill the position. I was notified several weeks before my time was up that Mr. Jack Sinclair from Calgary had been hired to replace me and that he would arrive early for an orientation.

Mr. Sinclair had been a mail carrier and really did not know what all was involved in running the office. When he arrived I proceeded to show him the ropes. After I had covered the whole operation I gave him the combination for the safe and asked him to open it to make sure he felt comfortable with it. He said not to worry; he wasn't concerned about it as long as he had the combination.

Well, the big day finally arrived when the officials from Edmonton came to do the big switch over. They audited the books, checked everything else out, and gave the post office a clean bill of health. It was time

CANADA POST OFFICE

ANNUAL EFFICIENCY REPORT

Date of Last Report...............1-10-67...............

Payroll No. ....
Paylist No. ....
Office and Date

La Crete, Alberta
1st October 1968

Name Mrs. Tena Friesen, La Crete, Alberta, Semi-Staff Grade 3

1. Date of appointment: Temporary .....29-8-63..... Permanent .....29-8-63.....

2. Present class title: .....Postmaster, RV-SCB-5..... Date .....1-10-67.....

3. Present salary .....$5020.00..... Date .....1-10-67.....

4. New Salary .....$5180.00..... Date .....1-10-68.....

5. Concise statement of regular duties All phases of operational and administrative postal duties

6. Ratings: Outstanding .... Above average .... High average ...X...

   Average .... Low average .... Below average .... Unsatisfactory ....
   (Make a full separate report and give your recommendation of action to be taken.)

7. Explanation of Rating: - .....Operation of office is very good,.....
   .....financially, operationally and administratively.....
   .....Good public relations.....

8. Suspensions since last report, if any. *(State length and reasons)* ....

9. Times late since last report - No. .... Time Lost ....

10. Absences since last report - No. .....nil..... Days Lost .....nil.....

11. Has employee passed required examinations during past year? .....n/a..... If so,
    state date and percentage obtained

	Distribution	Written Questions ....
	Postal Guide	D.O. Procedure ....
	Financial Procedure	U.M.O. Procedure ....

12. Has employee rendered meritorious service? .....yes..... Increased in usefulness in the Service? .....yes.....
    (yes or no)   (yes or no)

13. Do you recommend salary increase? .....yes.....
    (yes or no)

....
Signature of Immediate Supervisor and class

....
Signature of Head of Staff or Office
SUPT. OF OPERATIONS

Note — This form is to be prepared in triplicate annually - original to Headquarters - one copy to be handed to the employee with an explanation by the Postmaster, District Director or other delegated responsible officer, and one copy signed by the employee for employee's file. Employee is to be given every opportunity to discuss his ratings with a responsible officer.

22-54-021 (6-67)   39/45 3   8587
LA CRETE
23   1968 Signature of employee and date
ALBERTA

200

328

for me to put my signature on the papers to make the switch legal. Before Mr. MacDonald, one of the officials, handed me the pen he said, "Mrs. Friesen, you realize that if you don't sign the papers, the job is still yours." I told him that I understood that. That was the closest any one had come in those twelve years of telling me I was doing a good job. I was to learn the true value of commendation in the years to come.

My first day off the job dawned bright and beautiful; a day I had looked forward to for three months. I was going to allow myself a day all to myself, celebrating a day free of responsibilities. Carl had gone to work and the children were at school. I was still in my housecoat, enjoying a cup of hot chocolate when a knock at the door startled me. I couldn't figure out who would knock on my door at this hour, as it was only a few minutes past nine o'clock. Mr. Sinclair had sent a patron to my house and asked if I would come and show him how to open the safe, as the combination wasn't working for him. His customers simply had to wait until I had made myself presentable and made it to the post office. This was kind of a bummer, but it was yet morning and I would still have all the rest of the day – I thought.

It was early afternoon and I was sitting on the porch step enjoying the warm sunshine when a pick-up truck drove into the yard. It was Mr. Jacob J. Froese needing help with filling out some forms. Mr. Froese was a kind elderly man and a pastor at the Old Colony Church. I respected him very highly. Mr. Froese was plagued with crippling arthritis and needed a cane for walking. He was experiencing difficulty climbing in and out of his truck, and he carried a small stepping stool with him. He would open the door of his truck, put the stool on the ground to aide him in getting out. This was a real effort for him. He told me he had gone to the post office, not knowing there was a new postmaster there, but instead of asking him for help he drove to our house. Most of the elderly and the English illiterate felt comfortable with me because I could relate and explain to them in the German language. Mr. Froese was always grateful whenever I helped him; I always did it willingly and today would be no exception. I asked him to come into the house and I would help him. Somehow, that day, I felt more satisfaction in filling out forms than I had ever done before.

Later that afternoon the neighbours little girl was pulling her little red wagon, picking dandelions on our lawn. I was watching her through the window when she came knocking on the door. When I answered, she asked me if I wanted to buy some flowers. I asked her how much she was selling them for and she said 25 cents apiece. I kindly told her that I wouldn't buy any this time. She seriously informed me that they would be more expensive the next time, so I decided to purchase one while the sale was still on, and I made her day. It was the cutest experience I'd had in a long time and she helped make my day. Carl came home from work and asked how my first day off the job had gone. I told him it had gone very well, and I related my day's experiences to him.

Forty-Eight

New Horizons

Life away from work was quite different from what I had expected. With whole days to myself I discovered I really didn't know how to manage free time well. I was used to routine at work and I would have to learn to develop new plans for life at home. Keeping house didn't require much of my time anymore, as we had running water, electricity, forced air heating, and even a clothes dryer. I started needle work, embroidery, and tried some other woman's things like knitting, but none of these brought me much satisfaction. A group of ladies met weekly for knitting sessions and they asked me to join them. I bought wool and knitting needles and was serious about being part of it. I started to knit a sweater and, after I unraveled it for the eighth time, I decided that knitting was not going to be my pastime. Although I had given it a fair shot, I believe I was the only one who didn't succeed.

On many occasions we had picnics and barbecues with family and friends, and occasionally we took the children on fishing trips. Winter brought its own entertainment when we'd go skating and sledding with the children and were frequently joined by members of our extended family. Usually about two weeks before Christmas, on a Sunday afternoon, we'd take the children and head for the sand hills to cut down a Christmas tree. After Carl had mounted the tree, we all decorated it together and it became an important part of the Christmas season.

We kept up the Mennonite tradition of setting up bowls (like some

Craig and Jimmy Unrau and the highlight of a fishing trip - catching the big one.

families put up stockings) on Christmas Eve. We wrapped one gift for each of us, placed them under the tree and opened them on Christmas Eve. The children's gift was often a pair of pajamas, a colouring book and crayons, or a story book. There was extra work involved preparing for Christmas, which kept me busy for several weeks, but when all the excitement was over it was back to keeping house! I must admit that I felt there had to be more to life than keeping my furniture free of dust and having supper ready by six o'clock. I was home alone all day.

In February an opening for the secretary position came up at the La Crete Public School. Since jobs were few and far between, I decided to apply for the job. After several days, Mr. Ettinger, the principal, called me in for an interview. The day after the interview he asked me to come back in and asked if I would consider the library instead of the secretarial position. Jessie Derksen, who was the librarian, was much more interested in secretarial work and had asked to switch positions. I was thrilled with the proposal, accepted the offer and was hired to work in the library. I'm certain Mr. Ettinger never knew that he was instrumental in fulfilling my life's dream.

Mrs. LaFond was a teacher/librarian in charge of the library, and I began working under her watchful eye. The small country schools had been closed down except for Buffalo Head Prairie. All students were bussed to La Crete which gave the La Crete Public School a population of about 800 students, grades one to twelve. Mrs. LaFond was teaching Library Skills as well as other classes, leaving me in charge of the library in her absence. She took it upon herself to train me the day I started work, covering every area of that library from shelving books to cataloging books. This experience, no doubt, prepared me for all the responsibility I would accept later on.

The Fort Vermilion School Division built a new school in La Crete, Sandhills Elementary School, which opened in October of 1977, housing Kindergarten to grade three. Several afternoons a week, Mrs. LaFond went over to the new school to teach her classes, leaving me in charge for entire afternoons. With such a large student body there was always a class or two in the library. At recess and noon hours, the place filled up with students, leaving me to deal with discipline problems, which I wasn't particularly fond of nor trained for.

A little more than a year after I started work, Mrs. LaFond resigned and the school division decided not to replace her. Instead, they handed the reins over to me. I found it difficult to understand what was happening. She had trained me well and I understood the work involved, but to take charge and oversee the whole operation was more than I had bargained for. How could I possibly do all the work I had done before plus take on everything else she had done in the library? To say that I was overwhelmed was an understatement and the overload signs were everywhere for me. I had felt so secure working under her supervision, and whenever there was a problem she took charge and dealt with issues.

Grades K-3 had moved to the new Sandhills School lessening the load somewhat, but it was still a heavy load. I would either sink or swim! With the year-round help of many high school students, I managed to stay afloat. The school had a work experience program in place, allowing students to earn extra credits. Almost daily several students were assigned to work one or two periods a day helping me with all the menial

Going home after a day's work at the library.

tasks, like carding and shelving books and filing library cards. Students who could type also helped me with typing catalog cards. Some students volunteered their time at noon hours, either shelving books or filing cards, and I was very grateful for all their help. I don't know how I could have survived without them.

Since I was working at the same school where the children were attending it made life much simpler and easier for all of us. We all went to school together in the morning and home again at night as my hours coincided with school hours. Both Carl and I were working for the school division and our hours were practically the same. We had our evenings and weekends free; two to three weeks at Christmas, ten days for Easter, and two months in the summer. It was a good arrangement, which worked very well for our family life.

Our family in 1977; Carl, LaDawn, Craig, me and Louise.

Forty-Nine

Church Conflict

During all this time when our lives were taking different turns, the same held true for our church. The Bergthaler church was still a fledgling church and, even in this small congregation, the people came from various doctrinal teachings and church backgrounds, causing division among them.

Many people were unhappy about the way the church was changing. This caused ripples, which turned into waves and, gaining momentum, it resulted in a full-fledged storm. The biggest problem was that, for the most part, people were not ready to accept change and they stood by their convictions.

Mr. Jacob Dyck, who had moved with his family from Swift Current, Saskatchewan, had been elected as a pastor in the church. A short time later he was elected as their leader, the bishop. Mr. Dyck was leading the church forward spiritually and this did not fare well with many parishioners, thereby causing a split in the church. Mr. Dyck had a burden to bring the congregation into a relationship with Jesus Christ.

The Reverend Mr. Buhler from Saskatchewan, who had been so faithful – taking many trips in poor road conditions, volunteering his time, encouraging the people in the faith and mentoring them – was called once again to make the trip and deal with the problem. After many discussions, debates and brotherhood meetings, Pastor Dyck and his followers relinquished the church building to those who opposed him and found other meeting places, but kept the Bergthaler name. Mr. David Wall, a bishop from the Sommerfeld Church at Swift Current, Saskatchewan, came to lead the people who had chosen to stay and they took on the name, the Sommerfeld Church. I was a young Christian and neither Carl nor I were well versed in church politics or doctrine, therefore we were unable to make wise decisions. My parents had chosen to go with the Bergthaler group, and Carl's parents had chosen to stay with the Sommerfeld group. We were torn, and decided to refrain from going to church for some time.

During this time I made up Sunday school lessons for the children and we read Bible stories to them – doing our own thing on Sunday mornings. Somehow, it didn't feel right to stay home from church. After some time we chose to go with the Sommerfelders, but we soon realized that the church had regressed from where it had been before the split. Although we kept going for some time, we felt that our needs weren't being met. The decision of the leaders and the brotherhood was to refrain from leading electricity into the building and, therefore, there were no lights or loudspeakers. When we came to church and couldn't get a seat fairly close to the front, we couldn't hear the message and ended up going home totally empty.

When someone in the community passes away, the Mennonite tradition is that family and friends gather in the church for singing in support of the grieving family. After the singing, the funeral arrangements are usually made. When the singing happens in the evening, it means lighting many lanterns to light up the building – enough for the people to read the words of their song books. Today, 50 years later, the building is still not serviced with electricity.

We had to fight the children every Sunday morning to get them to church. I had so many unanswered questions and didn't know where to turn for help. One Sunday morning I struggled with the text of the message that had been presented. I read the passage over and over but I needed an explanation. We were well acquainted with the Andrew Knelsen family who had moved to La Crete the year after we did. Mr. Knelsen had been elected as a pastor with the Bergthaler church but had chosen to stay with the Sommerfelders. I knew him on a personal level as our family had spent much time together with their family before I got married. Still I struggled with asking him for answers and, in the end, I chose not to. Who was I to ask the pastor questions about scripture? It simply wasn't done. We were weary of making this huge effort every Sunday morning, feeling defeated and discouraged and again we decided to stay home from church.

One Sunday morning we had slept later than usual and, when we got up, we discovered that LaDawn was not at home. Louise and Craig informed us that she had gone to the EMC church, which was new in town and was located just down the street from us. Carl and I both knew and understood that we were responsible for the spiritual training of our children, and we were at a crossroad. LaDawn was thirteen years old and, having felt unfulfilled at the church where we had taken her, still had a deep desire for the things of God.

My brother John had been elected a pastor in the Bergthaler church under Bishop Dyck's leadership and was elected to serve as the bishop when Mr. Dyck passed away. As a pastor, John had a difficult assignment. He and Marge were raising a family of nine children without a salary from the ministry and time was seldom his own. His pastoral services were always in demand within the church families and in the community. (In the late 1990s, John and Marge spent several years ministering to the Mennonites in Bolivia. They went again in 2004–2005 but only for about five months.) We knew we would feel at home with John as the leader, so we wasted no time and started attending the next Sunday.

The blessings and spiritual benefits we received there were far beyond my expectations. The church services were still mostly in German, but Low German. It was a big improvement when we could all understand the message. Singing was mostly in English and it stirred my spirit. The singing at the Sommerfeld church was still strictly from the *Gesang Buäk* and their church service was still in High German. We were pleased that now, the children's Sunday school classes were taught in English and they worked from lesson books, which was a huge encouragement to them.

The church also offered adult Sunday school classes, which Carl and I attended every Sunday morning. It was here that a whole new way of studying the Bible was opened up to me. I had so many questions that had built up over the years, and I'm certain everyone in our class must have got tired of my questions. But I was so excited that I didn't care what people thought. Here was the chance for dialogue and potential for spiritual growth. I had been a child of God for almost twenty years and never had the nourishment to mature spiritually. I will be forever grateful to the Bergthaler church for their adult Sunday school program.

Carl and I also got involved in a Bible study group, which kept going for many years. It was here that my faith reached new heights and took me into a much deeper level in my Christian walk, but I still had unanswered questions. One question in particular that I wanted an answer for was, "Why do we celebrate three days at Pentecost?" The Mennonite tradition, which has taken on sacred dimensions over the years, is to celebrate three days at Christmas, Easter and Pentecost – Sunday, Monday and Tuesday, with church services conducted each morning

Since childhood I had been taught about all the major events in the Bible, at home and in Sunday school. I could understand the reason for celebrating Christmas, as there were pictures of the baby Jesus in a manger in Bethlehem, pictures of the angels announcing to the shepherds the birth of the Christ child, and the wise men following the star that led them to Jesus. I also understood Easter as there were pictures in our Bible story books about Jesus dying on the cross, the empty tomb, and the risen Christ as well as pictures of Jesus' ascension into heaven. But why were we celebrating three days at Pentecost? When I was still living at home and we'd come home from church after a Pentecost service, I would at different times ask Dad, "Why are we celebrating Pentecost?" His answer was always the same, "The Holy Spirit was sent down from heaven." Yes, I had heard that many times, but who is the person of the Holy Spirit? I had been taught that the Trinity consisted of three persons – the Father, the Son and the Holy Spirit. I believed it was the Holy Spirit that kept my conscience free. I was very sensitive and recognized immediately when I had stepped out of line, crediting that to the work of the Holy Spirit. Since there were no pictures available, I simply couldn't grasp the full meaning of it; therefore, I couldn't identify or get a mental picture in my mind. I was desperately searching for an answer.

Each year, many of the Bible study groups in our church shut down for the summer months, although our group chose to keep going all year round. Our group consisted of six or seven couples, and we alternated meeting in our homes, giving it a personal touch. One beautiful evening in June 1983, our Bible study meeting was held at the home of Pastor Peter and Margaret Knelsen. Carl had chosen not to come this particular evening, so I went on my own. It was one of the longest days of the year, when the sun sets at about eleven o'clock and dusk follows. In all the years I had lived in northern Alberta, these long, beautiful June evenings had never ceased to amaze me, and this particular evening would have special meaning. Our key verse for the evening was Ephesians 5:18: "*Do not get drunk on wine, which leads to debauchery. Instead be filled with the Spirit.*" It is a command, but how could I fulfill it if I didn't understand it? After our study was finished I still couldn't grasp the meaning of this verse in its entirety and almost sensed a feeling of frustration.

As I was leaving to go home my soul was perplexed. I had only traveled a short distance, and I had just turned south onto the road that runs past the John Derksen and the John Hiebert farms. This stretch of road had tall trees, all leafed out in their various shades of green, lining the roadsides. As I was driving, enjoying this beautiful evening, suddenly a spirit of tranquility engulfed me. I can't find any words to explain what happened next, but I remember that I was standing in the middle of the road. I couldn't recall that I had stopped the car, neither that I got out of it, but I remember standing in the middle of that dirt road lifting my arms to heaven and praising God. I don't know how long I stood there; time didn't seem to matter. There are no proper words to describe or explain my experience. I had never seen the world more colourful; never before had I seen the sky so blue or the grass so lush and green, and never before had I heard the birds sing so sweetly. I was in awe. God had not allowed any interference, as no vehicles had passed by to spoil this sacred moment, and I regard that spot on that dirt road as sacred to this day.

Ephesians 5:18 leaped off the page and I understood it. I had been filled and empowered by the Holy Spirit. After this experience I was able to understand portions of scripture I had struggled with many times, and I was able to quickly memorize Bible verses and remember where they were found. Scripture teaches in John 14: v26 *"... the Counsellor, the Holy Spirit, whom the Father will send in my name will teach you all things ..."* I experienced peace, contentment, and a feeling of selfworth I had never known before. I understood why there was no picture of the Holy Spirit. The Bible's description is that it's like a mighty rushing wind. I experienced it, and it is like the wind. You can feel it, and you know it's there, but you can't see it.

I still felt there were missing pieces to the whole puzzle of the Christian life. I had been raised and trained in a legalistic church, a legalistic community and, to a degree, in a legalistic home. At times I felt I was drowning in legalism. So many rules of the church simply didn't make any sense to me, especially if there was no scripture to back it up. I often studied the Bible on my own and the more I studied the more questions I had, especially when I studied the Books of Galatians, Ephesians, and Romans, which address the topic of God's grace.

It wasn't until some years later that I caught a glimpse of God's grace and began to see the whole picture. Since I was raised and trained under the umbrella of legalism, I was very faithful in instilling this in our children. When the children were teenagers, they recognized before I did that the dos and don'ts of religion – behaviour modification – can never fill the void that every person is searching to fill. Carl and I were adamant about enforcing rules and rebellion crept into our family life as a result. Had I understood even a little of God's grace, it would have spared us and our children many heartaches. The rules and regulations for producing obedience may change actions and deeds for a while but they can never change the heart. We were trying to produce the Christian life, and we were expecting our children to do likewise by doing all the right things out of fear rather than out of love. When I understood what the cross had accomplished, I also understood that our inner desire shifts from "I MUST perform and do good works to be right with God," to "I WANT to do good works because I am already right with God." It's a heart transformation. The Bible calls it grace – a foundational truth on which to build our entire Christian life.

Grace sets our spirits free, and we are no longer in bondage to the law or traditions to produce the Christian life. In John: 8:32, Jesus said, "... and you shall know the truth, and the truth shall make you free." In John 8: 36, He says, "So if the Son sets you free, you will be free indeed." Galatians 5:1 says, "It is for freedom that Christ has set us free. Stand firm then, and do not let yourself be burdened again by a yoke of slavery." (The law). I am so grateful for this freedom, and my desire is no other than to do God's will. When disappointments, heartaches, trouble or strife come my way I can still experience a 'Peace amid the storm.' In Phillipians 4:7, the Bible tells us, "And the peace of God, which transcends all understanding, will guard your hearts and your minds in Christ Jesus." My new-found understanding just whetted my appetite to learn and understand biblical truths and to know God more intimately.

Some of that was realized when, on a number of occasions, we went to visit LaDawn and Isaac (I will tell the story of their marriage later) in Montana where they are serving with and living on Youth With a Mission's (YWAM) branch campus of the University of the Nations, and Carl and I were privileged sit in on their teaching sessions. They had various teachers come to teach on certain topics, usually one topic being taught for a week at a time. I started to develop growing pains as I tried to understand and comprehend the depth of the messages that were taught. I had never been exposed to such powerful teaching before and more pieces of the puzzle were starting to fall into place.

Fifty

Farming

The history of the Mennonite people has always had its roots firmly planted on family farms. Carl and I both grew up in families that had a strong attachment to "the soil." Although there were often difficulties, the lifestyle was carefree and there was no need to carry a lunch bucket or answer to a boss. Carl had struggled with farming fever for all the seventeen years we had lived in town and he wanted desperately to move to the country and try to make a living off the land. He was interested in the land that bordered the property where his parents lived in the Buffalo Head Prairie area, which was approximately fifteen miles from town. This land had been surveyed upon our request after six or seven years of lobbying the government. We couldn't understand why it took so long to consider our request. One day we were notified that a homestead land sale was coming up in the community. The condition the government set was that every parcel of land for sale had to be a viable farming unit comprised of three quarter sections or more. The land we had lobbied the government for was coming up for sale and consisted of three quarter sections.

We were excited and applied for it, knowing the government had all our correspondence regarding this land in their files, and we felt confident that the decision would go in our favour. When the announcement was made, the land had been awarded to someone else. We were devastated. We received a letter informing us that we could appeal the decision. We did send in our letter of appeal together with a copy of all of the previous correspondence we'd had with the government concerning this land. When the appeal decision came back we had been awarded two quarter sections out of the three section unit. One quarter was hilly and rocky, and the other quarter had the creek running across it as well as the Forestry Tower Road, so many acres were lost. The best of the three quarters, which had the potential for making it a viable farming unit, went to a farmer whose land bordered on this quarter. In all the 50 plus years I have known Carl I have never seen him more discouraged or feeling more defeated and betrayed. In the weeks and months that followed we discovered more than we ever cared to know.

Discouragement aside, we would try to make the best of what was dealt to us. We knew we wouldn't be able to make a living off this land, but we decided to try and farm anyway. We were still thankful that we would be able to move out of town. The children were growing up fast, and the time had come that they wanted to spend more and more time around town with their friends. We were uncomfortable when we didn't know where they were.

That first winter we had 230 acres cleared, and we planned to move to the homestead in the summer. Abe and Edna Wiebe, a couple we knew well, were in the process of building a new house, so we inquired about

We moved this house onto the homestead.

their existing house. They had built the new house too close to the old one and therefore couldn't torch it. They told us we could gladly have it for moving it off their yard. We couldn't believe our good fortune. We had planned to build a house that first summer, but it didn't materialize. We had highly underestimated all the work that needed to be done and the time it would take to do it. We moved the house and started to make it livable.

At one point someone had started to tear down the house, which meant it needed to be fixed up again. Carl worked hard all summer getting the ground level and the cement blocks laid for the foundation as well as building a driveway. Glenn and Pat Grandgenet, our friends from Edmonton, came up for ten days in August. Glenn was a great help to Carl. The last week in August some of my family and some of Carl's family came to help us pack and move, as well as wash out the entire house so it was ready to be rented. We had signed a contract with the Fort Vermilion School Division to rent it commencing the early part of September. Carl and I were both employed with the school division and felt rather fortunate, as we both had two months off in the summer. I don't know how we would have managed otherwise.

Hind sight is 20-20, and we soon realized we had been too hasty to move. We had no water or sewer, no electricity or telephone. We didn't have the heat going for quite some time except for the heat from the propane oven, and it rained practically every day in September – we were forced to cope in the cold, dark, clammy atmosphere.

Every minute of every day seemed to be taken up with work, and at times, it seemed like there wasn't enough time to burp after a meal. This experience took me back 25 years when I had moved with my parents to the ruthless hinterland of northern Alberta. It was inconvenient, but I could cope. LaDawn, on the other hand, was at the age where it was a must to have a shower and get hair washed every morning before school, adding to an already stressful time. We hauled water from the neighbours and heated it on the propane stove. LaDawn needed to be ready for the school bus by eight o'clock – another setback; riding the bus for almost an hour before she got to school.

Craig and Louise adjusted more easily to their new surroundings. They both had to adjust to a new school, as we transferred them to the Buffalo Head Prairie School only a few miles away. LaDawn had no choice of schools, as the BHP school only went up to grade 9 and she was taking grade 10. Craig and Louise caught a later bus. I had to leave for work before they got on the bus, and they were home before Carl or

I. Considering the primitive conditions we were living in, I didn't think I could handle another day of this. I had gone through hardships growing up, and I wasn't convinced that I wanted to subject my family to any more than necessary.

After agonizing over the decision I would have to make, I did what I needed to do. After three and one-half years in the library at La Crete Public School, I handed in my resignation and felt, under the circumstances, it was the right thing to do.

Carl had to build corrals and shelters before he could move the animals. He purchased a big red barn, which had belonged to John F. Driedger, for $800.00 and moved it onto the yard. This barn served us very well at milking and calving time and often as a shelter. Carl was so overloaded with work that he also gave up his school bus driving job.

After a while things started falling into place. We got the heat going, as well as a big mantle lamp to give us light. In October we dug a well and got good drinking water at sixteen feet. That was one less headache – no more hauling water except hauling it from the well to the house, which was done in buckets. This chore fell mostly on Craig and Louise's shoulders. We had bought four new galvanized buckets for this purpose, so whoever hauled the water in the winter put the buckets on a sled and brought the water into the house. Water always spilled over while hauling it, making the pathway, which was a bit sloped, icy and slippery. One winter day when the path was very icy it was Louise's turn to bring in the water. Since it wasn't her favourite job, she allowed her frustrations to kick in. Twice she tipped the whole load but went back a third time. It happened again! She kicked the buckets and they went flying. We still had no water in the house, but we did have four very badly dinted, brand new water buckets. Later we used big plastic barrels, with lids and that worked much better. With no electricity, I went to one of my sisters, either Mary or Babe, to do the laundry. We got telephone service in October, but we had to wait until February for the power company to provide us with electricity.

The house was spacious throughout. The main level had two bedrooms, a large living room and a bathroom. A lean-to had been added to the main part of the house, and it served as a kitchen and dining room. A small porch was attached to the lean-to. The children were all excited to have their own bedrooms. LaDawn and Louise occupied the two large bedrooms upstairs while Craig has his own downstairs. I must admit that, over the years, I quite enjoyed that old house if I didn't dwell on its transparency, especially in the winter.

Carl put a new ceiling into the lean-to part of the house, and I painted it white. When Sears sent out their clearance sale catalogue, I ordered many rolls of wall paper – our choice was limited to mainly pastel floral designs. We put new linoleum into this part, making it feel very homey with the wood fires burning. The rest of the house didn't need as much work, although the walls in every room were a depressing, dark chocolate brown paneling. I went to work and wall papered all the rest of the rooms and was very proud of the result. I sewed new curtains from my old orange ones, strung them up, and added another colour to the confusing décor. I really felt like I had given this baby a face lift and didn't realize that Carl despised the wallpaper designs. I needed to remind him that the wallpaper had been on sale. I didn't discover that he detested wall paper, period, until months later. It was a little too late. He was always afraid to hurt my feelings, and sometimes I didn't find out until much later that he really wasn't excited about what I had done.

For the most part our marriage was going very well; we had adjusted well to living under the same roof. There was one area, however, that

Carl's family, taken after his parents and two brothers had passed away.
Standing in the back row: Sarah, David, Pete, Frank, George and Marge.
In the front row: Carl, Agnes, Jake, Kay and John.

Grandma and Granddad with their family of twelve boys. Dad is the third from the left in the back row. Uncle Abe, who passed away in 1947, is first in the front row. This photo was taken circa 1936.

Carl and me a few years after we moved to the homestead.

still needs continual guardianship. This conflict stems back to the homes in which we were raised. I was raised in a home where the motto was, "Never leave until tomorrow what you can do today." My dad was always in a rush, and I think he must have been born in a hurry. The saying went that Grandma just jumped over the cradle and another son had joined the family. Dad came from a family of fifteen boys, (three died in childhood), no girls. "There's work to be done so let's get this thing over with and let's get on with the program."

With only boys in the family, Grandma was probably justified in always being in a hurry. So my dad passed this undesirable trait onto me, which I have struggled with all my life. But, oh, being able to work quickly comes in so handy when there are deadlines to meet. Carl, on the other hand, came from a home that was much more laid back, and he didn't get terribly hot and bothered when things didn't get done. Both traits can be equally damaging or rewarding depending on circumstances. One day Carl had a doctor's appointment in town, and he wasn't coming in from the garage, although I had reminded him not to forget. I went to check and see what the hold-up was and asked him, "Carl, what are you doing? You have an appointment to keep." He said, "I'm teaching Craig how to weld." Most of the time he had more patience with the children than I did which was a good thing, but finding and keeping a balance is an ongoing struggle.

Although Louise and Craig coped fairly well, they did have a few adjustments to make with the move to the homestead. Louise was never a difficult child, so I'm sure that at times we were blind to her needs. I think the most difficult thing for her was to change schools. She was very unhappy at her new school as she had left all her friends behind. We ended up switching her back to La Crete Public. The next year, however, the school division made it compulsory that students were not allowed to attend a school outside their district unless parents provided transportation. This didn't make much sense to us, as the bus came into the yard to pick up LaDawn anyway. We had no choice but to switch Louise back to Buffalo Head Prairie School.

Craig on the other hand, could never have been happier than he was with the move to the country. The first fall we lived on the homestead the rabbit population was at its peak, and he and his cousin Terry were on a rabbit hunt continually. One night they decided to butcher several of the rabbits and fry up the meat. Craig persuaded me to try some, and I actually found it quite tasty. He loved the outdoors and the bush and spent many hours in the forest, sitting on the creek bank until long after dark during beaver hunting season. In no uncertain terms, he gave me strict orders not to call for him, as it would chase the beavers away. I was always afraid of the dark, and I couldn't handle the thought of this twelve-year-old out there by himself until long after the sun had set, the hungry bears having just emerged from their winter sleep. He never feared the dark, and he simply couldn't understand why I was so concerned.

Goose hunting season came to be the highlight for Craig in the fall. As soon as the season opened, he was cutting down willows to make his blind (a natural screen in which to hide when hunting). Craig preferred the morning hunt – that meant setting up the blinds and decoys the evening before to get the geese acquainted with the surroundings. He usually went hunting with friends or his cousins – often Carl accompanied them. Since Craig preferred the morning hunt it meant getting up around four or four-thirty in the morning, depending on the distance he needed to drive to a good hunting field. This was supposed to be fun? I didn't get it!

Craig always wanted me to accompany him on a hunt and, one day, he finally persuaded me to go. The alarm clock rang at 4:30 a.m. It was drizzling rain and I don't think I had ever been less enthusiastic about anything in my life that was supposed to be pleasure. I got dressed real warm and drug my feet all the way to the vehicle. Carl, LaDawn, and several of Craig's buddies joined us.

When we got to the hunting field, Craig parked the vehicle out of sight near some bushes, trusting the geese would not detect any danger. We all settled inside the blind and quietly waited. As the sun was starting to rise we faintly heard the geese honking and the guys started to call them in. Peeking through the blind, we could see them coming in our direction. It had quit raining and the sunrise was a spectacular sight – the surrounding forest was dipped in autumn gold; the geese silhouetted against the orange sky. The honking got louder as they came closer and we could see the famous V formation of the geese. I was in awe of this moment – witnessing nature as I had never seen it before. But, then, the serenity of the moment was shattered by shot-gun blasts as the geese came directly overhead. Many came down. We took them home, plucked their feathers, then butchered them and enjoyed a good supper. I made many pillows over the years from the soft down. It had been a good morning and I began to understand how this event could get into your blood and become addictive.

In the winter Craig set some traps and caught fur-bearing animals to earn some spending money. During chore time one morning we discovered that our good milk cow had taken its last breath. Carl had the difficult assignment of hauling it out to the field. Now, Craig despised anything to do with chickens, be it cleaning the chicken coop, chicken dinners, or gathering the eggs. One of our laying hens always pecked him, cocking one eye as chickens do, and giving him that puzzled look when he went to gather the eggs while she was sitting on the nest. He vowed the next time she pecked him he would ring that chicken's neck and use it for coyote bait. It wasn't until years later that he told me he had done just that and used it to bait the trap he set by the dead cow. He caught quite

Mom and Dad's 50th wedding anniversary, July 19, 1981.

a few coyotes but the crafty wolves were not lured into the trap. One day we watched four timber wolves feeding on the dead cow, disregarding the chicken. We all took turns looking through binoculars from the upstairs window as these beautiful animals dined on what had been our precious milk supply.

On hot summer days, LaDawn, Louise and Craig often went swimming, together with their cousins, in a dugout about two miles from home. I was usually terrified because they hadn't learned to swim, and the potential for drowning was very real. Before leaving on one of their afternoon swim trips, Craig told me I had said, "Be careful and don't drown. If you do, I won't let you go swimming again." I still don't believe I said that, but it's his word against mine. The children all learned to swim in that dugout.

Mom and Dad loved to come to our new home. I had a close relationship with my parents, but I felt it was more than that. I believed they were reliving their past to a degree, especially the first while that we lived on the homestead. We used the mantle and coal-oil lamps for light, and we were heating the house with wood. Frequently, Dad would be ready to go home, but Mom was in no hurry. She would sit beside that wood heater just enjoying the wood heat, and she simply wasn't ready to go. Somehow,

I felt they were connecting the past to the present and found comfort in it. On July 19, 1981, Mom and Dad celebrated their 50th wedding anniversary together with family and friends.

Some years later we got well acquainted with our neighbours, Mr. and Mrs. Isaac Klassen. Mrs. Klassen was Mom's first cousin, and I felt a real kinship there reminding me of going to Grandmother's house years ago. She was still cooking on a wood cook stove year-round, rekindling my memories of days gone by. They collected rain water from the roof, led it into a cistern, mounted a small hand pump on the kitchen counter and drew up the water for their needs. Mrs. Klassen was always in the process of concocting some health remedy, which did seem to keep them healthy. She picked and dried rose hips, the seed of the wild rose. The flesh of the rose hip is loaded with vitamins and is very sweet after a good frost. She dried these on brown paper behind the wood cook stove and, later, used them for making tea. The whole atmosphere in their home reminded me of *The Little House on the Prairie* series by Laura Ingalls Wilder. Carl and I still love to go visit them in their home, and it takes me back 50 years in time.

The second winter we lived on the farm, Carl again went back to driving school bus, but that same winter he needed back surgery and was flown to Edmonton for it. The doctors kept him in the hospital in High Level until they could arrange a flight, but I went home. The next day the hospital staff informed me of the time the plane would leave. I was torn between going with Carl, or staying home to look after everything. I phoned Jake and told him about my situation. He told me he would take me to High Level if I wanted to go. I needed to make up my mind in a hurry – the plane was leaving in a few hours. I knew that family and friends were only a phone call away if the children ran into trouble. LaDawn was almost seventeen years old and quite capable of taking charge. I decided to go with Carl. Jake took me to High Level, and when the plane left it was minus 54 degrees Fahrenheit. Ice fog was thick and visibility was nil, so I was quite concerned about Jake heading back home as the truck had started to sputter on the way up. But he made it safely home.

The cold snap lasted for quite a long time. Margaret and Fred popped in one day to visit us after we got back home after the surgery. We had a small wood heater in the living room where Carl was recovering. Margaret told me I would have to take the ashes out of the stove, as it was half full. I told her that I couldn't let the fire go out. It was bitterly cold outside and at times, it felt like the wind just slowed down a bit when it hit the house. It would have to wait until the weather turned milder. There were times when the weather turned warmer very suddenly. We lived at the foot of the Buffalo Head Hills, and we enjoyed many chinook winds in the dead of winter that often didn't reach far beyond our area. One winter morning when I was driving to town the thermometer read plus 40 degrees Fahrenheit. I had driven only a few miles when I noticed a very distinct cut-off of the warm winds. The hoar frost had all disappeared from the trees up to a certain point, and then they were white and heavy with frost again.

Carl's parents lived about a quarter of a mile from where we later got our homestead, and one Christmas morning, when we still lived in town, the temperature had dropped to minus 40 degrees F. Mom and Dad Friesen were to host the family Christmas celebration on December 26 like they did every year, but because of the extreme cold temperatures, Mom phoned all the family and asked us not to come. She reasoned it was too cold and she and Dad did not want to worry about all of us being on the road with all the small children. They thought it wiser to celebrate Christmas when the weather turned milder. When we woke up the next morning the mercury had climbed to plus 40 degrees, an overnight change in temperature of 80 degrees. We did celebrate Christmas on December 26, and the children had a great time playing in the snow and making snow men with the wet, sticky snow.

Fifty-One

More Jobs Available

I was home by myself most of the day and I began to feel the urge to study. The University of Athabasca was offering courses via correspondence. I enrolled in several courses and I rather enjoyed studying by correspondence again. After some time, though, I realized if I was going to be serious about earning a teaching degree it would take up too much of my time. The children were still living at home, and I wasn't ready for this huge commitment. I put the project on hold.

After some serious thought, I went to the Buffalo Head Prairie School and applied for a substitute teaching position. For various reasons, teachers were often away, and they needed adults to take charge of their classes. I rather enjoyed the students and was on call for quite a number of years as a substitute.

Working with children at the Buffalo Head Prairie School was not the only thing that I worked at during that time. During my stay with Ged and Beulah Baldwin I had spent about a week at Sokoloski's, who were good friends of the Baldwin's. We had never kept in touch, but Mrs. Sokoloski remembered where I lived. She was employed with Elections Canada and was responsible for Peace River North. She called me one day and asked if I'd be interested in taking responsibility for enumerating the Buffalo Head Prairie, Savage Prairie, and Tompkins Landing areas for an upcoming election. I told her I would take the job. I wasn't totally sure what it all entailed, but I soon found out. I had to travel to every household in these areas and try to get everyone over eighteen years of age onto a voting list, making sure their names, addresses and phone numbers were correct. The worst of the job was coming face to face with every man's dog. When people weren't home, I had to brave the task of knocking on their doors while putting up with dogs that were ready to climb out of their skins. I never got bit, though. When election time came around I was responsible for setting up the polling station, and finding someone willing to sit beside me from 8:00 a.m. to 8:00 p.m. – a boring job, as not many people came out to vote. I did this for quite a number of elections, both provincial and federal.

In the summer, the church ran a Vacation Bible School program and help was always needed. I started out helping with baking cookies for snack time and later I helped out in the kitchen. One year when the need for a grade 7 teacher arose I volunteered to fill the spot. I was quite familiar working with students of this age group, as I had often been called in to supervise a junior high school class at the BHP school. I related well to junior high students, and I taught grade 7 VBS for quite a number of years. Many children from the community attended as well as all the children from church, before the Bergthaler church expanded, placing a huge responsibility on the organizers to find enough teachers. One year there were forty people on staff, not to mention all the mothers at home baking cookies and the mothers who were baby-sitting, freeing others up to teach. It was a huge undertaking for the organizers and the workers, but there was the assurance that planting the seed of the Word of God would produce good fruit in the years to come.

Our lives were continually changing, and some changes were more difficult to cope with than others. It was June, 1982, and LaDawn was graduating from high school. Having applied for college in Grande Prairie, and scheduled to leave in September, we knew she would only be home for the summer. She had already met and fallen in love with her husband-to-be, Isaac Dyck. He was a fine young man, and we approved of her choice.

When it came time to move, she borrowed Isaac's truck, backed it up to the house and starting loading her belongings like it was an every day affair. She left home for college in the same fashion she had left the house to start grade 1, anxious to try new things. Quite a number of her classmates also went to Grande Prairie to attend college, making it a little easier. We had given her roots, and now the time had come to give her wings. She would have to learn how to fly on her own, and I remember praying, "Lord, if she flies too high, please clip her wings." She was the first one to leave home, and I really struggled with it. What made it more difficult for me to understand was that she had no second thoughts, tackling this big change head-on, like you just do what you have to do and don't look back. Everything worked out very well; she and Isaac were married the next summer and settled down in Grande Prairie. We knew the days of her coming home to live were over, and it seemed so empty just knowing she had moved out for good.

The government ran a home care program in La Crete and they were advertising for workers. I applied for the job and was hired. I wasn't particularly fond of my job description – basically cleaning and spending some extra time with my clients, but I thought I'd give it a try. I really enjoyed working with the older people, actually bonding with them, and found that part of the work rewarding. It didn't give me any satisfaction, though, spending all day cleaning people's houses and toilets, especially when I got home and was faced with cleaning my own. I didn't feel particularly blessed with this job, so my eyes were ever open for other opportunities. The cost of farming, especially on such a small scale, was mounting – there was always an unexpected cost somewhere. It didn't take very long before Carl and I realized we would both have to earn a wage to support the farm if we were to continue living there and enjoying country life.

Fairview College was setting up a campus on the Buffalo Head Prairie school grounds to expand their adult literacy program and they were looking for instructors to teach basic literacy. I was immediately interested. I had experienced first-hand during my years in the post office, the number of intelligent, illiterate people who were living in a silent prison, experiencing so much hidden pain due to circumstances beyond their control. When I got notice that the job was mine, I was thrilled to have the opportunity to help these people. Numerous others who were literate also attended – brushing up on grammar, sentence structure and spelling. I found this job very rewarding.

Fifty-Two

Summary Excursions

During our busy schedules we always managed to find time once or twice during the summer to go on fishing trips together with my sisters, Mary and Babe, and their families. Occasionally some other members of the family joined us, and we always ended up having a great time. For many years, fishing was really good at the Chinchaga River, which is half way between High Level and Rainbow Lake. Usually, the river at the place where we camped was so shallow we could walk through the water to the other side.

One summer day we had again packed up all our camping and fishing gear and headed for our favourite fishing spot. Since we were late getting away we scrambled to set up camp before dark. We had not finished setting up, but were already in the process of feeding the children and getting them ready for bed, when we noticed the river rising. Some of the men had gone to gather firewood along the river bank and when they returned they said, "The water is rising fast and we're in trouble." One of the men pounded a stick near the water's edge to give us an idea of how much the water was rising. It was rising fast and we knew we had to get out. We all scampered around for all we were worth, packing everything up again and heading out. By the time we left, the trail leading down to the river was totally submerged, and we weren't able to detect all the big rocks hidden there. It was a rough ride, but we all made it safely to dry ground. It was an inconvenience, but how thankful we were that it didn't

Craig and Carl with their catch at Chinchaga.

happen in the middle of the night when everyone was sleeping. Somehow I felt that God was always looking after us, and especially in times like these.

When, after a number of years the fish population at Chinchaga started to dwindle, we started camping at Machesis Lake near High Level. By this time our families had grown up and most of them had families of their own – the extra hands came in handy when organizing the campout. There was no fishing here, but the men folk rented canoes and, at different times, everyone enjoyed canoeing on the beautiful lake. At sunset we watched as the sun disappeared behind the trees and we enjoyed the colourful reflection in the water. At night we built a big campfire, and

A successful day of fishing at one of our favourite spots, Little Buffalo River, NWT.

Craig with his 22 lb. jackfish.

Carl with a good catch.

Me, Mary and Babe with our pilot, John Lonsdale, and another good catch.

sat around eating goodies, roasting marshmallows and enjoying "Spitz"– cracking sunflower seeds – while visiting and singing until everyone started falling asleep. We spent so much time together that a special bond developed within our families.

In later years we started traveling to the Little Buffalo River near Fort Resolution, Northwest Territories, where the fishing was excellent, especially at the mouth where the Little Buffalo River flows into the Great Slave Lake. On one of our fishing trips we caught about 70 fish in a twenty-four hour period, the majority of them big ones. We were a large group, and were each allowed three in possession. We needn't have worried anyway, as we fried up many of them for supper each night. At one point our friend, Jae Penner, now my niece Kelly's husband, was in the boat with us and since he was the only male, killing the fish automatically fell to him. I remember him getting a bit frustrated as we were hauling them in faster than he could kill them. He didn't get much fishing done!

Louise had made many friends in town, and she was also close to several of her cousins. She loved pajama parties, and usually once or twice during the summer, she had all her friends over. One afternoon when she was making arrangements for one of her parties, a bear ventured into the yard. It wasn't uncommon, as we had a bear in the yard every summer for the first six or seven years we lived on the homestead. The girls had decided to sleep in tents, but Carl and I felt very uncomfortable with that idea, especially with a bear hanging around. We had a camper shell on the back of the pick-up truck – Carl backed it up to the house near our bedroom window and the girls bedded down in there. The biggest thrill about a pajama party is, of course, the privilege of staying up late, eating special treats, music, and just the joy of having fun time with friends. Needless to say, Carl and I didn't get much sleep that night due to the noise, but we wouldn't have had much sleep either had they slept in a tent. At least our minds were at ease and the girls were having fun.

Louise was a model teenager, and she never gave us any trouble. When the children started going out on their own we had an agreement to leave a note where to contact each other if necessary. Curfew time at our house was eleven o'clock and we expected everyone to be home by then. One evening Carl and I had gone to my sister Mary's to have coffee with her and Jake, and, of course, we left a note. Their phone rang at eleven o'clock and Louise wanted to talk to me. She seriously informed me that it was eleven o'clock and we still weren't home. Her understanding was that the rule applied to everyone and she was about to enforce it!

Carl and me with the bear he shot a few feet from our house.

Fifty-Three

Abandoned Moose Calf

Spring. The time when birds and animals have their babies and are busy feeding and protecting them. Wild animals fiercely protect their young, but occasionally nature interferes and with instinct as their guide, they will abandon their offspring.

This was the case one spring day when Johnny Wieler, who lived at West La Crete, discovered an abandoned moose calf. Why it was abandoned still remains a mystery. He kept close watch, but the mother did not return. The calf was getting very weak, lying in the hot sun all day, without any nourishment. Johnny knew we had lots of extra milk on the farm, and asked Carl if he would consider taking it home. He did but it gave us much extra work. We bottle fed him at regular times, just like a baby. When he was hungry and came crying, we dropped whatever we were doing and took time to feed him. We knew it was illegal to harbour wild animals and Carl took precautions to keep us out of trouble. He contacted Alberta Fish and Wildlife on numerous occasions, leaving messages, but they never responded. We had done our part and didn't worry about it anymore.

The baby moose needed lots of attention and thereby provided much entertainment. He adopted us like a mother and followed us around just like a puppy. He and the dog were often in competition, both laying claim to the porch deck. During an electrical storm one day when a bolt of lightening flashed, followed by a crash of thunder, both of them headed

Our baby moose.

for the deck at the same time. It was three steps up but the moose made it there first and the dog had to find another place – they were equally afraid of thunder storms. It was not unusual for the moose to walk straight into the kitchen when the door was left open, especially when he was hungry; steps were not a hindrance to him. He ate watermelon just like a human, only eating the red part of the melon.

Spring turned to summer, and I had a beautiful garden. The moose loved the garden more than I did, so we frequently locked horns. We kept close watch of the garden and often had to chase him out of the corn patch. He was a crafty, sneaky little rascal, and we discovered him lying down behind the corn patch one day feeding undisturbed, which got to be his habit. Since we couldn't see him feeding anymore, one of us had to keep watch continually. When I caught him again I was at my wits end. The children were very attached to him, just like Carl and I were, but enough was enough. I came into the house and told Carl, "This is it. Something has to be done." We knew we couldn't let him roam, as he was already wandering away from the yard at times. Hunting season was coming up and we knew he would be meat on somebody's table the first

Craig feeding watermelon to the baby moose.

day of hunting season.

Craig said, "I'm going to phone Al Oeming and see if he wants a moose." Dr. Al Oeming operated a game farm a short distance out of Edmonton and called it "The Alberta Game Farm." Later, when he was no longer farming tropical animals, he renamed it, "Polar Park." His game farm boosted the tourist industry in Alberta. Dr. Oeming had raised a cheetah from birth, which became his traveling companion. He traveled across the country and internationally, visiting schools and lecturing students on wildlife, especially endangered species; always bringing his pet cheetah with him.

He toured northern Alberta and was scheduled to visit the Buffalo Head Prairie School. The students were excited knowing he would be accompanied by his pet cheetah. As part of his lecture, Dr. Oeming described an endangered animal; its habitat, size, colouration and how many were left in the world and then asked the students if they knew which animal he had described. During his lecture at the BHP school he described the black-footed ferret. He was not finished describing the animal when Craig gave him the correct answer. He was pleased and mentioned that

Craig and two other students with Dr. Al Oeming and his cheetah.

in all his years of lecturing in Canada and internationally, Craig was only the eighth student to have the correct answer after he described the black-footed ferret. Dr. Oeming asked to have a photo taken with Craig. This incident hit the newspaper and radio; it was good to know that a grade 6 student from the back woods of northern Alberta was able to answer a question about an endangered species.

Craig had this little experience with Dr. Oeming, and felt he could lift that telephone receiver and talk to him. I got his phone number, and Craig dialed him up, got him on the line right away and asked him if he wanted a moose. He told Craig that he had wanted to get one for a long time, but strict government regulations usually posed a problem. As a game farm owner, he certainly had to go through a lot of red tape to legally take possession of and transport the moose. Dr. Oeming called us to arrange a time for pick up, although he needed a medical examination of the moose before he could transport him. Dr. Bob Gainer was the veterinarian at Fort Vermilion, serving all of La Crete as well. Carl knew him on a personal level due to sharing a mutual interest in caring for sick animals. Dr. Oeming and Dr. Gainer were also well acquainted; Dr. Gainer readily agreed to do the examination and the arrangement was made to meet at our house for supper and then load the moose later.

That clever little prankster knew something was up and hid in the

Louise, Craig and LaDawn taking turns feeding the moose at the game farm.

bushes surrounding the house. Our pet name for him was 'Moosie Baby', and he always came when we called him, but not this time. All of us joined in the search and eventually found him camouflaged so well we wouldn't have found him if someone hadn't stumbled over him. Dr. Gainer gave him a check-up, the men loaded him into a big crate on the back of the truck, and he was off to the game farm.

Several weeks later we took the family on a short holiday. We toured the Storyland Valley Zoo, Fort Edmonton and other places of interest. The second day we headed for the game farm, as we were anxious to see the moose. When we spotted a group of animals, one in particular looked like a moose but he didn't look like *our* moose. No sooner had we called his name, however, when he came running towards us. He had grown so much in such a short time that we hadn't recognized him. When all the tourists had left and the gates were closed for the day, Al Oeming invited us to stay for supper and offered us the privilege of watching his staff feed all the animals. He allowed the moose to come out of the fence; we fed him and he followed us around the park. Al Oeming officially named the moose 'Craig' and turned him loose on forty acres of bush land in the park. Some time later, on several occasions, Al Oeming appeared on the Alan Thicke Show with "Craig" promoting the protection of wildlife.

Fifty-Four

Life on the Farm

Our land had been cleared of roots, plowed and cultivated, and so began the cycle of seeding and harvesting. Farming was on a very small scale, but we were still always thankful for whatever the land produced. We raised almost every kind of farm animal for a number of years; horses, cows, pigs, sheep, dogs, cats, turkeys, ducks, geese and chickens. We even had a mother hen who had hatched her own baby chicks and was fiercely protective of her brood. One day when a strong wind came up, she was scampering for shelter; her tail feathers standing straight up as the wind pushed her, her babies peeping and trying to keep up until she found a safe place. Springtime was such a wonderful season when all the babies arrived, keeping us all very busy.

The animals served many purposes and helped us keep food on the table; the chickens with eggs and meat, the sheep with wool, and the ducks and geese with meat and down for pillows. The cows provided us with meat, cream, butter, cottage cheese and milk. There were times when we couldn't get the milk when we needed it. We had a calf whose mother produced enough milk, but was always sneaking milk from our milk cow. We had to do something. I went to the barn yard, took the measurements of the cow and sewed a bra! I had a bit of trouble getting it to fit right but in the end I was convinced that it would solve the problem. At chore time we noticed the calf enjoying an illegal breakfast and the cow was still kicking, trying to remove the frayed material still hanging from her

Carl enjoying harvest time.

back, some of it tangled around her legs. We would have to find another solution.

Carl and the children usually helped with chores, although there were times when it wasn't possible. One winter morning I was left to do the chores and the pathway was slippery. We had a downward slope just before we came to the house and, returning from the barn, I had forgotten about it. I was carrying a big bucket of milk in one hand and a bucket of eggs in the other when BANG, down I went, spilling the milk while the eggs went flying in every direction. I uttered a few words unfamiliar to my everyday vocabulary, which I wasn't famous for, but it was only the dog and me, and he had much more important matters to tend to. I discovered immediately that he was an "egg suckin' hound" and he was having himself a party "all by hisself."

Craig was experiencing pain in his legs which seemed to increase as the day went on then reached its peak at bedtime; more so in early spring when he was traipsing through the bush and slushy snow wearing rubber boots. One evening after he went to bed he called me and asked if I would massage his legs. He occupied a bedroom upstairs after LaDawn left home, and I needed to walk up the stairs, which was an effort for me, as I was waiting for knee-replacement surgery. I took some lotion up with me

A morning's work gone to waste.

and started massaging his legs, when all of a sudden he ripped a loud one that almost blew me off the bed and I was beginning to choke. I was very upset when he started to laugh and he couldn't quit. I let him know I was upset and made my way downstairs.

A short while later, he called again and begged me to finish the job. I told him I wasn't coming up again if all he would do was blow hot air. He promised he wouldn't do it again and was very sincere in his pleading as he said his legs were very sore. My motherly instinct, to take care of my hurting child, kicked in and I went back upstairs. No sooner had I started to massage his legs when it happened again. He went into fits of hysterical laughter and I had had it. He knew better than to ever ask me to rub his legs again.

In the spring Carl sheared the sheep, and then came the awful task of washing the stinky wool. Mom and Dad came to help, as they had forgotten more about washing wool than I was likely to learn. We needed soft water, which meant waiting for the rain to come. We heated the water in the *Miea'grope* and washed the wool outside in big galvanized tubs as it needed many washes and many rinses. When the wool was clean we carefully laid it out to dry in the sun. In the winter, when I had more free time, I carded the wool with a hand carder. One spring when Carl had sheared thirteen sheep, I found the task too big for me. I very quickly decided to take the clean wool to Mrs. Letkeman who was in the business of carding wool and making wool comforters. Today we are still using and enjoying the comforters she made.

We raised our own animals on the farm to supply us with meat year-round. Every fall we butchered our pigs in the old traditional way; a steer got strung up and at times was supplemented by a moose. The children also enjoyed butchering season. Chicken butchering bees were much hard work and a lot of fun. We had a group of regulars – mostly extended family – that worked well together. Everyone seemed to find their own area of expertise and the operation went quite smoothly. We established an assembly line of sorts. Equipment was already set up outside, close to the well at the barn, and the *Mieaʾgrope* was full of boiling water when the workers arrived. First order of business was the honourable job of decapitating the chickens. This was done by stretching the chickens necks between the two spikes pounded into a large block of wood and lowering the axe swiftly and with considerable strength. This job usually fell to one of the men, but if LaDawn and Craig were around, they sometimes did

LaDawn and me trying to stay in good spirits while performing the worst of the worst of jobs - gutting chickens.

this job, too. LaDawn was well acquainted with every aspect of butchering chickens as she wasn't afraid to get her hands dirty and gutted her first chicken when she was six years old.

The birds were dipped into scalding water and handed over to the plucker operator to have all the feathers removed. This handy device saved hours of work. Before the days of chicken pluckers, this was done by hand. At this point they were brought into the building where the butchering was done. The tedious task of removing the pin feathers was followed by singeing the hair before the feet were cut off, and then they were plunged into large vats of warm soapy water to be washed. After several rinses they were ready for the smelliest job of all – removing the innards.

Several more rinses followed and they were placed in large bins or barrels of cold water which was continually changed until the fryers were completely cold. Meanwhile several people were working at cleaning the gizzards and feet – delicacies by some standards. With a good crew and an early start, we could easily have 100 chickens in the final water before lunch. The rule at our house was that chicken was not served on butchering day as it was all rather too vivid – both sight and smell. A good beef roast and all the trimmings and a pot of *Borscht* and *Mooss* were the common order for the day. And of course a great dessert like Saskatoon pie or cinnamon rolls finished the meal.

After lunch it was back to work; bagging chickens, hauling them to the deep freezer, and cleaning up the considerable mess that this day always entailed. At the end of it we were usually tired, had heard a few new jokes and the latest news, and had a deeper sense of camaraderie. There is nothing like bonding through guts and gore!

One fall evening when Mom and Dad came for supper, I had left doing the chores until after dark. Dad said he would come with me as Carl was busy combining. There was still a fairly large mud puddle sitting near the house from the rain several days earlier. On our way to the barn I warned Dad about it, and we managed to walk around it. By the time chores were done it had turned very dark and, walking back from the barn, Dad was concerned about the puddle. He said, "Tena, I don't want to step into that mud puddle." I took his hand and told him, "I'll lead you around it." We could see the lights in the house, but I misjudged where the puddle was. I led him and we both walked right through it. He was less than impressed! I explained to him that that's what happens when the blind lead the blind. They both walk through the puddle. We all laughed about that later.

The private road going into our yard was very curvy, with natural bush on both sides. It led to the creek, which we had to cross to get to the main road. Many times on Sunday evenings Carl and I would go for a walk in this romantic setting and enjoy God's wonderful creation. At different times we drove to the back quarter, checking the crops and walking among them as the late evening sun cast a shadow over the hayfields, announcing that the darkness would soon be moving in. At times, slices of light were still shining through the trees as the sun was sinking lower and lower beneath the horizon, turning the poplar trees lime yellow. How we enjoyed these beautiful summer evenings.

One year we had so many wild strawberries on the back quarter that the tractor tires turned red while driving in the field. One couple picked about 50 ice cream buckets that summer, and many other people picked as well. Picking berries was more fun when many of us went together. One morning several of my sisters and nieces came berry-picking with us. We packed a picnic lunch, and while everyone seemed to be having a great time, I couldn't really enjoy myself, as I constantly kept watch for bears. We didn't see any that day. The next day, however, when we headed back to the strawberry field, a big bear was sitting on the tractor but quickly darted into the forest when we arrived on the scene. Carl had parked the tractor right beside the path near a big strawberry patch. I must have sensed his presence the day before. The bear had thoroughly enjoyed the strawberries judging from the evidence he left behind.

It wasn't just bears that enjoyed Carl's little tractor. Our dog was very faithful in guarding it. Occasionally, Carl left it out in the field, and that's what he had done the day we "lost our dog." It was the weekend, and the weather was hot when we noticed the dog was nowhere around. We couldn't recall seeing him for quite some time so we started calling him, but he didn't respond. All of a sudden Carl remembered: the tractor. He went to the back quarter and, sure enough, the dog was lying by the big wheel of the tractor, guarding it. He was our faithful dog!

One year Isaac and LaDawn came home to help with the harvest. Carl and Isaac were out on the back quarter combining around the clock. As with any good farm wives, we brought meals and snacks out to the field so that production could keep going. This one afternoon, LaDawn and I were ready to head for the back quarter to bring the guys a snack when she decided to take the wheel of Craig's Chevy Blazer which was outfitted with roll-bars and said to be 'un-rollable.' We were half-way across the summer-fallow field when suddenly I remembered and said, "Oops, we forgot the coff … " I wasn't even finished speaking when LaDawn cranked that baby around without slowing down one iota. The dirt flew as she dug eight inch ruts in the dry fallow swerving in the tightest circle that Bronco could manage. When we straightened out and I had finished screaming, I reprimanded her sharply and in my frightened and flustered state, I said, "Just forget it!" Without blinking an eye, she cranked that wheel again and we repeated the scenario leaving another set of eight inch trenches and much displaced fallow for Carl to smooth out.

When LaDawn noticed that I was trembling from head to toe, she gently turned around and headed back home to pick up the coffee. She assured me we were safe because we had roll bars but, I wasn't convinced. I was still pale by the time we reached the guys but LaDawn had had the time of her life – testing the limits. Ripping around in vehicles had always been a thrill for her.

Fifty-Five

The End of a Journey

Mom had been quite sickly for a number of years, always in and out of the hospital due to her diabetic condition. She was physically weary and worn from a lifetime of hard work and the disease that destroyed her body. The doctors had discovered too late that she was afflicted with diabetes, and the dreaded disease had already started to perform its destructive work, damaging her heart, kidneys and her eyesight. Her vision had deteriorated greatly over the years, but she was not prepared to give up her hand work. She braided strings from used material and later stitched them together to make rugs, which she donated to charity. She couldn't see well enough to thread her needle anymore and Dad's eyesight was also failing. Whenever someone visited, the first thing she asked was for someone to thread her needle. She was determined to be productive until she simply couldn't work anymore!

Mom had been hospitalized again and, early in the morning on November 24th, Dad got a phone call from the hospital calling all the family in; the doctor was certain he would lose her. She had slipped into a diabetic coma and was drowning in fluids. It was very difficult to watch her suffer so terribly. The night staff had not been very vigilant and at shift change they found her in this condition. With aggressive treatment she miraculously survived. When it looked like Mom would recover, at least to a degree, the family started to go home. John was the pastor in our family, and we always leaned on him in times like these. Before John

Mom, with Al "Boomer" Adaire, Member of the Legislative Assembly (MLA) for Peace River North, during his visit to La Crete, showing him the rug she made.

left, he asked Mom if there was anything in particular she would like him to pray for. She said, "Yes, please pray that all my family; children, grandchildren, great grandchildren and all that will follow, will meet in heaven some day." John prayed a powerful prayer, and I believe it still resonates in the heart of God, as this prayer is in constant progress working in the lives of our large, extended family.

It was May 26, 1986, Jake's birthday, and many of our family had gone over to help him celebrate the day. Mom was quite sick already, but she couldn't possibly miss one of her children's birthdays. We spent a good evening together and when it was time to go home she said, "Tena, I want to go home with you for the night." I didn't know how to respond, as this was quite unusual. Dad persuaded her to go home and told her she could pack a few clothes and they would come to our house in the morning, which they did.

I believe Mom's body told her that she couldn't fight much longer, and I believe that she had this unspoken request that she wanted to spend her last days at one of her children's homes. She had chosen our home. They were a very difficult three weeks, more so for Mom than for anyone else, as she knew she had lost the fight, but, still wanted to stay. We had family at our house around the clock for several weeks taking turns sitting by her bedside.

Many times sleep would not come to her, and in the darkest hours of the night she reminisced and told us many things she had never shared before. One night, when one of my sisters and I sat with her, she told us about an incident with her mother hen and baby chicks. A sudden storm had come up and had blown the chicken coop door shut and the hen couldn't get her babies to safety. Mom said she looked out the window and saw the mother hen with her chicks come to the house, wanting in. She said the thought had crossed her mind, "What if I reach the shelter of heaven's door and Jesus won't let me in." She said she took the brood in until the storm passed.

Esther, who was serving with Missions Outreach International, had come home to visit Mom. One evening in particular stands out in my memory when our whole family was at our house at the same time. Mom asked if we would all come and stand beside her bed so she could see all of us at the same time. She told us she could part with everything here on earth, but she couldn't get herself to part with her family. This was one of those lucid moments, and we all knew how much she loved us.

Mom peacefully reached the end of her journey on June 19, exactly one month before her and Dad's 55th wedding anniversary. (It is interesting to note that Mom passed away on June 19, 1986, 33 years to the day since we had left our home in Saskatchewan. Her funeral was held on June 23, the day we had arrived at our homestead.) I shed many tears, but the special number, "Tears Are a Language God Understands" which Abe and Anna Bueckert sang at her funeral, comforted me. She had led a productive life but the time had come to leave her cares behind. Both Carl and I have never regretted that we opened up our home when she needed us so much. I only had to look back in time and remember how much she sacrificed for me, and I counted it a privilege to serve in this capacity. We were a large family, and we often had our differences in opinions, be it politics, religion, red or green tractor, Ford or Dodge, Toronto Maple Leafs or Detroit Red Wings; but in times like these we all pulled together, laid our differences aside, and found great strength and comfort in being part of a large family.

Fifty-Six

Highlights

Carl and I had been excited and looking forward to becoming grandparents for quite some time. We were still surprised when the phone rang early on Christmas morning and Isaac and LaDawn announced the birth of a baby boy, Jeridan Alexander James. There was no way I could go back to sleep. I think we were just as thrilled as LaDawn and Isaac. This was the first Christmas without Mom, and Dad had come to spend the night with us, as did Esther, who had come home for Christmas. After I got up, I cooked breakfast, and we all headed to High Level to see our precious Christmas gift. Jeridan was an adorable baby, and we felt honoured to be his grandparents. There were so many firsts with our first born: LaDawn was our first child, changing our life forever, the first to start school when we had to learn how to let go, the first to go on a field trip in grade 6, trusting her into someone else's care. She was the first to graduate from high school, the first to get married, and now, the first to give us a grandchild. We were to have nine more of these exciting experiences as we had ten grandchildren in ten years.

Carl and I had reached a milestone in our married life – the 25 year mark. Our children threw a party to celebrate the occasion, inviting our families, relatives and friends, including friends from my Peace River school days. I was so surprised and pleased to see Anne (Sheard) Goldbeck and her mother Flossie, and Alice (Yurkowski) Budney, another one of my school friends. Many people came and we felt honoured. It truly was

Enjoying our precious Christmas gift - Jeridan Alexander James -
Christmas 1986.

a reason to celebrate, as the Lord had blessed us with 25 wonderful years
together and a beautiful family.

Craig and Louise were both teenagers and a big help on the farm
and around the house, giving me more free time. Carl had worked hard
leading water and sewer into the house, which was a great improvement
and time saver. With extra time I again felt an urge to go back to studying.
I applied for several courses, typing and bookkeeping, from the Granton
Institute of Technology in Toronto. These courses were offered by correspondence, and, again I was in my comfort zone – reminding me of
correspondence school when we first moved to northern Alberta. I may
have been a bit older, but once again I was a student!

Our family at our 25th wedding anniversary. In the back, LaDawn's husband Isaac, Craig, Carl and Louise. Seated are LaDawn holding Jeridan, and me.

Fifty-Seven

A Library Career

A new secondary school, housing grades 4, 5 and 6 was built in La Crete in 1987 and named Ridgeview Central School. I was hoping that a library position would come up when the school opened, but that wasn't the case. Running the library in these smaller schools fell on the shoulders of the secretary. There was no way the secretary had the time to start up a new library, although the Fort Vermilion School Division had hired a central librarian to oversee all fourteen schools in the division. All the new books for the school had been ordered, but they still had to be readied for the shelves, a very time-consuming job. Her time was divided fourteen different ways; the few hours she could spend at any one school a month just didn't cut it for Ridgeview's situation.

It wasn't until November that the FVSD decided to hire someone to take over the responsibilities of the library. It was also at this time that the division decided to hire librarians for every school that did not have someone in charge of the library. This meant that the Buffalo Head Prairie School, which was only four miles from home, also had an opening for a librarian's position.

Near the end of the school term in 1984, when the enrollment reached well over 200 students and projections were even higher, there was serious talk about hiring someone to take charge of the library in the Buffalo Head Prairie School. In September, of the same year the first private school opened and approximately 70 students left to attend the private school, ending all possibility of the school division hiring someone to take over the duties of the library. There are presently seven private schools operating in the Mennonite community with no certified staff. They follow a Christian-based curriculum and are allowed school time to teach the students German and religion. There are also a large number of students enrolled in home schooling.

I was really interested in the Ridgeview library position. The library was beautiful; very spacious with large picture windows. The place was modern and looked very inviting with all the new shelving and furniture. I applied for the job, but, with no guarantee I would be hired, I applied for the Buffalo Head Prairie position as well, hoping to get one of the jobs. I was granted interviews at both schools, and I felt they had gone well – now the wait. I was ready to go back to work, especially in the library. With four years experience at La Crete Public, I felt capable of taking charge of either library without any assistance.

Mr. Ed Dyck was the principal for the new school, and I was hoping to get a phone call from him. Several days after the interview, Mr. Dyck phoned to inform me that the job was mine. I was pleased, to say the least. A little later, that same afternoon, Mr. Dan Maxon, principal of the Buffalo Head Prairie School, also called to say he had hired me for the BHPS library. I was ecstatic and had to pinch myself to check if I was dreaming or not. Both positions were for three hours a day; we would have to come up with a schedule that worked for both schools. I was excited about going back to work, as I loved the library and enjoyed working with students. I knew I was facing a full load, but I was willing to tackle them both.

Both positions seemed overwhelming for me, but the Ridgeview assignment, which included setting up a new library, took me to a level where I experienced frustration and, at times, despair. I gave it all I had, but I could only accomplish so much in three hours a day and the teachers were waiting for the library to open. Mr. Dyck would frequently come to encourage me and see how I was progressing, and he sensed my frustration. He decided to lobby the school division for additional help until the library was up and running. When his request was granted the job took on a new meaning for me, and I began to find enjoyment in it.

The Buffalo Head Prairie Library was suffering from neglect, as the secretary over the years simply didn't have the time to handle two jobs. It didn't seem as overwhelming, as I could take more time re-organizing the system. What satisfaction I experienced bringing that library into good health! I was always thankful for all the parent volunteers at both schools.

They were rewarded for their volunteer work at Awards Day at the end of the school year but I really don't think that any of them understood how very grateful I was for their dedication and commitment. The way the libraries were run back then was very time-consuming compared to the computerized systems used today.

The Fort Vermilion School Division belonged to the Peace Library System, which provided many services to the schools, but since our division was located so far north we could not make use of many of the services they offered. They did, however, provide a two day library conference each year that was usually held in Grande Prairie, which I found very valuable. My superiors were very supportive and encouraged me to attend. I was always anxious to learn more about the library and usually felt I had gained more knowledge which I could apply to my jobs, making the trip and the time spent very worthwhile.

Every year, various book publishers set up booths to promote their books and several years after I started work, SAIT (Southern Alberta Institute of Technology) in Calgary, was promoting their library program, available via teleconferencing. I think I was more excited than I'd ever been about learning new things. I would have an opportunity to get more training in a field I thoroughly enjoyed.

A personal friend, Mary Jane Hollier, who had taught at La Crete Public School when I was the librarian there, was now employed in the Fort Vermilion School Division office, representing the librarians. Mary Jane attended the conference, as did some of the other librarians, and she encouraged us to enroll in the program. When Mary Jane got back to work she addressed our interest to the superintendent of schools who could see the benefits for every library in the division, and offered to pay for all the courses. I ordered several courses immediately and was excited about studying. It took the better part of three years to complete all of my courses, but I earned my library certificate with honours. I didn't find the courses difficult, as I had quite a number of years of hands-on experience. Still, I felt it was a real accomplishment.

My job was rewarding in many ways. I worked alongside many beautiful people. When I was given an extra hour a day at each school, it made a big difference. Mr. Dyck, from Ridgeview School, asked me to draw up a library skills program and teach it to the classes. One section of the provincial achievement tests had numerous questions on library skills and, since it wasn't taught as a subject, many students scored poorly on this section. Teaching these classes allowed me more interaction with the students. Reading to them was part of the program, and it created a challenge now and then, especially with classes of 30 grade 7 students.

For the most part students were very attentive. However, one afternoon, as I was reading to the class, one of the boys, who had a reputation for getting himself into trouble, decided to challenge my authority. When he disrupted the whole class, I asked him to come and sit beside me. Not a good idea! He was now in a better position to make faces and make the other students laugh. After a few minutes I asked him to sit at a table behind some book shelves so he couldn't see the rest of the class. I told him I didn't like doing this, but after class we would have to see Mr. Dyck in his office. When the bell rang for recess he came up to me and said, "Mrs. Friesen, I wasn't really that bad, was I?" I knew without a doubt that he wasn't interested in paying the principal a visit. I took the time to explain to him what a difficult situation he put me in, and he promised he would never do it again. We settled the issue right there. He respected me after that and never gave me any more trouble. This student came from a troubled home, which made me more sensitive to his needs.

Mr. Dyck was my mentor all the years I worked under his supervision. I'm sure I learned more in those years than the students did. I highly respected him and the way he carried out his responsibilities. He made every staff member feel needed and important in the operation of the school, and he knew how to bring unity into the school atmosphere.

When it was time to go home, I often watched through the large windows as all the 200-plus students headed for the school buses. Many times I took the time and prayed for the safety and protection of all the students. I made it a point to pray for all the bus drivers, who were always on the road with their precious cargoes.

The Buffalo Head Prairie School was a country school and an entirely different atmosphere prevailed there. Teacherages had been built on the school premises to provide housing. The staff living in this little community, along with the rest of the staff, formed unique bonds. We found many reasons to celebrate – sometimes for no reason at all, except that we enjoyed being together! We had corn roasts, barbecues, pot lucks and, occasionally, it was just time for some Chinese food. One time, Ann Thompson, one of our teachers, announced to the staff that they had ordered a puppy which was going to be conceived that day, and she thought we should celebrate the conception. A joke, of course! But such was the lively family atmosphere we worked in.

When I had completed my studies and received my librarian's certificate, Ron and Lorna Joch hosted a surprise party for me at their home to celebrate the occasion. They brought much stability into that school, as they had taught there for many years. They were always willing to help anyone, and Ron stood by me many times when I needed help in the library, especially computer-related. When a killer frost was predicted in the early fall, all staff members enjoyed a bouquet of flowers on their desk when they arrived for work in the morning, compliments of Ron and Lorna's beautiful flower garden. Carl and I have been very thankful for their friendship over the years. Another pillar in the Buffalo Head Prairie School was Peter Janzen who taught until his retirement, and after 40 years, is still contributing, occasionally teaching the children and grandchildren of his first students.

There is much stability in all the Mennonite schools stemming from stability in the homes. Students, with few exceptions, come from two-parent families and, generally, parents are concerned about the quality of education for their children. The schools have a very high percentage of parental support. Most parents had a concern about the content of library books, and I valued their input. They stood firm that they did not want their children to read material containing witchcraft, sex scenes, nudity, necromancy, using the Lord's name in vain, or violence, and requested character-building books and Christian reading materials that portrayed good moral values.

On December 11, 1949, a major newspaper in Toronto announced: *"Crime comics are no longer produced or distributed in Canada. A new Criminal Code amendment bans any periodical that 'substantially' comprises matter depicting pictorially the commission of crimes, real or fictitious."* The comic Batman (plus 25 other titles) were banned. I often wonder how different our country would be if the government had continued to take a stand to protect our children and young people from materials that corrupt the mind.

The content of books that parents requested further enforced the values that were taught in the home. I still needed to balance the library collection, making sure students were exposed to all genres of literature. There was a high degree of unity between staff and parents. Some of the parents from the Buffalo Head Prairie School made a wall hanging, which hangs in the school entrance. It reads:

GUIDING HANDS

I dreamed I stood in a studio
And watched two sculptors there
The clay they used was a young child's mind,

And they fashioned it with care.
One was a teacher, the tools she used,
Were books, music and art.
The other, a parent – working with a guiding hand,
And a gentle loving heart.
Day after day the teacher toiled
With a touch that was deft and sure.
While the parent laboured by her side,
And polished and smoothed it o'er.
And when at last their task was done,
They were proud of what they had wrought.
For the things they had molded into the child,
Could neither be sold nor bought.
And each agreed they would have failed
If each had worked alone.
For behind the teacher stood the school
And behind the parent, the home.

Author Unknown

Once a year Secretary Week rolled around and the secretaries were honoured with a bouquet of flowers. Anyone who has ever worked in a school setting knows that the secretaries are worthy of this honour. Their multi-task position keeps them hopping all day; running errands, taking care of students in the infirmary, phoning parents, bandaging a sore finger – not to mention all the office work waiting for them. When Mr. Dick McLean came to take over the principalship at the Buffalo Head Prairie School he definitely recognized the secretary's workload, but he also recognized the work that all the rest of the staff were doing to keep that school running smoothly. He wrote a note of appreciation to every staff member thanking each one for their contribution to the school of which the parents and community were so proud. He had a way of letting every staff member know they were valuable. One morning he popped his head in the library door and said, "Good morning." He told me he was having a very busy day and would likely not have time to say "hi" later. I learned so much from my superiors during my library career that I'm sure I came out a much better person.

My highlight of each year was the annual trip to Edmonton to purchase books for the schools. Encyclopedias at the BHPS were ten years old or older except for one set, which was five years old. I remember discarding

A busy day at the Buffalo Head Prairie School library, December 1990.

a book called, *China Today*, which had a copyright dating back 30 years. It was time for an update, and I embraced it wholeheartedly. I was thankful when the superintendent, upon the request of the principal, allotted extra money to update the reference section. The principal also gave me a healthy budget for the first few years to upgrade the rest of the library. Over the years I have often thought back to my high school days when I worked so hard for the goal I had set for myself. I don't know that I could have ever been more fulfilled as a teacher than I was as a librarian. Perhaps I had landed among the stars!

During my library career I also served on the community library board for about 15 years. There was more involved here than in a school library. Writing policies, applying for grants, organizing summer programs, delivering books to the older folks and shut-ins (a traveling library) were all part of the assignment. This was a joint effort within the board and I found it a very rewarding experience as well.

At this time I was in charge of the church library for about 15 years as well. This library was on a much smaller scale, but very challenging. It was, of course, strictly Christian literature. Regardless of circumstances, I found this library much more difficult to operate. Some of the parishioners were very conservative while others leaned more towards liberal views. In a large congregation there are definitely opposing views on topics like grace, prophecy, speaking in tongues and eternal security. It was difficult to have a balanced collection, as not all the people were at the same level of spiritual maturity. Therefore, many could not understand the various doctrines, resulting in close scrutiny of new library books. It was a joy, however, to see the excitement on the children's faces when they came to sign out books and videos after church.

Fifty-Eight

History Relived

The Mennonite pioneers of the La Crete area have a very rich history well worth recording. Jan Gleysteen from *Preservings*, the quarterly magazine that records the history of the Mennonite people and their faith, states, *"A people who have not the pride to record their own history will not long have the virtues to make their history worth recording; and no people who are indifferent to their past need hope to make their future great."*

Talk had been circulating amongst a group of people who, for some time, had been toying with the idea of getting the history of our pioneers recorded. It was in March of 1987 when the first meeting was called to see if enough people were interested in pursuing an undertaking such as this. Quite a number of people showed up for the meeting, and an organization, the "La Crete Area Then and Now Society" was formed. That same evening, a committee was elected and I was voted in to serve as the treasurer for this project. Little did I know the job I was about to undertake far exceeded the description of a treasurer.

After a short while, we all knew there would be much extra work involved in getting the history of our people recorded, as most of the pioneers and their families were unable to read and write English. It was decided that six subcommittees would be set up, placing someone in charge of collecting the histories for designated areas. I took responsibility for Savage Prairie and the Buffalo Head Prairie areas. To begin with, our committee decided to set aside certain evenings, and get word out to the people that we would help them write their histories. We set up in the La Crete Community Hall and many people took the opportunity. Not every one could attend, so I called the people in my area, as did the others for their areas, and offered to come to their homes to help them. Some people were not interested, as they could see no value in recording their stories. Others simply found it too difficult to relive all the hardships and tears they had experienced. Still, many others shared their stories willingly.

We knew it was crucial to get as many histories of the early settlers as possible to get an accurate picture of all the hardships, loneliness, and even hunger, they had faced and endured. We wrote letters to the people who had pioneered here but had moved on. We were thankful for their responses and the many pictures we were able to collect that supported and enriched the stories of these early homesteaders, giving insight into what life was really like during these very difficult pioneer years as well as the years that followed. After throwing ideas around for the name of the book, the name chosen was, *A Heritage of Homesteads, Hardships and Hope.* I felt that the title was very appropriate, as I could identify with all the struggles my family endured in this northern wilderness. My parents had homesteaded, faced many hardships and yet they had never lost hope.

The early pioneers who had chosen to stay when so many families migrated to other countries to preserve their lifestyle, had no choice but to adjust to change. They had come to this remote area to live in peace, far-removed from civilization; to live a lifestyle the Mennonite people had treasured for centuries with freedom to raise their children and worship God without any government interference. Ironically, in the process, they became the stepping stone that ushered in civilization and paved the way for the progress they had hoped to escape.

When the Mennonites moved from Saskatchewan to the La Crete area in the 1930s they were not interested in continuing village life and did not pursue it. However, when the Mennonites from Mexico joined this group at La Crete, they intended to set up their villages like they had previously done wherever they settled. In Manitoba and Saskatchewan the government had granted the Mennonites a "hamlet privilege," which allowed them to settle in villages and fulfill the requirements of the Homestead Act. The requirement was to live on the homestead for six months of the year for three years and to bring ten acres of land under cultivation each year. In Alberta, however, the hamlet privilege was not extended to them. This marked the end of village life for the people who had chosen to move to Alberta.

When the Mennonites from Mexico emigrated to La Crete, they prematurely named areas designated for villages from the river crossing at Tompkins Landing to the river crossing at Fort Vermilion, and were disappointed when the hamlet privilege that had been granted to them in Saskatchewan was not extended to them in Alberta. The names they had chosen for the villages were, of course, existing village names. The Tompkins Landing area was Neuanlage, Buffalo Head Prairie was Rosenfeld, West La Crete was Schoendfeld, the area where the town of La Crete now stands – and surrounding area – was Rhineland, and the area near Fort Vermilion was Blumenort. It is interesting to note that the name Blumenort has stuck for that area. (Please note that the envelope that carried our wedding invitation letter to the West La Crete families was addressed to Schoendfeld - see page 261.) This group settlement arrangement had stood the test of time and, therefore, the Mennonites must have concluded that it was good. Their motto over the years has been, "If you remain united, you will be strong."

Today La Crete is a thriving community situated in the heart of some of Alberta's richest farm land; the fastest growing and the most northern agricultural community in Canada. The Mennonites are an industrious people, progressive and self-sufficient. The sacrifices the early pioneers made paved the way for future generations to enjoy a standard of living that compares with any other area in Canada today.

In 1953, when I moved to this community with my family, there was one small building, which served as a store. It housed a few groceries and was situated along what is now Main Street. Over the years, schools were built and busing was provided so all school-age children were able to attend school. More churches were built, giving the people central places to worship. Roads were constructed and graveled and, years later, they were paved. A post office and a grocery store were built and, one by one, more businesses popped up. Electricity and telephone services became available as did banking, dental and medical services. A bridge now spans the mighty Peace River near Fort Vermilion, to provide access to the outside world year round. Senior housing complexes were constructed as well as a senior citizens lodge and a long-term care facility to accommodate the growing senior population. A Fairview College campus, sports arena, golf course and the Municipal District office were also built. The people are enjoying a comfortable life style today, and I feel a satisfaction that I experienced first-hand the development of this wonderful community. It was a rewarding experience for me to be involved in bringing the history of La Crete and its people to fruition.

Fifty-Nine

Our New Home

It was evident that changes would continue to happen in our home as the children grew up; LaDawn had left home five years earlier. She and Isaac had moved and settled in High Level, making it possible for us to see them more often. Craig was away at work most of the time, but came home between jobs. When Louise graduated from high school, she chose to go to Briercrest Bible College in Carenport, Saskatchewan, where Esther was on staff. It was the long weekend in September when Louise left home to go to Bible school. Carl and I moved her there, and helped her unpack and get settled in. It was a difficult transition for all of us. Louise was under the weather with headaches and sore throat, and I found it very difficult to leave her there. Everything was strange for her, and I struggled not to pack her back up and bring her home again. Louise had a close relationship with Esther, easing my concerns somewhat, but both Carl and I struggled with the situation.

When we arrived home an empty house awaited us. For 30 years, our life had centred around our children. Now they were all on their own and Carl and I were left alone in the big house. It was much too quiet and, at times it seemed like our voices echoed to the farthest corners of the house. It took us a while to get used to the idea that the children had all left home.

Louise's good friend, Suzanne Unger, got married in October. We sent Louise the plane fare to come to the wedding, and we were able to see her again. She came home for Christmas, and we met in Edmonton at Easter time, both coming half way. We were glad when that year was over. The following year she went to work at the bank in High Level where she met and fell in love with a wonderful young fellow, David Friesen. They married the next summer. Louise didn't even have to adjust to changing her last name! We feel so blessed with the choice of husbands our daughters made, and we are proud to call them our sons.

During the time when Louise and Dave lived in Edmonton, LaDawn and Isaac, and Carl and I happened to visit them on the same weekend. We decided to go shopping and after spending some time in the mall, we all sat down for refreshments. I didn't realize that I was in for a very frightening experience. After resting for a few minutes I decided to use the wash room. I usually clung very tight to my purse in a public place, making sure no one would steal it and the girls always teased me about this, saying I was even more of a target with the obvious way I guarded that bag. No sooner had I sat down to some very serious business – when all of a sudden my purse, which was sitting on the floor, began to move. Someone in the next stall had very stealthily taken hold of its long strap and was attempting to steal my purse! Anger kicked in! I tried to grab that purse, and skinned my knuckles in the process. I was determined to catch the culprit, so I didn't worry too much about using paper, or pulling my pants up all the way. I didn't care who saw what, but no one was going to get away with this. When I burst through that bathroom door I was horrified! There stood Louise, doubled over in fits of laughter until she almost 'peed' her pants. I didn't see anything funny about the whole thing, and, of course, when Louise told her clever trick to the rest of the gang – and mentioned that I had actually sworn at her – that was reason for hoots of laughter. Today I can actually laugh when she re-tells the story. With the encouragement and influence of additions to the family, pranks were on the rise.

Our old house had served us well, but it seemed to get considerably colder every year despite the many layers of wall paper I had given it over time. In January of 1991, when U.S. President George H.W. Bush decided to invade Iraq, starting the Gulf War, I was scheduled for knee surgery (another one of five.) I was terrified of going to Edmonton, thinking that the bigger cities may end up being a target, and I struggled with keeping my appointment, but courageously, I did. I felt so secure living so far north in times like these.

It was another cold winter and our house was extremely cold, especially the floors, as the house sat several feet off the ground with no basement. After the surgery, while I was recuperating, I sat around much of the time and had trouble keeping my feet warm, which gave me more pain in my knee. To ease the pain, I warmed my feet in a tub of warm water, and then wrapped them up in blankets. On cold winter days when we had a bath, it seemed at times like we would have to hurry and get out before the water froze in the tub. The little bit of wood shavings that had been left in the walls for insulation must have disappeared completely. One day Carl said, "We have to do something. This is too hard." I asked him what we were going to do, as neither one of us had seriously thought about making any changes. As it turned out, events further north were to answer my question.

Grimshaw is Mile O on the Mackenzie Highway, which was completed in 1948. When we moved from Saskatchewan to Alberta in 1953, the highway was still an inadequately maintained, narrow, gravel road. The highway, however, opened a direct land route from Alberta and southern Canada to the waterways, the people and the natural wealth of the Northwest Territories.

The Pine Point Silver Mine in the Northwest Territories, owned by Comenco, Ltd., was formed in 1951. In 1958, when Mr. John G. Diefenbaker came into power with a Conservative government, one of his first achievements was to build a railway to Pine Point to accommodate the silver mine there, and production started in 1965. By the mid-1980s, depressed prices caused economic difficulties for the mine, so they shut down their operations in 1987.

Carl and I had heard that Ed Walisser had moved 180 houses out of Pine Point after the silver mine shut down. Many of these houses were moved to his property on the outskirts of Manning, and we knew of several people who had bought one. The price of a house was $25,000 which included moving it onto the basement and leveling it.

I had another appointment in Edmonton to follow up on my knee surgery, and on the way home we stopped to check out a few houses. We both felt we would never get a better deal, so we started to throw some figures around. Carl made a big sacrifice to improve our living conditions when he sold his precious herd of cattle and received a cheque for $12,000. I had received a $10,000 inheritance cheque from Dad, which I had deposited in the bank, and it had accumulated $1,000 in interest. We had enough money to make the basement, so we went ahead and bought one of the houses.

The house was moved in July, and Carl and I both worked very hard until we were able to move in. The floors were all hardwood except for the kitchen and bathroom. We stripped and refinished all the floors as well as the cupboards and baseboards. We laid new linoleum in the kitchen and bathroom, installed forced-air heating, took out a wall and repainted the whole house. I mentioned to Carl, "I want to wallpap … " He didn't let me finish speaking before he commented, "Not a chance!" I came to the conclusion that he really wasn't that fond of wallpaper, but the house was beautiful without it. Again, we received much help from family and friends. Dick and Janet McLean came to help us a lot with finishing baseboards and trim as well as moving furniture. After twelve years in that old house, we moved in to the new one. It was November 7, my birthday, and we had reason to celebrate.

One evening, shortly thereafter, the Buffalo Head Prairie School staff gave us a surprise house-warming party. They stealthily drove into the yard without their lights on and stayed out of sight. Carl was at the barn doing chores and Dad was resting on the couch while I was cleaning up supper. Suddenly, I was startled when I heard strange noises around the house – and then singing! Dad and I were both a little frightened. Dad said, "Tena, there's something very wrong here and we have to find out what's going on." We had no clue what was happening, until I saw the top of Valerie Clark's head in the dining room window as she tried to sneak to another location – then the lights came on! Oh, how we appreciated this special evening, celebrating with friends.

The site where the town of Pine Point once stood is located about 30 miles west from the camp site at the Little Buffalo River near Fort Resolution, Northwest Territories. This was our favourite fishing spot for many years. On one of our fishing trips we went exploring at the old town site and discovered that all that was left of the town were sidewalks, streets and the graveyard. We wondered where our house would have stood. In several places large poplar trees were growing right through the paved streets. The place wasn't even a ghost town – it was history!

Several years later, in 1994, when I had my total knee replacement surgery, Louise and Dave were living in Edmonton. Marita, their oldest daughter, was 18 months old and a real live wire. I had my surgery at the end of June and Jamison, their second child, was born on July 1; their home was a busy place *without* the addition of a patient in the house. Jamison was a model baby reminding me of the picture of the Gerber babies on the baby food jars.

I was in Edmonton for much of the summer for therapy. Carl helped as much as he could; taking Marita to the playground, playing with her and running errands like shopping for groceries. After a while, when I started to feel better, Carl went home to take care of things there. Louise packed up the two little ones daily and took me to my therapy appointments. We were so thankful for Louise and Dave, and I don't know how we could have made it through that ordeal without them. This time, coming home to recover in a nice warm house was a lot less stressful.

Sixty

Mennonites in Mexico

When the Mennonites migrated to Canada from Ukraine in the 1870s, they came with the firm resolution to restore and continue a way of life which they considered the sacred expression of their religion. They negotiated a *Privilegium* – a "charter of privileges," with the federal government and agreed to the conditions the Canadian government set forth. For generations the Mennonites in Russian Ukraine had been granted "special status" when they settled in "foreign colonies," living as non-citizens under special arrangements by the ruler of that country. When they migrated to Canada they came with the understanding that the Canadian government would recognize their group as a separate community within Canadian society. They once again became subjects.

In Ottawa, on July 23, 1873, the Minister of the Department of Agriculture signed the *privilegium*, extending many privileges to the Mennonite immigrants. The two privileges that had always been granted to Mennonites whenever they sought a new homeland – and their reason for finding a new homeland – were the exemption from military service and the freedom to educate their own children.

Archival documents reveal that when the Minister of Agriculture asked the Governor General to sign the *privilegium* and make it law, the Governor General refused. He demanded to add a phrase, "as permitted by the laws of Canada." This, to all intents, changed the whole promise made to the Mennonite delegation. Government officials quietly put the signed document away and did not inform the Mennonite people until 50 years later when the school crises arose.

The federal government did not honour the *privilegium* and shifted responsibility for education to the provinces. When the school crises arose in 1917–1918, the provincial governments had the jurisdiction over education and didn't honour their agreement either, compelling all children to attend the English public school. When the Mennonites refused, the government applied pressure by imposing fines. My grandpa Neudorf paid $27.00 per child per month, which was a large sum of money in those days. Grandpa only paid the fine for one month then sent the boys to school. In addition to paying fines they were required to pay taxes to support the public schools. In some cases drastic measures were taken; people were given jail sentences and livestock and property were seized and sold at public auction to make up for the unpaid fines.

Not all Mennonites, however, were opposed to public education. *"Those Mennonites who in the 1870s had gone from Russia to the United States instead of to Canada had been unable to obtain similar assurances of military exemption from the American government. As a result, the Spanish-American War (1898) created anxiety among some U.S. Mennonites and led them to explore emigration to Canada."* [14] Some of the Mennonites who chose to leave the US and settle in Canada were instrumental in getting the public schools started. They wanted their children to learn the English language. Mr. Jacob Boldt wrote a letter to the Deputy Commissioner of Education on January 31, 1903 to pursue the possibility of getting public schools started in the Osler area. As a result, the Altona School District was formed and the Altona School started operating in 1904. This is the school I attended and six of Mr. Jacob Boldts' sons were our neighbours in Saskatchewan.

It was at this time that the government also introduced conscription. The First World War was difficult for the Mennonites. Germany was Canada's enemy and the German speaking Mennonites were considered to be suspect in their loyalty to Canada. After negotiations by Mennonite leaders, the federal government exempted the young men from military service with the option for alternative service. Some, however, joined the military while others chose to work as conscientious objectors in bush camps, parks and hospitals.

With these harsh actions against the private schools and the young

---

14 Excerpt from *Subjects or Citizens?* Adolph Ens p 172

January 31st, 1903.

Dear Sir,

Although not personally acquainted with you I should like to hear your advice regarding our school district. We emigrated from Minnesota and settled here in Saskatchewan 3 miles West of Osler. We have lived on our land for about 1½ year, and we were advised of the school taxes while in Minnesota. I have 6 of my own children to go to school but there is no district school in the neighbourhood. Our neighbours are mostly Mennonites from Manitoba who simply are against any other school and we are hardly enough people here for an election of a school board. Under these circumstances, I should like to have your advice in the matter. If the object can be reached only by more votes becoming available, there will be but little hope for us, as the land here is, so to speak, all taken up, but the people are not yet all living on it. Is there no possibility of having a district organised, and if so, would the village be included in the district, or would it be the land outside the village only which would comprise the district ? I am rather unacquainted with the school laws here. In Minnesota all the lands were divided into districts. I do not know how to start this matter, as I do not know English well enough, I can speak it fairly well but cannot write it, and I should much like to have my children learn it better. Hoping to receive your advice in the matter, I remain,

Yours truly,

Jacob J. Boldt.
Osler, Sask.

Letter printed with permission from Dennis Boldt, Osler, Saskatchewan, from Altona School District No. 859 Page 16

men having to serve in the war in one way or another, the Mennonites made appeals to the provincial and federal governments. When the ruling did not go in their favour, they began to prepare for mass migration.

"From 1919 to 1921, representatives from three Old Colony groups from

the Winkler area in Manitoba, and the Swift Current and Hague areas of Saskatchewan tried to work together. So did groups from the Bergthaler family of churches. They were the Chortizer and Sommerfelder from Manitoba, the Sommerfelder from Swift Current and the Bergthaler from Hague, Saskatchewan. Seventeen delegations traveled to Argentina, Brazil, Mexico, Uraguay and Paraguay to search for a country, where the government would again grant them their religious freedom. Only two countries, Mexico and Paraguay, satisfied their conditions.

From 1922 to 1927, approximately 8000 people from Manitoba and Saskatchewan uprooted and left Canada for Mexico and Paraguay. The Old Colony people, about 6,000 in total, chose to move to the northern highlands of Mexico since the government was quick to guarantee the religious and educational freedoms they sought. The Manitoba Old Colony Mennonites settled in the San Antonio valley (Cuauhtémoc) in the province of Chihuahua; and the Hague, Saskatchewan, Old Colony Mennonites settled near the village of Patos in the province of Durango. The rest, the Bergthaler church families, moved to Paraguay." [15]

After the church delegates had gone to check out the land, they made a deal with the Mexican government. *"On September 6, 1921, the Old Colony people from Manitoba purchased 60,000 hectares of land in Chihuahua State which became the Manitoba Colony. The Swift Current delegates purchased an adjacent track of 30,000 hectares which became the Swift Current Colony. The price of each was $20.40 U.S. gold per hectare."* [16]

They chartered thirty-six trains with approximately forty-five cars per train and hauled all their machinery, building material, livestock and people to their new homeland. Once in Mexico, they aimed to preserve their cherished heritage and the institutions that were a part of it. They continued the village system with the house-barn units, the school system, church organization and the total way of life to which they were accustomed.

Over the centuries, with the Mennonites dedication to the soil, they have generally flourished and experienced economic success wherever they have gone. Mexico was no exception, although the seed grain they brought with them, to their dismay, did not grow well in the desert-like soil conditions. They applied their farming skills and brought thousands of acres of land under cultivation and discovered which crops could be grown that would provide a livelihood for them. They had to learn by

---

15 *Subjects or Citizens*, Adolf Ens, p. 214, and *Global Anabaptist Mennonite Encyclopedia Online*.
16 Excerpt from *Mennonite Historical Atlas*, p 146.

bitter experience, and it took many years of hard work and much money, resulting in many disappointments and financial difficulties before they attained a level of success.

With all their experimenting, the Mennonites discovered that apples, corn and beans were cash crops and would provide a living for them. Many experimented with making cheese and, by the turn of the century, there were 24 privately-owned cheese factories in the colonies with one of the factories employing more than 100 workers. Thus, dairy became a main source of income.

The Mennonites are a very skilled people. Without any training in a school, college or university, they invented bean and corn harvesters; and manufactured sawmills, hammer mills, harrows, cultivators, machine parts, trailers, gas heaters and kitchen ranges. An apple packing facility, which included washing, drying, waxing and packing the apples, was also designed in the colony. They mill and market rolled oats to all parts of Mexico and also have a national market for their cheese, produce and machinery. [17] With their self-contained, self-sufficient religious and economic lifestyle, they turned the mountainous, desert terrain of northern Mexico into a breadbasket.

Roman statesman, orator, and writer, Cicero (106–43 B.C.) states, *"Natural ability without education has more often raised man to glory and virtue than education without natural ability."*

In the spring of 2002, the President of Mexico, Vicente Fox, visited the Mennonites in the La Honda colony in Zacatecas, which totals about 5000 residents. It was the 80th anniversary of the Mennonites arrival in Mexico. *"A reception was held in the yard of Jacob and Liesa Giesbrecht. The yard was fenced and a security screen with a metal detector was put in place. Soldiers were stationed at various points in the colony as guards. A Mennonite meal of fried Wrenatje and Komst'borscht and other Mennonite foods were served, which the President thoroughly enjoyed. The President entered the Giesbrecht home to wash his hands, at which time he was presented with various gifts, and then shared the meal with the people. It was estimated that about two-thirds of the residents of the La Honda colony attended the event including ministers and deacons from the Old Colony Church. In his address to the people the President stated, 'For us in Mexico you are a model in work, an example in family life, and a model in morals, which we value highly.' "* [18]

---

17 Information taken from the film, *Mennonites in Mexico.*
18 Excerpt from *Preservations* No.21, December, 2002.

The Mennonite migration from Manitoba and Saskatchewan to Mexico in the early 1920s and in the years following has affected generations of families for many years, and is still felt today. Families were torn apart when some members decided to stay while others moved. The same was true when quite a number of families decided to return to Canada years later and other members chose to stay in Mexico.

Carl's parents, as well as many of his aunts and uncles and their families, had been caught up in this move, although they didn't move until 1928. They stayed for eight years then returned when life got too difficult. Crops there had failed, and they experienced desperate times, so they were thankful to plant their feet back on Canadian soil.

During that time in the mid 1930s and the early 1940s when Carl's family moved back to Saskatchewan, many other families were experiencing the same desperation and left for La Crete, joining the Mennonites who had moved there from Saskatchewan in the early 1930s. There were several other reasons why some people felt the need to leave Mexico.

"In 1936, the Mexican government closed down all the private schools in the Cuauhtémoc and Durango settlements. After several months of tense negotiating with the government, the church leaders were able to restore their earlier promised freedoms – which they still have today." However, the seeds of distrust had been sown. There was still no threat of public schools in northern Alberta, so they felt confident they would be able to continue their valued way of life. Another reason to leave Mexico was the political unrest in the land. *"The threat of a revolution was looming and mass demonstrations were being held with shouts of, 'Down with the clergy, lift high the Revolution.' Eventually this wave of communism was controlled and the country was spared the tragedy of a revolution."* [19]

The Mennonites had intensified their traditions while in Mexico and brought them back to La Crete with them. Since they were now a majority in church membership, it changed the religious landscape of the Old Colony Mennonites at La Crete. When they freighted all their implements to Mexico, the worldly rubber tires were removed and replaced with steel wheels. Although some people at La Crete were driving cars, no cars were allowed on the church yard, only horses with buggies or sleighs.

Carl's parents were able to bring all the family back and Carl was born shortly after they returned. Over the years some of Carl's relatives also returned to Canada while others stayed in Mexico. Some returned for economic reasons, first as migrant workers but later settling permanently

---

19 Excerpts from *Perservings* No.29, 2009.

in the Leamington and Alymer, Ontario areas as well as in Manitoba and southern Alberta. They experienced no problem relocating in Canada, as they were Canadian citizens/British subjects, either by birth or by naturalization.

As the years went by, land shortage in Mexico continued to be a problem as the increase in Mennonite population in the 1970s approached four per cent per year. As the number of landless people increased and poverty became a factor, the search for land accelerated. When word spread that a huge tract of land was available in Texas, USA, where they would again be able to live in solitude, Mennonites in Canada and Mexico were more than willing to pack up and move yet again.

In 1977, approximately 70 Mennonite families from Mexico and 60 families from Ontario (who had returned to Canada from Mexico) all from Old Colony background, undertook settlement ventures at Seminole, Texas. In 1979, another 40 families joined them. The Mennonite families from Mexico and Canada pooled their savings and made a down payment of $455,000 on 6,400 acres of ranchland in Gaines County located 20 miles southwest of the small oil town of Seminole. (Seminole serves as the county seat for Gaines County.) Accounts about the price of the land vary, but most estimates range from $1.7 million (*Time Magazine*) to $2.6 million (*Washington Post*). Their intention was dryland farming (farming without irrigation), but precipitation proved inadequate. When the farmers began to dig wells to irrigate their crops, they were informed by the oil companies that they had no right to the water since they (the oil companies) owned water and mineral rights to two-thirds of their property. Lack of sufficient water supply resulted in the liquidation of some of their land … but more problems were on the horizon.

Early in 1977, when the first colonists arrived, they believed that having purchased land in the United States, they would be allowed to enter the country as legal immigrants, but they were not. After all, they had been assured by the real-estate agents that legal status would be automatic with the purchase of such a huge tract of land. Form letters from the Immigration and Naturalization Service (INS) started arriving, threatening deportation. The Mennonites were informed that their visitor permit visas had expired and that they had 30 days to leave the country.

"One of the main players instrumental in rallying public opinion around the Mennonite cause was former mayor of Seminole, Bob Clark. He had been approached by some of the group's leaders about their plight. According to Clark's statement to the Odessa American, he had never had any experience dealing with immigration laws and therefore referred them to

411

a lawyer and then called Rep. George Mahon for help with the problem. Since this would require special legislation, Mahon referred Clark to Sen. Lloyd Bensten, because a bill like this would go through the Senate more quickly than the House. Chances of such a bill passing the Senate were slim. However, Mayor Clark and the people of Seminole made sure the media heard of the Mennonites' plight. Newspapers, TV stations, and periodicals of every kind heard of the story and jumped in. This caused a public outcry of proportions that even the people of Seminole had not counted upon. Mayor Clark received hundreds of letters from all across the nation and the world, asking what they could do to help and voicing their support for the group of Mennonites that had ended up in such dire straits. Later, Mr. Clark donated his large collection of letters to the Southwest Collection of Texas Tech University where they can be seen today. Many letters contained money to help with any legal costs or land payments that needed to be made.

Under pressure from across the country, politicians in Washington were forced to take action. Senator Bensten introduced a bill which would give the Mennonites special treatment and allow them permanent residency in the United States. With support from various Mennonite organizations from Ohio and Pennsylvania, the bill passed the Senate on August 2, 1979, the House of Representatives on October 2, 1980, and President Jimmy Carter's signature 17 days later made the bill law.

In 1986, most of the Mennonites became citizens at a ceremony that was also attended by Senator Bensten and others who had been instrumental in helping the Mennonites." [20]

Those whose immigrant status had not been confirmed were supplied with a green card or work visa and legally allowed to live and work there, provided they abide by the laws of the land. Although they are not citizens of the United States, they are residents and therefore they must pay taxes.

"The immigration issues had been resolved but it was clear, that without water rights, there was no future for the Mennonites on the ranch they had purchased. Eventually some of them moved back to where they had come from and others moved into the town of Seminole where they took on various jobs. They had no trouble finding employment on the numerous farms and ranches in Gaines County and surrounding areas. Many have since started up their own businesses and today the Mennonites in Seminole, Texas are thriving. The Mennonite population in 2006 was approximately 5000. They set up their churches and private schools along with their villages, although they show only a trace of the village-type lifestyle that has followed

---

20 Excerpt from *25 Years of Mennonites in Seminole, Texas*, 2002 pp 11 and 12.

the Mennonite migrations from country to country. Currently, an increasing number of families are enrolling their children in public schools embracing the English language, and leaving the more traditional education methods behind. Styles in clothing are also changing from the traditional Mennonite dress to "American" style clothing, making it more difficult for the group to maintain its' own sense of identity.

Despite the fact that the Mennonites have faced many difficulties and challenges in their move to the small oil town of Seminole, they have managed to prosper and grow and are continuing to have a major religious, economic and social impact on the community." [21] Some of Carl's relatives from Mexico were part of this migration.

During the course of our frequent visits with Carl's brother John and wife Betty in Lethbridge, the conversation would often turn to Mexico. One of our visits resulted in the idea of traveling to Mexico together to visit John and Carl's cousins, and from that time on we started discussing the possibility of making the trip. John was twelve years old when he returned to Canada with his family. Since he had spent eight impressionable years there, he could relate to the life style of the Old Colony Mennonites.

In the spring we decided to meet in Edmonton to make arrangements and plan a date for the trip. Financially, Carl and I felt we were able to take this trip. We had filed our income tax returns with a local man who worked out of his home, and our return showed we would be refunded a little over $2000. We were excited, as now we would even have a few extra dollars to spend. We looked forward to connecting with Carl's relatives and see first hand the Mennonite colonies where Carl's family had settled and lived sixty years ago.

We left Lethbridge on July 12 in John and Betty's camperized van. We were compatible travelers; all of us were early risers and we were all ready to call it a day in late afternoon, which gave us time to find a good restaurant and enjoy a relaxed supper. We usually hit the road between 6:00 and 7:00 a.m., drove for several hours and then stopped for breakfast.

We stopped at any points of interest along the way – museums and historical sites. We spent several hours at the site where Lt. Col. George Custer and the 7th Cavalry were defeated by the Lakota Sioux and the northern Cheyenne Indians. The Indians were outraged over the continued intrusions of whites into their sacred lands in the Black Hills; they

---

21 Excerpt from *25 Years of Mennonites in Seminole, Texas 2002,* and *Global Anabaptist Mennonite Encyclopedia Online.*

joined forces and went to battle. The battle took place near the Little Bighorn River in Montana in 1876. We viewed the battlefield where Custer and his men fell.

We visited the museum where the artifacts of Billie the Kid, including his famous rifle, were displayed. Billie the Kid was the teen-age outlaw and a true figure of America's Wild West. He was the famous cattle rustler and leader in the 1878 Lincoln County cattle war in New Mexico. He was shot and killed in 1881. Carlsbad Caverns in New Mexico was another place of interest. We toured the cave marveling at its most unusual giant formations.

We always found time to shop. One day when we hit a big city, John said, "Let's find us a mall." Was my hearing failing me? I wasn't sure, so I asked Betty if I had understood him correctly, as I found it quite unusual for a man to suggest finding a mall. We drove around for quite a while until we found one. Yes, he was serious, although he didn't make many purchases. When he got tired, he and Carl found a coffee booth and visited, while Betty and I found our treasures.

Carl's cousin, Hilda Friesen, had worked as a nurse in the Mennonite colonies for a number of years and had connected with some of the cousins in Mexico. She gave us the name, address and phone number of one of Carl's cousins, Maria Schmidt, and her husband, Ben. Hilda said they would be glad to see us. When we hit the city of Cuauhtémoc, Chihuahua, Mexico, we felt lost. Indirectly, the Mennonites are credited for building the city. When the Mennonites arrived in 1922, Cuauhtémoc was a railway station surrounded by a few houses. Now it is a bustling city of more than 100,000 inhabitants.

We couldn't ask for directions, as none of us knew enough Spanish to communicate. All at once I spotted a man across the street and said to Betty, "That's a Mennonite." He was wearing green overalls, and we later discovered that all the men wore overalls in many different colours. They were easily distinguished from their Mexican counterparts. We walked across the street to talk to this man and he gave us directions. He was a little surprised when we spoke to him in German, but we had no problem revealing our identity. Ben and Maria were surprised and pleased to see us when we finally arrived, and we enjoyed a good time with them.

The *Kleine Gemeinde*, the name of an Evangelical denomination meaning "Small Denomination," and the EMMC, Evangelical Mennonite Mission Conference, had planted several churches in the colonies at Cuauhtémoc, and change had already started to come within the Mennonite community. When we discovered that Ben Schmidt was serving as a lay pastor in one of the churches, we knew we would be sharing some common ground.

When we drove into the Mennonite settlements in Mexico, I was fascinated to see they had set up the same village pattern and copied the village names from the reserves in Saskatchewan and Manitoba that the Mennonites had brought with them from Russia. I had been too young when we moved from Saskatchewan to Alberta to understand the village structure or the significance of it. Group settlements were important to the Mennonites to protect their way of life. Therefore, village life provided the stability to uphold their cultural and faith endeavours.

John was anxious to find the place where he had lived with his family while in Mexico. As we were traveling down one of the village streets, the van started giving us some trouble. John and Carl went for help, but Betty and I stayed back. The sun was beating down mercilessly on the van and when we needed some relief, we decided to knock on the door of a house a few yards from the village street. A middle-aged lady answered the door, and we started visiting. We discovered during the course of our conversation that she was the daughter of the school teacher, Mr. Wall, who taught John while he lived there. The Walls lived on this same yard and John was able to connect with his former teacher. We all felt this was a divine appointment, and we concluded that we never would have met him or his wonderful wife if the van hadn't given us trouble. The Walls were very hospitable and invited us to come back for *Vaspa* the next day. Their granddaughters had done some special baking for this occasion and we felt honoured. Mr. and Mrs. Wall had been adults when they moved with their parents to Mexico and, when they started to reminisce we knew they could relate to Canada and to some degree, to us.

Mr. Wall informed John, that the school which he had attended still stood at the original site. He willingly took the time to show John and Carl the school and John relived his early school years. With directions from Mr. Wall, John and Carl found their grandparents' graves. With further help they found the place where Carl's family had lived. We were thrilled to hear that the house was still being occupied and the people who now lived there were quite willing to give us a tour. John was excited to relive more of his childhood memories. We picked apples and apricots in what used to be Mom and Dad Friesen's garden, and I decided to pick an apple for each of Carl's siblings. Not being familiar with regulations at the border crossing, I innocently declared them and, of course, left them there.

Ben and Maria Schmidt, who hosted us for the duration of our stay, took us out for dinner one day. The restaurant was fairly new and looked very modern, but it was practically empty. We inquired about it and they told us that there was no money now as the crops weren't harvested yet. Using credit cards was not a way of life for them, and likely they hadn't been introduced to it yet. What a blessing!

Ben and Maria organized a family get-together where we had the opportunity to meet many of Carl's relatives and their families. We experienced joy from this reunion, but at the same time we experienced great disappointment. Moral decline had begun to make its way into the Mennonite community at Cuauhtémoc; some of Carl's cousins and their families were not excluded. Horse travel had been replaced with vehicles the year before we came, and some of the young people did not know how to handle their new found freedom. There was infidelity, alcoholism, drug abuse and debauchery, not only among the young people but the married people as well. I could not comprehend what had happened to these people, who had, with great pain, pulled up their roots to search out a country where they would not have any interference worshiping God; free to pursue a lifestyle that would be honouring to Him. It appeared they were no longer clinging to God for their needs but were desperately clinging to tradition, likely the result of a spiritual drought that had taken hold over the years, allowing tradition to trump scripture. All the worldly pressures these people had tried to escape had lain in wait for them, manifesting themselves when the time was right. Pain, despair and hopelessness were evident in the eyes of many women, while the men seemed indifferent to the needs of their families.

These were our people, and I was deeply troubled. It had been four generations since the migration to Mexico and Christianity had been watered down to a large degree due to the fact that High German – the language the Mennonites use for church services or when reading the Bible – had been watered down. Teaching skills were passed down without any upgrading. Many could not read the scriptures for themselves, and many who could read could not comprehend what they were reading. To this day most of the people speak only Low German, making it more difficult to understand High German.

Opinions and traditions had been passed down through the generations, and neither gave the people any strength to live the Christian life. It appeared that these people had lost the very purpose for which they had first come. At our family get-together, one of Carl's cousins asked me about Carl's mother. She was concerned whether or not Mom had remained faithful to tradition; faithful to wear her head scarf, apron and

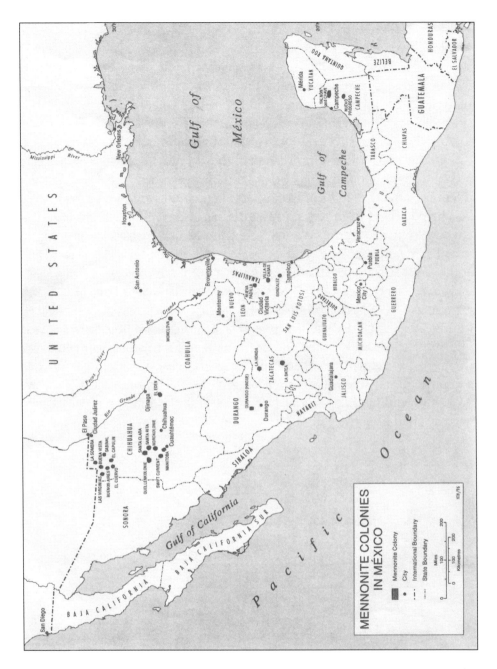

long sleeved dresses. She was so relieved when I informed her that Mom Friesen had not changed her style of dress. While the majority held to this view, it was encouraging to know that Evangelical teaching had started to make its way into the Mennonite colonies and perspectives were changing.

By 2004 there were 70 Mennonite colonies in Mexico. On our visit to Mexico, I experienced first hand, the Mennonite way of life as it was in the 1800s when they migrated to Canada from Russia. Other than the fact that many people, especially the youth, had given in to destructive lifestyles, they maintained their culture; village life, traditional clothing, speaking only the German language, private schools and a determination to uphold their culture. This was the highlight of the trip for me.

The time we had set for visiting family was nearing the end, and I had mixed feelings about leaving. Some of the women had freely shared their dilemma, how they felt so lost and defeated, and I wondered how I could be a help to them from so far away. This trip cost me some sleepless nights after we returned home. We left and enjoyed our trip back, stopping to spend some time at the Grand Canyon, another wonder of the world, and at the Hoover Dam in Arizona, which is a human masterpiece.

When we arrived home I was so thankful for a safe trip and all our experiences. We had a month's mail waiting for us, which we checked immediately. Included in the pile was a letter from Revenue Canada informing us that a mistake had been made in filing our income tax, and we needed to return the refund cheques plus a few dollars more. We had a great trip and we would never be sorry we went, but chances are we probably wouldn't have enjoyed shopping quite as much had we known what awaited us at the end of our journey.

Sixty-One

Mennonite Homecoming

Fewer than 20 years after the first migration of Mennonite people from Ukraine to Manitoba, Canada, the large block settlement the government had reserved for Mennonites was filled up. Mennonite representatives lobbied the Saskatchewan government for land in the Rosthern area, which was granted in 1895, creating the Rosthern reserve which included Hague and Osler. Many families moved from Manitoba, settled on these lands and started over. They set up their villages and their cherished lifestyle continued.

In August of 1995, people from the Hague and Osler districts were planning a celebration commemorating the 100-year homecoming of the Mennonites from Manitoba and their settling in Saskatchewan. Since both sets of my grandparents and my dad had been involved in this move and both my parents had grown up in one of the villages, I was excited about this celebration.

Over the years I had developed a keen interest in the history of the Mennonite people and was anxious to discover more about my roots. This homecoming was going to be a big event, and Carl and I decided we wanted to be a part of it. I was anticipating meeting some of my school friends from my Altona School days, which I did. Erma (Boldt) Funk and Helen (Klassen) Bergen were both present, together with their husbands. We had a great time reminiscing about our school days. Erma and I seemed to pick up where we had left off some forty years earlier, and Erma's husband, Mel, and Carl connected like they had always been friends. We've since become good friends spending time visiting on the telephone and in each other's homes. I also met many other classmates and it was great to reconnect and converse at an adult level, catching up on all the years since our move north in 1953. It would have been easy to pretend that the forty years had not elapsed if we hadn't all aged so much.

The main highlight of this centennial celebration was the unveiling of their history book entitled Hague-Osler Mennonite Reserve 1895–1995. Many people had worked very hard, spending many long hours assembling this 728 page book. I had been involved in producing the history book of our community, so I could appreciate and identify to some degree with the undertaking of a huge project such as this.

Various activities had been planned for the reunion and the one that held the most meaning for me was the tour of some of the remaining villages. Neuhorst, the closest village, only two miles from where we had lived, and the Neuanlage village, where Dad had grown up, were part of the tour. We stopped at a museum site where a newly moved house-barn was going to be restored. Saturday evening was a planned program where many people presented the audience with their musical talents and other forms of entertainment.

The food was plentiful and good, and we all enjoyed wonderful fellowship around the tables. Sunday morning marked the church worship service, which we could all identify with. Our culture stems out of a faith which the Mennonites have struggled to maintain for over 500 years. As a result, the church service held a lot of meaning, especially when everyone joined in to sing, Nun danket alle Gott – 'Now thank we all our God, with hearts and hands and voices' – for preserving our heritage and the faith of our fathers – the Christian faith.

Former Altona School students at the Mennonite Centennial Homecoming in August 1995.
I am standing in the centre, adjusting my dark glasses.

Sixty-Two

A New Venture

With Craig getting married and leaving home for good, Carl and I were now the sole occupants of the house, but we still kept very busy with one thing or another. Craig married a beautiful and talented young girl, Twila Roll, and we experienced no difficulty in calling Twila our daughter. They settled down on an acreage right across the road from us. It was great to have family live close by.

Margaret Krahn, who was the secretary at the school where I worked, was a very talented and artsy person and she persuaded me to paint with her at the school on Monday nights. I found myself getting involved in art classes without ever planning to do so, knowing I didn't possess any natural talent in this field. She also connected with and persuaded several other people to join us, and we formed a painting guild. Four of us – Margaret, Rosalind Petzold, Lynda Washkevich, and I – made up the core group, with many others joining us at different times. Occasionally we had as many as twelve interested people in one evening.

Mr. Lee McCullough, the art instructor at La Crete Public School that year, was on a year's medical leave with much extra time on his hands. When he discovered that a group of us were meeting regularly for painting sessions, he offered to come out and teach us some painting skills. We took him up on his offer, and we all had a great time. Most of us experienced and played around with water colours and it was good to have all that constructive criticism.

We had various artists come out at different times to give us workshops, and, one summer, Margaret, Rosalind and I traveled to Jasper to attend a workshop on learning how to paint mountains. A talented artist and art instructor from Edmonton offered a two day water colour workshop, and I felt privileged to be able to attend. We had a lot of fun, and I learned many new skills, which I could apply to my limited knowledge of art.

One evening Mr. McCullough brought some mat board frames with him and showed us how our picture would come to life when we put the frame around it. It really did make a difference and we were all enthused. Out of this experience came the idea of ordering a few mat boards and a small manual mat cutter, just to encourage our painting group. I had a few connections and decided to make some phone calls. Carl's nephew, Randy Neufeld, owned and operated a photography studio in Lethbridge; I decided to give him a call. Carl and I had visited him in his studio at different times, and I was certain he would be able to answer some of our questions. He directed us to Folkgraphis Frames in Edmonton. When I spoke to the manager there, he offered to send some mat and frame samples. We had a lot of fun putting some mats and frames around our paintings, but it didn't take long and we had other people asking if we could frame pictures for them. I had ordered a small mat cutter from an art shop in Edmonton, but that would never do for custom framing.

On one of our trips to Edmonton we stopped at Folkgraphis Frames just to check things out and ask a few questions. Nabiel Debach, the owner, took us seriously and offered to train both Carl and me without cost, providing we would purchase all our materials from him. We needed to think about this one. After discussing and debating the matter we decided we couldn't go wrong. There was no dollar figure to meet in our purchases and the training could do none other than benefit us. We decided we would go for it.

The training in Edmonton lasted a whole week. We were frustrated at times, as there was so much to learn. We were thankful that our instructors were very patient and understanding. Carl is a perfectionist by nature, and I could sense immediately that this kind of work interested him. He was fascinated with the glass cutter and the thumb nailer, as well as the mat cutter. I was also intrigued with the mat cutter and spent many hours learning its many uses. When our week was over, Carl and I were hooked, and before we left for home we had purchased all the machines and supplies to start a picture-matting and framing business.

Folkgraphis supplied us with all the mat and frame samples, so we were ready to go except for the legalities of finding a name and getting a home business license. Our basement had ample space and was ideal for this particular home business. We went back to Edmonton many times to attend Folkgraphis' annual two-day workshop in the years since we've started the business. It seems like there is always so much more to learn. Both Carl and I enjoyed the work, and we could do this in our spare time and in our own home. As business increased, I found I had less time to paint, but took the time to teach the grandchildren a few basic lessons in water colours. I was happy with the few pictures I did paint, considering I was an amateur, and of course I framed them!

Sixty-Three

Death ... A Part of Life

Dad was a picture of good health practically all his life. His first overnight hospital stay was in 1995, at age 85 years when he was airlifted to Edmonton to have a pacemaker put in. His granddaughters Sheryl and Valerie, both registered nurses, were able to accompany him on the flight, taking care of his needs and giving him assurance that he was in good hands. Bill, and his wife Sara, brought them all home by car several days later. Mary and her husband Jake took Dad in for several weeks until he could manage on his own again.

When Dad went for his annual medical check up in 1997 the doctor was suspicious and ordered some tests. He discovered colon cancer and booked Dad for surgery in Grande Prairie. Dad was traumatized and needed someone to coach him through this difficult time. I was working, but I was able to arrange for a few days off. It tied in with the long weekend, giving me five days. Jake had a very compassionate nature and he always volunteered when a need arose. Together, we took Dad to Grande Prairie and stayed with him for a few days after the surgery.

I needed to get back to work, but Jake and I both felt we couldn't leave Dad alone yet as he was still very nauseous, hooked up to the IV and in need of bathroom assistance. Valerie volunteered her time again and came to stay with Grandpa and coached him through the rest of his stay. Dad felt very comfortable to have Valerie looking after him. The doctors were very positive that the cancer was contained and, therefore, did not

Dad surrounded by his family on his 85 birthday, October 23, 1995.
Standing, from left to right are me, Martha, Bill, Annie, Jake, Babe and Helen.
In the middle row are Leonard, Margaret, Dad, John and Esther.
In the front are Betty, Pete and Mary.

suggest additional treatment.

Dad had been very lonely for quite a number of years as Mom had passed on twelve years earlier. He had married again to Mrs. Aganetha Wiebe, a lady with whom our family was well acquainted, but she had also passed on. Carl and I tried to make as much time for him as we could in our busy schedules. In the last years, Dad parked his car for the winter months as he felt uncomfortable driving on winter roads. This meant he couldn't visit his family whenever he felt like it, and, thereby he lost a measure of independence. Carl and I often took him to our house for the weekend, and I took him home Monday morning on my way back to work. Dad loved to spend time with his grandchildren and great-grandchildren.

Many of the family and his friends often dropped in to visit him. However, one day I learned there was a big difference between dropping in and going for a visit. I often dropped in after work and occasionally I would ask Dad if he had any visitors that day and he usually said, "No." Later I discovered that several people had dropped in, and I decided to

Dad reading to his great-grandchildren, Jamael and Marita.

ask him about it the next time. He told me that people drop in but they don't come for a visit. He taught me a lesson that day. It's quite easy to drop in at our convenience and feel that our duty is done, and no doubt he must often have felt we were dropping in out of duty rather than out of love or concern. We all had our busy schedules, but I knew I had to examine my motives. I only had to think back to all the times he and Mom were there for me.

Carl was always so good with Dad, spending hours playing games with him, and he was so patient with me when I suggested spending time with Dad, especially on weekends, which was the only time we could spend time together ourselves. The qualities that drew me to Carl fifty years ago are still the qualities I admire in him today. He is always patient and understanding. One day, as I was thinking about Dad's situation, the question came to my mind: When I am old and lonely will my children come to visit me? Will it be out of love or out of duty? I then realized the example Carl and I were setting would be an example and model for our children and grandchildren to follow.

Dad recovered completely from his surgery but, eight months later he suffered a stroke, which paralyzed his right side. Thankfully he did not lose his speech. He did not want any extra medical help and refused all forms of treatment. He said he was tired and he wanted to go Home. He could not handle the thought of someone else taking care of his personal needs. The Lord granted his request and took him home three weeks later.

Dad had led a full life, and I was able to accept his death as part of life. A children's book called, *Freddie the Leaf* by Leo Buscaglia, Ph.D. explains death in such a positive way. The leaves must all fall off the trees at the end of the season so new ones can take their place. I realized I would soon be approaching the season when I would need to make room for the next season's growth. I had a traumatic experience with death as a young child when Uncle Abe died, and through many experiences in the years that followed, I had become somewhat acquainted with death. Carl had lost both of his parents, three brothers, several nephews and other family members. I had lost my little brother Harry, my mother and now my dad as well as my nephew, Joel. I am thankful that I am now able to view death from a different perspective.

Sixty-Four

Tumbler Ridge, British Columbia

It had been known for many years that there were coal resources in the Peace District. Some exploration had been done and it was discovered that the coal seams were very thick. The geographical location of the coal deposits could create a problem for mining the resource, so it was deemed not feasible, economically.

When a global energy crisis loomed in the 1960s, the government accepted applications for exploring the coal resources. Exploration increased dramatically as mining exploration crews began surveying the region. By the late 1970s, fifteen coal deposits had been identified. Forty studies were commissioned by the government to ascertain the viability of developing the coal and the development of the town of Tumbler Ridge, British Columbia.

In 1981, an agreement was signed to allow mining of the coal resources. The Japanese steel industry was identified as the prime potential customer. Two big mines were developed, the Bull Moose Mine and the Quintette Mine. Huge camps were constructed to house the workers. By the fall of 1982, the plan for the town was laid out and the construction of Tumbler Ridge began. By November 1, 1983, the first shipment of coal was on its way to market. By the late 1990s, world coal prices declined to a level where production was no longer economical; the Quintette mine ceased operations in 2000 and the Bull Moose mine in April of 2003. [22]

---

22 From *Tumbler Ridge–Enjoying its History, Trails and Wilderness*, Charles Helm, 2001.

When the mines closed down there was no more work for the miners and the majority moved out in search of employment elsewhere. Houses were put up for sale and prices reached an all-time low. It appeared that Tumbler Ridge would become a ghost town. In the late 1990s, we heard a rumour that there was a possibility the mines would be shutting down and on one of our visits to Dave and Louise in Grande Prairie, Dave informed us that the mines were indeed closing down and the houses were selling for unbelievably low prices.

We didn't take notice, as Carl and I were still busy farming and working our day jobs. The idea of moving off the farm hadn't even entered our minds. In 2002, talk again began circulating about the price of houses in Tumbler Ridge. My sister Helen and her husband, Jim, had just recently purchased a house there, and it sparked an interest. In April we went to my nephew Dennis Wiebe's wedding in Grande Prairie. After the wedding, we decided to take a run out to Tumbler Ridge to see their house and tour the town. We pulled in at 11:00 p.m., spent the night and then started touring the town in the morning. We had only a few hours to spend, as Carl and I had to be back for work on Monday morning. The price of houses was unbelievable. During our tour we started counting houses with 'For Sale' signs in the window and quit counting when we reached 50. There were still all the other houses for sale that were listed with real estate agents.

We purchased this house in Tumbler Ridge, BC in June 2002.

We really had not come with intentions to make a purchase, although we spotted two houses that we were interested in viewing. After touring both houses we were impressed, to say the least. We focused our attention on the house that was situated on the green belt, a large open area with natural forest all around. It was located in a cul-de-sac and therefore had no street traffic. When we returned home we discussed the opportunity of buying a second home at a very reasonable price and decided to go ahead with the purchase. By the end of June the deal was complete.

In August, only two months later, Craig and Twila purchased a house in Tumbler Ridge as well, and they moved in October of the same year. Craig was able to find work for his oilfield maintenance business and therefore was able to spend more time at home with his family.

We had completed a major renovation project on our house in town a few years earlier. The rent money we collected for more than twenty years helped us through many hard times. We decided now was as good a time as any to sell it. It was a beautiful setting, very privately situated on a double lot surrounded by tall spruce and maple trees, which we had planted when the children were small. We put a 'For Sale' sign on it and sold it shortly after.

I was still working an eight hour day between the two schools, and I started to feel it weighing heavily on me. I loved my job, but it was the driving to work every day that was getting to me. I had to travel the

Ridgeview School where I worked for 17 years.

433

highway every working day in every kind of weather. Winter driving, especially, was getting me down. So many times I was fighting the elements driving in fog, snow storms, icy roads, poor visibility, minus 40 degree temperatures and often dangerous road conditions. After prayerful consideration, I resigned from my position at the Ridgeview School. The Lord had protected me on the highway all those years, and I was grateful for that. I had found fulfillment in my work and felt privileged to have had the opportunity to work with so many wonderful people, staff, students and parents and I formed a lasting friendship with many of them.

We had rented space in town and moved the framing business there for a while. The overhead cost was so high that we moved it back home when only half of the lease agreement had expired. We were fortunate to get out of the agreement when someone else was looking for space to rent.

I realize that life will have its ups and downs, but I wasn't prepared for the disheartening phone call that came unexpectedly one day. Jake had been diagnosed with colon cancer, and the doctor was booking him for surgery. After his surgery, Carl and I drove to Grande Prairie to visit him in the hospital. I was relieved to find him so up beat. He was so hopeful for a complete recovery that he encouraged my heart. When further tests indicated that the cancer had spread, however, Jake and Mary sold their farm and moved the family into town.

Frequently Jake dropped by the framing shop and we would visit. We reminisced, but he also talked with difficulty about his future. The former Altona School students were planning a centennial celebration of the Altona School, which had opened in 1904. One day when we were visiting, our conversation turned to this upcoming event. He said, "Tena, I won't be around to take that in." I felt helpless and couldn't find any words to respond. His body was telling him that he wouldn't be around much longer unless the Lord performed a miracle.

Jake was interested in Tumbler Ridge and the house we had purchased. We had bought some furniture at a yard sale and a used washer, dryer, fridge and stove at a used appliance store. We had taken a few dishes, pots and pans from home and were able to spend weekends there, but we really weren't set up to stay for any length of time. Carl and I were going out to Tumbler Ridge for the Labor Day weekend, as Erma, my Altona school friend and her husband Mel, were coming out to spend the weekend with us. We invited Jake and Mary to join us as well. They thought it would be too many people, and chose not to come.

On one of our visits, Jake had mentioned to me that he likely wouldn't get to see Tumbler Ridge. When I went home after work that day I mentioned it to Carl and we decided we would make another trip to Tumbler Ridge if Jake and Mary could arrange to go. They decided to come. Jake was not well that weekend and he couldn't enjoy it. His health was starting to take a downhill turn.

Sixty-Five

Celebrating 50 Years in Alberta

Fifty years had passed since our family had stepped onto Alberta soil to carve out a living in the sparsely inhabited boreal forests of northern Alberta. Life had been difficult with extremely primitive living conditions being our lot in life for the first twelve years. This was especially true for Mom and Dad and, of course, it affected all of us as well. Over the years, living conditions had improved somewhat. Mom and Dad had moved into town shortly after they purchased the service station. They now had electricity, although still no running water or sewer. There was a well in the garage that was attached to the living quarters of the restaurant which was a big improvement from hauling every drop of water that was used. Life had become less complicated and demanding as, one by one, we had all left home, leaving one less mouth to feed.

My brothers and sisters and I had worked very hard to establish ourselves and raise our own families. As difficult as life had been, time had not stood still. I think I could speak for all my siblings in saying that our family had been richly blessed. Firstly with a godly heritage that unites our family in a way that nothing else could. Secondly, with material possessions, in varying degrees, but God had provided for all our needs and after five decades it was time to celebrate.

Esther had settled down in Kansas, in the United States when she married Brad Friesen, an American Mennonite. Brad's grandparents had migrated to the U.S. in the late 1800s when about 10,000 Mennonites

This family photo was taken in July 1978, 25 years after we moved to northern Alberta. Standing are me, Margaret, Esther, Martha, Jake, Mary, Annie, Bill, Babe, John, Betty and Helen. Seated are Leonard, Mom, Dad and Pete.

settled there – the same time period that our grandparents migrated to Canada from Ukraine. Esther flew in for our big celebration while everyone else was within a day's driving distance.

I felt it was extremely important to have a family picture taken at this time as we all knew that Jake was not well. We had a family portrait taken before our move 50 years ago, and another one at the 25-year mark. Now it was important to take another family photo while we were still all here, except for Mom and Dad.

We started the celebration by taking family pictures at our original homestead. That day, Friday, June 19, 2003 marked 50 years to the day since we had left our home in Saskatchewan. Dave and Lisa Peters, who lived on the old home place, were very accommodating and allowed us time and space to relive our memories. We took the pictures in front of the famous summer kitchen, which still stood.

Jake and his wife Mary had purchased the Woodland RV Park just outside of La Crete, and they offered to host the event there. Pete and his wife Sarah offered to host a big dinner on Friday night for all the immediate family and their spouses. There was much time and work involved

Our family on June 19, 2003 - 50 years to the day since our move to Alberta.
In the back row are Pete, me, Helen, Martha, Bill, Mary, Babe and Jake.
In front are John, Betty, Annie, Esther, Margaret and Leonard.

in both undertakings, and we were all thankful for their generosity. After the meal we went to visit Mom and Dad's graves to honour them for the sacrifice they had made to enable all of us to live and enjoy a good quality of life today.

Our family was very well represented, although not all the nieces and nephews could make it out. The weather was unfavourable for most of the weekend, cool and rainy, and it dampened our spirits somewhat, but it didn't have the power to dampen my thankful heart. We had an outdoor church service on Sunday morning, and the pastor spoke on the importance of keeping family together. By nature, it's the parents' role, but now that Mom and Dad had passed on, that responsibility fell on us siblings. A strong bond unites our family, but the stronger bond of God's love is what ultimately keeps our family together. As I reflect on the years I was influenced by my parents and the example they set, my prayer is that I will have the same godly influence on my family.

Mom and Dad were no more perfect than many other parents, but despite their shortcomings, I feel blessed to have been raised in a home where we were taught strong moral values, a love and respect for God

The supper Pete and Sarah hosted on June 19, 2003. All our family are here with our spouses. Carl and I are at the very end and Pete and Sarah are on the left.

and where all of us knew we were loved unconditionally. Therefore, I am able to stand here today and call them blessed. They raised a family well in the worst of times – first the depression years, followed by the war and then years of pioneering in very primitive living conditions – never losing focus of their God-given responsibility for raising their family.

Over the years of raising my own children, I have prayed so often for wisdom and knowledge to perform a task which I felt unqualified for. I have concluded that if the result of raising the children will have produced law-abiding citizens, God-fearing individuals living the Christian life, I will have succeeded. I would like to include here a Mother's Day letter – one among the many letters and cards which I have received from the children and grandchildren over the years. This one was sent by LaDawn in May of 2002.

TO MOM, ON MOTHER'S DAY

There are so many things that come to mind when I think of you that it's impossible to articulate all my inner feelings and thoughts, so I'll try to share just a few. I want to take this opportunity to tell you how much I appreciate all you've done for me over the years and mostly who you are.

I don't know if I ever told you before that I admire so many things about you – first and foremost that you have not been content to be confined to the societal box where you live. This demonstrated itself in:

-Your determination to get a high school education, when, all the odds were against it.

-Your stand in wearing your hair and clothes the way you wanted rather than what was dictated.

-Your active role in the community, as a woman in different projects, from Community Library to the History Book.

-Your integrity in your work, and challenging those, who others may not, due to their position. You are not easily intimidated.

-Working outside the home when it was not the norm to do so and perhaps often feeling misunderstood in your motives/ need for doing so.

-You have been a woman ahead of her time in many different ways.

-Not only have you stood in the face of opposition, you have done so with much grace and quiet strength. And over the years the truth of your character is what is recognized.

I look up to you as an example in your courage to learn new things – from painting to computers and taking on challenging tasks like running a business. You have kept your mind active even though you are not as young as you once were.

I appreciate, too, very much; how you love us, your children, embrace our spouses and each one of the grandchildren for the uniqueness and gifts they are. I also appreciate your servant heart that empowers you to give in so many ways, even when you are not feeling well.

Most of all I admire and respect you for your deep faith and openness to embrace more of who God is … and in turn, passing this on to your sphere of influence. How often I thank God for my praying mother. Only in eternity will we see the path you paved in prayer in the lives of countless others.

I thank you too for your release, blessing and support in every way of the ministry God has called us into. How we value this gift. I thank you, too, for always being there to listen to me, and loving me unconditionally.

So on this Mother's Day, I want to say, I love you Mom! Thanks for being a great Mom, and thanks for being my friend.

With heaps of blessings,
Your daughter, LaDawn

Jake was beginning to have more bad days than good. Christmas was coming up, and it was Jake and Mary's turn to host our gathering. Carl and I offered to open up our home for the celebration. Then, if he got too tired, they could go home if they needed to. Jake was very sure they wanted to host it, and he probably felt that if he got too tired at least he would be at home. He joined us at the supper table and took part in a few activities, but he spent most of the evening in bed.

Esther had come home to visit Jake, and all fourteen of us were together again – but it would be the last time we would all spend Christmas together. Jake had fought hard and suffered much after completing three rounds of chemotherapy treatments. The time had come when his body wasn't strong enough to continue the fight. He never complained and wasn't discouraged, and he often requested for his family and visitors to sing, "I Won't Have to Cross Jordan Alone." His faith grew stronger as his body grew weaker, and he passed on into Glory on February 6, 2004. Jake's untimely death affected me deeply. We had shared such a close relationship all our growing up years and later. We had seldom been separated by more than a few miles or for more than short periods of time for more than 60 years.

Sixty-Six

Buffalo Head Prairie School Reunion

It had been five decades since the introduction of public schools in the community; another cause for celebration. We formed a committee of former students, parents and staff to organize the event, and I had great pleasure being a part of it. We got in touch with as many former students as possible and got them involved arranging for some of them to come to school and speak to the students, telling about some of their experiences at the first school. One of the former students recalled her first year in school, when communication between teacher and student was practically zero. She said they had lots of time to play – the teacher didn't understand German and the students didn't understand English. In later years, Mr. Nafziger, the teacher, became fluent in German, and the students became fluent in English. Two years after the school opened, Miss Sarah Lehn came to teach the lower grades, solving many communication problems, as she spoke German. She became a real asset to the school.

Before Christmas we organized a choir of former students, and they sang Christmas carols at the annual Christmas concert, the songs Mr. Nafziger and Miss Lehn had taught them 50 years before. When we realized that Mr. Nafziger was too ill to take part in the ceremonies, we contacted his son, Lowell, who lives in the U.S., and he flew in to represent his father.

The Nafzigers, despite the many hardships they endured, made La

Crete their permanent home. Mrs. Sara (Lehn) Harder, at the age of 90, came from Chilliwack, BC to take part in the celebration. She brought her photo albums of her 20 years at BHP school and, together with some school photos that were taken in later years, I made a photo gallery that was on display for the whole weekend. Mrs. Harder and Mrs. Nafziger came to the school the day before the event and spoke to the students, allowing them to ask questions about school in the early years. Lowell Nafziger also spoke to the students of his experiences at this first school.

The entire Buffalo Head Prairie community, consisting mainly of former students and their extended families, shared in a pot luck dinner. It was wonderful to see so many families participate. After the dinner everyone gathered in a tent that was set up for this occasion. There was a formal program to begin with, and later, people brought out their instruments and everyone joined in singing the many favourite hymns Mr. Nafziger and Miss Lehn had taught them. It was a beautiful evening in June, and as I was walking from the picnic tables to the school building my mind took me back all those years to how I had struggled for an education. Now it's available to anyone and everyone who is willing to give the effort. It's like it is being handed to them on a silver platter compared to my experience. Perhaps, because it's free, many parents and students still don't see the value of it.

PART FOUR

Our Sunset Years

Sixty-Seven

Retirement

Life is a continual cycle of changes, and we can neither escape them nor ignore them. We can accept and enjoy them, for every age has a special meaning. I have chosen to accept this chapter as the crowning years of my life. I have gained experience, knowledge, wisdom and memories that only the years can bring. Carl and I have sailed the seas of life together, often stormy, but more times very beautiful. We have experienced failures and successes, joys and disappointments and tried to never lose sight of God, the Lighthouse.

With the years I have reached a new vantage point where the values of life are better observed and evaluated. I understand now that many of my disappointments in life were God's appointments, conditioning me for eternity. Often times I view my life as the weaving described in the following poem.

THE DIVINE WEAVER

My life is but a weaving
Between my Lord and me;
I cannot choose the colours
He worketh steadily.

Offtimes he weaveth sorrow
And I in foolish pride,
Forget that He seeth the upper,
And I the under side.

Not till the loom is silent
And the shuttles cease to fly,
Shall God unroll the canvas
And explain the reason why.

The dark threads are as needful
In the Weaver's skillful hand,
As the threads of gold and silver
In the pattern He has planned.

Author Unknown

At other times I see my life as a painting that I've worked on all my days, thankful for the Bible, which has been my instruction guide and road map. I'm still adding to the painting and touching up areas here and there, and I often wonder what the finished result will be.

In August of 2002, Carl and I celebrated our 40th wedding anniversary, another milestone in our lives, surrounded by family and friends. God had richly blessed us all these 40 years and we were truly grateful.

Had it really been 31 years since Carl first stepped into that school bus to transport students to and from school? He had turned 65 and the school division allowed him to drive one more year after his 65th birthday. That year was now finished, and he parked that "big yellow beast" for the last time. It had been his faithful companion all those years, never getting tired of waiting for him regardless of weather or road conditions.

Carl spent the following year puttering around the yard getting things sorted out for an auction sale. Several years earlier, he had seeded the land to hay and rented it out, lightening the workload. Over the last few years the house and the yard seemed to get bigger as both our energy levels had diminished somewhat. Carl and I had spent many hours discussing and debating what we should do. We loved and enjoyed our beautiful place in the country, but it appeared that we had come to a crossroad in our life, and this chapter was coming to a close. We had worked hard building a home and a life on two quarters of bush land – put all our energy and money into it and trusted that it was a good investment.

Our 40th wedding anniversary, August 2002.

Carl drove the school bus for 31 years and received an award for more than one million kilometres of accident-free driving.

We set a date for an auction sale, which took us one step closer to the next season in our lives. LaDawn and the boys came home for about a month to help, and Louise and the children came for a week. Craig and Twila lived across the road from us; helping wherever and whenever they could. Mary and Babe came every day for a week, and Helen came to cook for the crew for that week. We had other members of the family help as well. My sister-in-law, Hilda, who lived nearby, was always willing and ready to lend a helping hand and we appreciated her help. Betty came to help for a day and Margaret came along to lift our spirits which was needed occasionally. Again I was so thankful for family.

I had a good idea of what I wanted to keep, but I wasn't always sure what was valuable to Carl. LaDawn and I started helping him sort things in the garage, and I soon discovered there were so many things he wanted to keep that I had considered junk. An old radio and tape player, which I had discarded long ago after it fell into a big pot of chicken noodle soup, meant a great deal to him. It sat quite nicely on the ledge of the kitchen range and, one day, for whatever reason, it landed in my pot of soup. He had messed around with it until he got it going again and was using it when he was working at the garage. (At the time I wasn't aware of this.) When LaDawn spotted this sun-bleached treasure she asked me, "Mom, is this garbage?" I said, "Definitely," and up it went onto the big truck with the rest of the valuables headed for the garbage dump.

Carl was walking towards the barn when he heard the thud of the radio landing on the truck box. He turned and asked, "What was that?" LaDawn replied, "It was just a piece of junk," to which he responded, "As long as it wasn't my radio!"

After a while Carl appeared on the scene and asked, "Where's my radio?" LaDawn replied, "Mom said it wasn't working anymore." At this point LaDawn and I looked at each other and decided this might be a good time to go fix lunch. Carl climbed onto that big truck and began digging to retrieve his treasure. We made it half way to the house before we just couldn't contain our laughter anymore. We were so tired we had a choice to either laugh or cry – we chose to laugh and we laughed until we cried. No sooner had he found it and got it going again, when Kitty Wells' famous "Honky Tonk Angels" echoed across the yard. It's still a good conversation piece today, and we often end up laughing just as hard as we did then.

We had purchased our property in Tumbler Ridge two years before our auction sale, and after prayerful consideration, we decided to move to this beautiful place. In April, I made another decision that I found very difficult. I resigned from my position at the Buffalo Head Prairie School.

The Buffalo Head Prairie School where I worked for 20 years.

Some of the Buffalo Head Prairie School staff singing a song they composed for me. I am the first on the left.

I gave my notice early, as I knew that my replacement would need some training to take over the library. Kathy Janzen, my niece, who had some library experience and an Early Childhood Development diploma – a real asset when working with children – was hired to replace me. She worked alongside of me for the month of June, and at the end of that time I felt very confident that she was capable of carrying on where I had left off. The principal made arrangements that I would accompany Kathy to Edmonton in September to introduce her to the book-buying venture. This had been one of the highlights of my job, and I felt privileged to enjoy it one more time.

We had a big house, with a big yard and, at different times, Carl and I hosted our staff social gatherings. It was time for our annual year-end picnic and farewell to staff that were leaving. We offered our home for this, one last staff social event whereby, we ended up hosting my own farewell. We had a great evening, but I had very mixed feelings. With the homey atmosphere that prevailed, it was like saying goodbye to another family.

We shared in a delicious pot luck dinner and had lots of fun later. The staff presented me with numerous gifts, and it was bittersweet. My last few weeks as librarian at Buffalo Head Prairie School included other events.

The last event that we hosted with my staff family from Buffalo Head Prairie School was our end of year picnic and my farewell.

The school council recognized my years of service and honoured me at the annual year-end awards presentation at the year-end picnic. Also, the Fort Vermilion School Division hosts an annual Long Service Award and banquet night when they honour their employees. I was awarded here for my years of service as well as my retirement. They had been good years – but the final stamp had been placed on my career!

Sixty-Eight

Altona School Reunion

In July, Carl and I traveled to Warman, Saskatchewan, to take part in the centennial celebration of the Altona School. It had been 100 years since the school first started operating in 1904. It was no longer an operating school as it had closed its doors in 1963, marking the end of another one-room country school. It was great to meet again with many of my former classmates. Several fund raising projects were organized to help cover the cost of the weekend. People donated items which were sold at a silent auction and a history book was put together. Former students were asked to submit brief histories of their lives, with pictures, which is truly a keepsake now.

Bus tours were organized to visit the whole school district and we relived past memories and saw again where all our classmates had lived. The bus tour ended at the Altona School site where one of the former students, Clifford Peters, now lived. With Clifford's permission, the committee had erected a cairn on his yard beside the road with the inscription: "In commemoration of our pioneers." Clifford and Sam Dyck, both former students, each gave short speeches, and the cairn was unveiled.

My friend, Erma and her musical band consisting of former Altona school students, entertained at various times during the weekend. I'm sure that Mr. Lepp, our teacher who taught us music, would have felt greatly honoured had he been there, knowing that someone had taken the music he taught us to a higher level. We shared time visiting and reminiscing, and Mr. Lepp's name frequently came up.

On Sunday morning we all gathered for a church service and a former student, the Reverend Bill Janzen, presented us with the message. The Altona School was only a small one-room country school, but it had been instrumental in the learning process that started many students on the road to discovering their talents.

Erma's band. Erma is playing the mandolin.

Former students of Altona School at the centennial celebration in 2004.
I am sixth from the right in the back row.

Sixty-Nine

The Big Move

Reality hadn't set in yet, even though our new adventure was about to begin. I had lived in La Crete for 51 years, and it wasn't easy to pull up my roots (I don't think I got them all) and move on. This meant leaving behind the life, the community, and the church which I had been a part of for all that time.

It was August and the packing began. Again, members of my family came to help with this big task, and I often wondered how people survive without family. I couldn't possibly survive without mine, and leaving them was the most difficult part of the move for me. I knew we would be only seven hours away, but the days of jumping into the vehicle and popping in for coffee or supper at one of my siblings' homes would be over.

Several days before our departure, Babe called and asked me which evening could she and Mary come spend some time with me. I told her Tuesday would be fine, but I wasn't sure what time we would get back from town as we had loose ends to tie up. When we returned home, the yard was full of vehicles and my counters in the kitchen were loaded with food fit for royalty. My brothers and sisters had planned this farewell evening for us, and Carl and I felt honoured and blessed. After a beautiful evening like that, it was even more difficult to leave.

On September 13, the moving van was loaded. I was totally ready to go, but Carl had a few odd things left to do, packing up the last of the tools

The home we left behind at Buffalo Head Prairie.

and securing windows and doors. I went to sit on the deck to wait until he was ready. We had built an addition to the house, including a three car garage and a large wrap-around deck several years earlier.

We spent many hours on that deck, shelling peas or sorting Saskatoon berries. On beautiful summer evenings we enjoyed sitting there, taking in the splendid view; the lawn surrounding the house, the garden, the hay fields, the forest and, to complete the scene, the beautiful Buffalo Head Hills. Many times we enjoyed a glorious sunset as it reflected on the shadowy forest and the giant hills. I captured the moments as I rolled back the years in my mind. In 80 BC, Cicero stated, *"Memory is the treasury and guardian of all things."* We had built this place up from virgin land to what it was today by the sweat of our brows, often mingled with tears when times got difficult. I viewed the fields, the pastures, and remembered all the land clearing, development and improvements representing so many years of toil.

It had been a hard but good life. The children and grandchildren had been happy here, enjoying country life and nature, playing at the creek, roaming in the woods and eating the fruits of my garden. On one occasion, when all the grandchildren were home, I had instructed them not to pull any carrots, as they weren't ready yet. Later, when I went in to the garden, I noticed that they *had* pulled carrots (about four inches long, greens included.) I confronted them and they assured me they hadn't pulled any. They were still too young to think about destroying the evidence.

The glorious days of spring made me lighthearted when pussy willows turned from pinkish grey to fluffy yellow and the sticky buds of the poplars looked ready to burst into leaf. When the ice broke up in the creek and the water started to run, we could hear it gurgling and rushing

462

as it made its way to join other tributaries. At other times the water sang a sweet lullaby as it flowed gently to its destination between the mossy, debris-laden banks. Numerous years in the summer when the skies opened up and showered us with three to four inches of rain in a period of a few days, the creek overflowed its banks and no one was able to cross the bridge. With difficulty we could get out the back way, but many times only with a tractor. This long way around led across a neighbour's yard – but it was the only way we could get to the main highway.

Heavy bush surrounded our yard, and the birds were very faithful from spring to fall in presenting us with their musical talents. In the summer months when the day dawned at around three o'clock in the morning, the birds announced a new day by echoing their songs through our bedroom windows. What peace I experienced then.

The bears frequently ventured into our yard, as though they belonged there too. With their natural habitat on our doorstep, they were right in their element.

Several winters, moose found sanctuary beside our house when the wolves were hungry and plentiful. It seemed like somehow they felt protected when they were near humans. One winter a cow moose with her calf were frequent visitors. They ventured away during the day but always found their way back until, one day, only the mother returned,

Moose a few yards from the house with the Buffalo Head Hills in the background.

and we knew there were a few less hungry wolves around.

The moose were getting braver and more annoyed with the dog, as he kept barking, trying to chase them away. On one cold winter night the moon was full and it was particularly light outside. I had gone to bed, but Carl was a bit perturbed by the irritable bark of the dog right in front of the house. He assumed the moose must be very close, so he kept watch. It was midnight when he came to the bed room and said, "Tena, you have to come and see this." Two big moose were standing right in front of our large dining room window, and the dog, only a few feet away from the moose, was very upset. Carl said, "Watch, they're going to charge." No sooner had he said that when the moose went after the dog, causing a big commotion, and the dog ran for cover. The moose must have scared him somewhat as he quit barking for a long time after.

I remembered the day when a bear attacked our faithful dog and we had to put him down; as well as the day when Craig brought home three orphaned Canada goose goslings, which we nurtured and wintered on the farm. It was amusing to watch Carl trying to teach them how to fly – running down our long driveway waving his arms, the geese following, honking and flapping their wings.

One spring, Craig brought home a brood of baby ducklings; as sweet as can be, but they were much work. After a while the novelty wore off and I was left to care for them when I had much more important things to do. When the time came to look after their needs again, I did! I loaded them up in the car, took them to the slough which was on the way to town and released them into the water. I had never seen happier baby ducks.

I could see the many bountiful gardens and still hear the garden tractor as Carl prepared the plot for planting every spring. The rich earthy smells of the newly tilled earth and the feel of the soft cool dirt between my toes

Our bountiful garden in July 2003.

lingered in my memory as well as the long summer evenings when Carl and I, together with the children, hoed and pulled weeds, forgetting all about time. One particular evening I mentioned to Carl that I was getting a bit weary. He looked at his watch and remarked that it was no wonder – it was almost eleven o'clock. The sun didn't set before then, so it was time to call it a day. In the spring our apple tree was a spectacular sight – loaded with white and pinkish blossoms, its fragrance drifting into the house through an open window and at other times, across the yard.

My memory took me back to the many warm days when LaDawn and Louise enjoyed reading and listening to their music under the shade of the big spruce trees in the yard, or the sound of the girls listening to music upstairs while doing their home work during the long winter evenings. I could still hear Louise dragging her furniture across her room upstairs, as she weekly rearranged it.

There were also the times when Craig and his friends skinned beavers beside the play house during the spring hunt, and the times when he and his buddies had knife throwing contests and I could hear the banging of knives hitting the walls of the granary. There were also the wonderful occasions when the grandchildren enjoyed birthday parties, playing with the baby puppies, having tea parties and water fights on the front lawn, as well as the time Carl and I made snowmen with them, when the snow

Our grandchildren celebrating Danielle's birthday.

Brittany, Danielle and Desirae playing with puppies.

Enjoying cold water on a hot summer day.

The grandchildren having a picnic on the front lawn at the farm.

Jeridan and Jesse having a mud fight after a heavy rain.

Jamael playing in the mud too.

Carl and our grandsons Jamael, Jesse and Jeridan making a snowman.

469

was wet and sticky.

So many memories flooded my mind. I thought of our grandsons, Jeridan and Jesse, as teenagers, having a mud fight after a heavy rain while Jamael was entertaining himself. They came into the house, still dripping mud, although they had attempted to clean up by hosing down outside. I was a little upset. I said, "You boys are going to clean up this mess." Jeridan's reply was, "Yes, we will, Grandma." I wasn't paying too much attention until I noticed that he had gone into my linen closet and was using a brand new white towel to wipe up the mud puddles. I practically lost it, and the boys were a bit startled at my reaction, as they hadn't seen me so upset before. Now it's a big joke, and the boys try to come up with ideas to get another reaction like that out of me. I relived the many picnics and barbecues we had with family and friends as well as the visits and game nights beside a cozy fire on cold winter evenings.

I could still smell the newly mowed-lawn and the freshly-mown hay as a soft gentle breeze filtered its scent into the yard from the surrounding hayfields. The honking of a thousand geese, breaking the early evening silence, was always a reminder that harvest time had arrived. They came flying low over the house in their V formation, landing to feed in the grain fields behind the barn. I could hear the sound of the tractor in the fields either seeding or harvesting; the cows mooing at milking time; the calves crying for their mothers when they were weaned in the fall; and Carl pounding iron at the garage repairing some piece of equipment. Now everything was still.

Carl joined me after a while and, one last time, we enjoyed sitting on that deck together. These were the memories of days gone by. Our quality of life had been great, and as we pondered all the years we had lived here, we knew it was time to move on. We had all the good memories of farm and country life, so we would close this chapter, start a new one, and trust that we would have many more memorable experiences to enrich our lives. Carl climbed into the moving van and I into our little white jeep, and we were off to our new home.

Seventy

Our New Home

The trip seemed very long. I was all by my self, with no one to talk to, and many hours to think as I followed Carl in the moving van. Somehow it didn't seem real. The stretch of road from Dawson Creek to Tumbler Ridge is a very scenic route, although we couldn't enjoy it as we were traveling this 100 kilometer stretch of road after dark. Not being familiar with all the hills, valleys, curves and wild animals on this narrow road, it was almost two hours before we saw the lights of Tumbler Ridge.

Helen and her husband Jim, had moved to Tumbler Ridge a few months earlier, and had rounded up a few people from church to help us unload. How grateful we were for their help. Craig and Twila and their four daughters had moved to town two years earlier; it was good to have family here when we arrived. Louise and Dave and their three children lived in Grande Prairie, so we were now only a few hours away from them. LaDawn and Isaac and their three boys were living in Montana; shortening our trip to visit them by about seven hours. Being closer to all our children and grandchildren would be a blessing!

The first winter kept us busy with renovations – taking out several walls, putting down new floors and painting. I am very happy with our smaller house which we have made into a cozy home. Our house is the very last one in the cul-de-sac with all natural forest surrounding it, so, for the most part, it is very peaceful. When I look out our dining room window it reminds me of the view we had from our dining room window on the farm.

We have many children in our neighborhood. Frequently, Carl and I watch them from our dining room window when they're playing in the water and having a lot of fun. We have a small coulee right next to our house, which fills up with water in the spring or when it rains. The children love to test the depth of the water, and occasionally their boots will overflow, bringing back memories of my childhood. The deer come to feed just a few feet from the house, and we never tire of watching them. We marvel continuously at these beautiful creatures.

Tumbler Ridge is surrounded by magnificent mountains, rivers and lakes, and good fishing and camping are within an hour's drive. Our friends, Kris and Willie Nelson, called us one afternoon and asked if we would like to join them on a fishing excursion. We packed our picnic lunches and in a short time we were at the lake. This evening stands out as a rare experience. The four of us were in the boat in the middle of the lake with no one else around. Tall mountains surround the lake, and a lonely loon was on the water, calling. With no breeze or ripple, the lake appeared like glass. There was something so peaceful and tranquil that I didn't want to leave. It reminded me of the scripture verse in Psalm 46:10, *"Be still and know that I am God."*

The spectacular Kinuseo Falls on the Murray River are over an hour from Tumbler Ridge, and, on several occasions, Craig has taken us, together with some friends, in his river boat to view the breathtaking sight. It was delightful to eat our lunch on the river bank where we got sprayed with mist from the falls across the river.

In 2005, LaDawn, Isaac, Jesse and Jamael were heading for Thailand, Ukraine, and parts of Europe for ten months to work mainly with the aftermath of the Asian Tsunami in Thailand, which hit at Christmas 2004, devastating many countries and affecting the lives of millions of people. Jeridan, their oldest son, was staying with us while he was working for Craig, trying to earn enough money to cover his school expenses. He was entering 'Discipleship Training School' with 'Youth With A Mission' starting in January. He was only two weeks past his 19th birthday and was heading to the Australian outback for his training. I could hardly handle it. He had traveled numerous times across the ocean with his parents, but now he was all alone. I tried to give him some advice, but I soon discovered he knew a whole lot more about traveling than I did. He was so confident about everything, just like his mother had been when she first left home. Carl and I took him to the airport in Edmonton and made sure

Carl and me at the spectacular Kinuseo Falls on the Murray River.

he caught the plane. After he got through the gates, he waved to us one more time and then disappeared around the corner. I kept standing there and watching until Carl said, "Let's go." I said I would like to stay around a little while longer, just in case he would need us for something.

We had experienced difficulty when the children left home. Now we felt the same pain when our first grandchild left to make it on his own. Jeridan made out just fine; after his training he flew to the Fijian Islands for an eight week outreach program, and then returned to Australia for several more months to minister with 'Impact World Tours Evangelistic Campaigns'. How blessed I was when he called from Fiji to wish me Happy Mother's Day. He had a great time serving the Lord in the field into which he had been called, and the Lord protected him much better than we ever could have.

Seventy-One

Forest Fire

The summer of 2006 was hot and dry. Electrical storms were frequent, but no rain accompanied the storms. It was a hot afternoon when we noticed some big, strange-looking clouds rise over the mountains that surround our town. We discovered shortly after that lightening had struck, and it appeared to be the start of a forest fire. Everyone kept watch as the choppers flew, attempting to extinguish the flames, and we felt confident that they would succeed.

LaDawn, Isaac, Jesse and Jamael had just arrived home from overseas, and they had to detour using the Chetwynd Highway, as the Dawson Creek Highway had already been closed due to the heavy smoke, and the fire had jumped the highway. They were all suffering from jet lag and it was time to settle in and rest. We went to bed knowing the fire had increased in size, and talk had been going around about a possible evacuation. In the morning my friend, Diane Reid, called and said they were packing all their valuables into their RV just in case. We hadn't really given it any serious thought, but after that phone call we started considering what we should pack into our motor home.

A sudden change in the wind had the fire heading straight for the town. At around six o'clock a gentleman knocked on our door and gave us an evacuation alert warning. He told us not to panic, but to eat our supper and start packing our valuables, just in case. I knew Jesse and Jamael loved ice cream bars, and since they had been deprived of many

Smoke over Tumbler Ridge, the start of the forest fire.

goodies for so long I had bought a whole case for them to enjoy when they returned. Enjoy them they did! We were all so busy running around that we hadn't noticed that they were eating them constantly. They told us later there was no way those ice cream bars were going to burn and go to waste, so they thought they may as well eat them – justifying their actions.

An hour after the alert warning, another gentleman knocked on the door and informed us that we had one hour to get out of town, as the fire was advancing fast. That hour is still a blur. We were thankful we had Jesse and Jamael to help us carry our valuables into the motor home. We had people's art work to be framed, so that was my first priority. Jesse and Jamael probably earned their ice cream bars in that hour.

We hadn't even given it a thought as to where we would go. Our friends, Irene and E.B. Johnson called us just before they left town and asked us where we were going to go. I told them we didn't know, but we had been notified that Dawson Creek and Chetwynd were setting up shelters. Irene and E.B. owned a big house on an acreage, just outside of Fort St. John, and they offered that we could all come and stay with them. Irene quickly gave us their Fort St. John phone number and their cell number and they were off. We discussed it and decided that this was a much better idea than staying in a shelter, as we had no idea how long this would last. We took them up on their offer, and, as soon as we were ready, we headed out of town.

We had to detour around Chetwynd, which made the trip several hours longer. We traveled in a caravan. Carl drove the motor home with Jesse; Isaac drove their van with Jamael, and LaDawn and I took our jeep. As we were going up a high hill we looked down into the valley below and saw a string of lights as far as we could see. The vehicles were practically bumper to bumper, mile upon mile, all heading for safer ground. We made it to Irene and E.B.'s place at about two-thirty in the morning and we were all too tired to function normally. Irene and E.B. had also called Helen and Jim and our friends Kris and Willie and offered them shelter if they needed it. They joined us in their RV's the next day.

The following morning we ladies went into town to shop for groceries, and we actually had a great time cooking, eating and playing games as long as we could block out of our minds that we may not have a home to return to. As we were to learn later, the winds shifted again and Tumbler Ridge was spared, thanks to the fire fighting crews and the prayers of many people. After four days we returned home and tried to get some semblance of order back into our home and lives.

Seventy-Two

Homecomings and Reunions

Reunions and homecomings are commonplace nowadays, but I was looking forward to a special one. It had been 44 years since I graduated from T.A. Norris High School in Peace River, and a big reunion was forthcoming. I was excited to meet again with many of my classmates I hadn't seen since my high school days. Carl and I took in the three-day weekend, which was well represented. It was great to spend time with my friends, whom I had kept in touch with over all those years – Pauline (Naturkach) Zeschuck and Anne (Sheard) Goldbeck, and to renew acquaintances with many others. An added highlight was reconnecting with Bonnie Plante – whom I had lost contact with after high school. Most everyone had made their mark in their communities and in their country. Many of the teachers had passed on, but some were present and they all received their well-earned honour that weekend.

The summer of 2007 was bittersweet. In May, a Neudorf reunion was organized at La Crete on my Dad's side of the family with well over 300 people in attendance. It was very rewarding to connect with so many relatives. Quite a number of my cousins, who, with some of their families, had moved to Bolivia in the late 1960s, had recently returned to Canada and attended the event. It was a great reunion.

At the end of May we traveled to Montana, to take in our grandson, Jesse's, high school graduation. On our way home we stopped in Lethbridge to visit members of Carl's family. Carl's sister Kay's health was

The T.A. Norris High School class reunion, 44 years after we graduated. I am standing to the right of the tall man in the back row.

deteriorating rapidly, so we spent some time with her. While on the trip we received a disturbing phone call telling us that my brother Pete was not well and the doctors were doing a thorough check. Several days later the disheartening news came that the test results were not good. Cancer had again reared its ugly head and struck another member of our family. The cancer was so far advanced the doctors did not suggest treatment.

The plans for a family reunion to be held in Kansas, where Esther had made her home, had been in the making for almost two years. The date was set for the first week in August. I had purchased my plane ticket and was scheduled to fly July 30. Carl's sister Kay passed away at the end of June, so we headed back to Lethbridge to attend her funeral. In the meantime Pete's condition had worsened, and the doctors weren't giving him much time. Carl and I made several trips to La Crete to visit Pete and his wife, Sarah (who is Carl's sister), and their family. Pete was hospitalized several days after he was diagnosed and didn't return home again. He had always been very active and upbeat – always working at something – and I found it heartbreaking to see him helpless and suffering so much.

I really wanted to go to Kansas, but I decided to take my eyes off my circumstance and concentrate on what I considered was more impor-

480

tant. I would not go as long as Pete was with us and left the timing in God's hands. After a heart wrenching struggle and much suffering, the Lord took him home on July 24, less than six weeks after he had been diagnosed. The funeral date was set for July 28. I had to leave for Grande Prairie the next day to catch my flight on July 30. God's timing was perfect, and it reminded me of the words of a song that is occasionally sung as a special number in church. When Mary had called for Jesus when her brother Lazarus was sick, Jesus was "four days late," but He was still on time.

Esther had flown in to visit Pete when he was sick, so she didn't come for his funeral. The timing here was perfect also. It was a great comfort to Esther that so many of us came; now she didn't have to grieve alone. We were able to share in all of Pete's sufferings and victories and were able to recall happy times as well as crying together. Esther and Brad had done much work to organize this big event and we enjoyed it as much as circumstances allowed. Sadly, I was becoming more and more acquainted with death, but, at times, I would still struggle with it. I got another clear picture of death when I read Henry Van Dyke's poem.

GONE FROM MY SIGHT

*I am standing upon the seashore. A ship at my side springs
her white
sails to the morning breeze and starts for the blue ocean.
She is an object of beauty and strength.
I stand and watch her until at length she hangs like a speck
of white cloud
just where the sea and sky come to mingle with each other.
Then someone at my side says:
"There, she is gone."
"Gone where?"
Gone from my sight. That is all.
She is just as large in mast and hull and spar as she was
when she left my side
and she is just as able to bear her load of living freight to her
destined port.
Her diminished size is in me, not in her.
And just at that moment when someone at my side says:
"There she is gone!"*

there are other eyes watching her coming, and
other voices ready to take up the glad shout:
"Here she comes!"
And that is dying.

My mind takes me back to all the reunions and homecomings I've taken part in over the years and the joys and blessings I experienced there. It is my prayer that all my family will be present at that last great homecoming where we will all meet again. As all of us siblings grew up, going out with friends during our teen years, starting to take responsibility for our own actions and making decisions without Mom and Dad's supervision, Mom could never go to sleep at night until all her children were safely in. A poem I came across years ago reminded me of Mom and the love and concern she had for us, her children.

ARE ALL THE CHILDREN IN?

I think oft times as the night draws nigh
Of an old house on the hill
Of a yard all white and blossom–starred
Where the children played at will.
And when the night at last came down
Hushing the merry din
Mother would look around and ask
Are all the children in?

'Tis many and many a year since then,
And the old house on the hill
No longer echoes to childish feet,
And the yard is still, so still.
But I see it all as the shadows creep,
And though many the years have been
Since then, I can hear Mother ask
"Are all the children in?"

I wonder if when the shadows fall
On that last short earthly day
When we say goodbye to the world outside
All tired of pain, and work and play
When we step into that Other Land

Where Mother so long has been
Will we hear her ask, just as of old
"Are all the children in?"

I believe that Mom's prayer, "that all her children and grandchildren, and all those that will follow after will meet in heaven some day" still echoes in the heavenly realm and is becoming a reality as one by one they are committing their hearts to Christ and one by one the Lord is calling them home.

Seventy-Three

My Faithful Guide

We have now lived in Tumbler Ridge for six years, and so far we are happy to call it home. We have experienced many positive things here. We enjoy the beautiful town with its lofty mountains, clear rivers and lakes, and the clean mountain air. We came from a farming community, which like most other farming communities, had embraced chemical farming with pesticides, herbicides and other chemicals filling the air from spring to fall. Breathing this contaminated air must have an effect on human health, and at times I wonder if it's not killing more than just bugs and weeds.

We love camping and fishing and are within an hour's drive of numerous beautiful lakes. We have a wonderful church family and have made many friends and live in a good neighbourhood. Both Carl and I agree that it would be difficult to leave all our friends, but at times my old home beckons me, and, on occasion, I have been tempted to answer the call. I choose, however, to be content wherever I live because I lack nothing. We've had struggles in our married life, financially, spiritually, along with heartaches in raising the family, but always I rested in the assurance that, when life got too difficult, the Lord would carry us through. Carl and I faced life's challenges together and grew wiser and stronger because of it.

So often I drew strength from the following poem and the power of its message has not dimmed with time.

FOOTPRINTS

One night a man had a dream. He dreamed he was walking
along the beach with the Lord. Across the sky flashed scenes
from his life. For each scene, he noticed two sets of footprints
in the sand; one belonged to him, and the other to the Lord.

When the last scene of his life flashed before him, he looked
back at the footprints in the sand. He noticed that many
times along the path of his life there was only one set of foot-
prints. He also noticed that it happened at the very lowest
and saddest times of his life.

This really bothered him and he questioned the Lord about
it. "Lord, you said that once I decided to follow you, you'd
walk with me all the way. But I have noticed that in the most
troublesome times in my life, there is only one set of foot-
prints. I don't understand why when I needed you most you
would leave me.

The Lord replied, "My precious, precious child, I love you and
would not leave you. During your trials and suffering, when
you see only one set of footprints, it was then that I carried
you."

Margaret Fishback Powers

Pastor Ken Campbell founded and organized an annual one-week conference here in Tumbler Ridge for five years until the Lord took him home. He named it 'The Wilderness Family Conference', and his theme was always the same; Calling Canada Back to God. Our nation was founded on Biblical principles but has plunged into social and moral decay, which gave him deep concern for our country. I felt privileged to take in this conference for several years, and I was blessed to meet Margaret Fishback Powers, the author of *Footprints*, at one of the conferences. She autographed her book, *Footprints, the True Story Behind the Poem that Inspired Millions*, for me. It was a great experience, and I was able to relate to her personally how many times her poem had inspired me and how often I had drawn strength from it.

With the Lord's guidance and direction, Carl and I have raised a beau-

Me with our first great-grandchild, Hunter Allen Craig.

tiful family; a family we love unconditionally and are proud of. The children have always been there for us when we needed them, and now the grandchildren are following suit. Most certainly we have made many mistakes in raising them, but we choose to focus on the end result, and I trust that the legacy we are leaving our children and grandchildren will be passed down for generations to come.

Dr. James Dobson says in his book, *Straight Talk to Men and Their Wives*, *"Lord, You know my inadequacies. You know my weaknesses, not only in parenting, but in every area of my life. I did the best I could, but it wasn't good enough. As You broke the fishes and the loaves to feed the five thousand, now take my meager effort and use it to bless my family. Make up for the things I did wrong. Satisfy the needs that I have not satisfied. Wrap Your great arms around my children and draw them close to You. And be there when they stand at the great crossroads between right and wrong. All I can give is my best, and I've done that. Therefore, I submit to You my children and myself and the job I have done as a parent. The outcome belongs to You."*

Over the years I have also claimed the promise, along with many other parents, in Proverbs 22: v6, *"Train a child in the way he should go and when he is old he will not turn from it."* I believe we have done that. Our children have all settled down, raising families of their own, and now the grandchildren are starting to leave home, to raise their own families, and so it will continue.

I have lived a full and rewarding life, and I'm now living in my sunset years. I cherish my yesterdays, as they are irreplaceable souvenirs of my journey through life, and I believe in my tomorrows, because tomorrows are what forever is made of. God has been my faithful Companion and Guide in my walk through life. He has carried me when the seas were rough and stormy, and walked beside me when the waters were peaceful and still.

When I allow my memory to view the entire canvas of my life, I know I would change many things if I could live life over again. The painting would look somewhat different, but art comes in many forms. I choose to see my life as a form of art with all the failures, successes, joys and disappointments woven together and etched into the canvas.

There's a special art to living,
And we learn it through the years,
It isn't automatic, it's the work
Of joy and tears,
Of friendships made and honoured,
Of dreams both sought and lost,
Of wisdom and experience
Hard-won, but worth the cost.

Afterword

2009 – Our Crisis Year

Much stress from 2008 carried over into 2009. I was experiencing much pain in my right leg – the knee in that leg had been repaired by knee replacement surgery fifteen years earlier. With my many visits to doctors the problem wasn't detected.

The winds of adversity had been blowing in our church family for over a year, but no one was prepared for what was to come.

On May 31, at 2:30 a.m. a terrible blast awoke the whole town. The house across the street from us blew up. Suicide was not ruled out. The man in the house was the only casualty, and it was nothing less than a miracle that no one else was killed or seriously injured. Some houses were ripped open, windows were blown out of many and people were thrown from their beds.

Initially, about 25 houses, ours among them, had to be reconstructed, but there were many more claims in a very short while. We received notice that we would have to move out completely before the reconstruction could begin. We didn't know where we were going to move to – at this time the insurance company had not informed us that they would relocate everyone. In the meantime, our friends, Walter and Diane Reid, offered that we could move into their vacant house.

Since I was in pain almost constantly, I couldn't begin to do all the packing. LaDawn came from Montana for two weeks to help with the huge task, Craig and Twila, the girls and my sister Helen also pitched in. The house was stripped and only the studs separating the rooms remained. The roof, siding, doors and windows were replaced as well as all the floors, ceilings and walls – in other words, we ended up with a brand new house. We were all so traumatized from this upheaval in our lives that our focus was not on the real tragedy. How sad that the future can seem so meaningless and hopeless for anyone, that facing a new day becomes unbearable.

The winds of dissention that were creating havoc and confusion in the church continued to blow and on June 18, when the hurricane unleashed its fury, our church took a severe beating. Many of my emotions that had not been put to a serious test before were severely tested. I had to deal with anger which I normally didn't have to guard, with forgiveness, and mostly with love. In John 13:35 Jesus said, *"Thereby shall all man know that you are my disciples – the love you have for one another."* His command in John 15:12 is to *"love one another, as I have loved you."* It was a difficult assignment when I witnessed firsthand how Christians can inflict so much pain on fellow believers. Those of us that remain are trying to pick up the pieces, rebuild and go forward.

With all this emotional and physical stress in our lives there was more to come. The pain in my leg was so severe that many times I simply couldn't walk and retreated to crutches and a walker. Again I went to the clinic – the doctor ordered an ultra-sound and the problem was discovered on July 8. My leg was in very rough shape and time was not on my side. My doctor referred me to a specialist in Kamloops who specializes in knee-replacement repairs and I had my first appointment with him on September 22. He ordered me into a wheel chair until he had a surgery date – he needed to reschedule surgeries in order to fit me in. Much bone had deteriorated and the bone beneath my knee was ready to break.

On our way to this appointment we got a phone call saying that my niece, Bobbi, was on life support in the Grande Prairie hospital. We were so shocked that we forgot about road signs, missed our turn-off to Kamloops, and were heading for Vancouver. Another phone call confirmed the worst – Bobbi had passed away. She was suffering from Crohns Disease and died as a result of the treatment. She was only 25 years old and seemed to have everything going for her in this life except for her illness. She worked as an occupational therapist in the hospital and was married to a fine young man; their future looked promising. But her life was cut short without warning. What a sad day when we attended her funeral in Grande Prairie.

Shortly afterwards, I received a phone call confirming a surgery date –

it was set for November 17. Because of all the pain I was experiencing, we decided to fly to Kamloops. I couldn't begin to imagine another trip in a truck for twelve hours, one way. LaDawn again came to my aide. She also flew into Kamloops to be with me during my surgery. My cousin, John Klassen (who I had spent much time with in Saskatchewan) married my friend Annie (Knelsen) who I had chummed with in the 1950s. They live in Kamloops and opened up their home to us. What a blessing that was! My surgery went well. The doctor gave me a new knee plus he needed to put plates below and above my knee. He informed me that it would take about two years for the bone to grow back so I'm relying on walking aids and will for some time. But my leg, as scarred up as it is, looks beautiful to me. I will be able to walk again and I have no more pain.

We knew that Carl would have to return home a few days after the surgery and take care of last minute things at the house. The insurance company wasn't going to pay storage rent any longer than they had to. They moved everything back into the house a few days before I came home and what a disaster awaited me. Boxes were stacked high throughout the house with only a pathway into the kitchen, bathroom and bedroom. LaDawn came back home and stayed for another week to take care of me and help unpack. Craig, Twila, Danielle, Brittany and Desirae also came alongside, kicked into high gear and got some order back into our house and lives. Initially, when I got home, all this turmoil didn't affect me very much. I was high on drugs, but not too long down the road … they began to wear off!

Three weeks after my surgery, on December 8, we got another phone call, this one telling us that my brother-in-law, Johnny, Babe's husband, had passed away. He had been suffering from what was believed to be Multiple Sclerosis (MS). He had been confined to a wheel chair for many years and had lost his speech which proved to be very difficult for him. He loved to visit and was always cheerful and upbeat, living life to the fullest. In the last years his eyesight deteriorated and he also lost use of more motor skills. It was difficult to see him suffer so much, but after he was relieved from all his suffering, it still hit hard. Death is so final but we have all the fond memories of the good times spent together.

Our year ended with all the children, grandchildren and great-grand-children coming home for Christmas. I was still very much a patient but I was so blessed with family who looked after everything.

The grieving continues. Recovery from the church crisis and my surgery are slow – but we are enjoying our beautiful new house.

Our family on December 25, 2009.
In the back row: Danielle, Dawn Amber, Andrew holding Jordan, Jesse, Jamael and Jeridan.
In the middle row: Jamison, Louise and Dave.
Seated: Craig holding Hunter, Twila, Carl, me, LaDawn and Isaac.
In the front are: Brittany, Desirae, Marita and Janaya.

Tribute To My Family

To My Children

LaDawn

You were a beautiful baby and a precocious child. You have matured and grown into a lovely woman of God. You are a pillar of strength in my life. Isaac, I want to thank you for being such a wonderful husband to LaDawn and a great daddy to Jeridan, Jesse and Jamael. I want to thank you together with LaDawn for raising the boys in a God-fearing environment that reflects the love of Jesus Christ in your everyday lives. You and LaDawn make a great team; an encouragement, strength and blessing to so many people in need of direction – people who need confirmation of their self-worth and their identity in Jesus Christ, at home and abroad. I trust the Lord will reward you for your endless labour of love.

LaDawn and Isaac have served the Lord with Youth With A Mission for fifteen years working from the YWAM branch campus of the University of the Nations in Lakeside, Montana, USA. Their work takes them around the globe and I've truly learned to "let go" and "let God."

Isaac and Jesse standing behind Jamael, LaDawn and Jeridan.

Craig

You were a contented happy child and you blessed our home in so many ways; your humour often saving the day. You're a lover of nature and sense the power of God in His creation when you roam the woods all by yourself. I want to thank you for being such a great daddy to Dawn Amber, Danielle, Brittany and Desirae. It's a great blessing to see how you love your girls unconditionally and how their response is likewise. I want to thank Twila also, for being such a great mom and grandma. Together you and Twila have raised a beautiful family. You are a wonderful grand-daddy to Hunter and Jordan Lee. I want to thank you for always standing by our side when we need you.

Craig and Twila live in Tumbler Ridge, BC from where Craig runs his oilfield maintenance business. Twila has the huge responsibility of taking care of all the paperwork from the home. They purchased horses giving the girls the responsibility of caring for them as well as the pleasure of riding them.

Danielle in the back, Twila, Desirae, Craig and Brittany, Dawn Amber in front.

496

Louise

You were such a delightful, cheerful child and your smile and laugh have always been infectious. You were the ray of sunshine that filtered through in our home on a dark dismal day. You have grown into a stalwart woman of God and I admire your strength in standing up for what you believe. You chose to home school your children even if it wasn't the most popular thing to do in order for you to instill in them the values and godly principles you believed in. You are a great mom to Marita, Jamison and Janaya. Dave, I want to thank you for being such a loving husband to Louise and a great daddy to your children. I admire you for the spiritual pillar you are in your home.

Louise and Dave have settled down near Grande Prairie, AB where they enjoy country life together with a menagerie of animals. Dave has worked in sales for many years for numerous different companies, always testing the waters with both feet and never afraid of a challenge. Louise is a stay-at-home mom and together she and Dave have created a very inviting atmosphere in their home where people love to come and spend time.

Jamison, Dave, Louise, Janaya and Marita.

To My Grandchildren

You are all so special and you make my life very interesting.
I am blessed by each one of you.

Jeridan

You are a true outdoorsman who loves being in the wild, hunting and fishing yet we can sit and have deep meaningful conversations over a cup of tea – a tradition that started before you went to school. We experienced the Lord's anointing on your life since you were a child. You had insight into many things and asked such deep questions that I would have to think before I could answer. We praise God for your obedience to His calling. I pray the Lord's blessing on you as you follow God's path, teaching in the School of Biblical Studies at the YWAM branch campus of the University of the Nations in Lakeside, MT and beyond. We were privileged to hear you teach through the book of Ezra and can see how your vision and passion for His Word will transform people's lives around the world.

Jesse

You are our inquisitive one, always questioning something you don't fully understand and challenging anyone who doesn't agree with you. Your loving personality and intelligence is attractive to all who know you and it shines through when you help me time and again with the same computer issues. Your strength of character makes you stand firm in what you believe. My prayer is that you will use your many giftings to their highest potential and bring glory to God.

You are a very interesting character who thinks outside the box. Musically gifted and talented in culinary arts, you have also been given a great sense of humor. You are the family comedian! How we all love to listen when you imitate high profile people, especially George W. Bush. The relaxing music you make on the ukulele and guitar puts my heart at ease. Working together with you in the kitchen can be a very interesting endeavor as there is usually only room for one of us. You love and live life to the full and enjoy travel, adventure and living on the edge. I know that God will use this to do great things in and through you. This is my prayer.

Jamael

Dawn Amber

I am blessed by your sweet gentle spirit. The good times we shared while cooking and painting are very special to me. You have grown into a gracious woman. You are a very good mother to Hunter and Jordan Lee and I sense the deep love you have for your boys by the way you care for them. I admire your courage to drive long distances on your own with two small boys. My prayer is that the Lord will give you and Andrew the courage and strength to raise the boys to become great men of God.

Andrew with Jordan, Dawn Amber with Hunter.

Danielle

You are our lover of nature. You believe that God put moose on this earth for a food supply which was evident when you shot your first one at the age of fourteen. I treasure our painting sessions where your artistic talent is clearly evident. Cooking is another highlight of times shared together. Your independence and determined nature can be a challenge but also stands you in great stead as you don't give up easily. Your bravery makes you capable of great things and my prayer is that you will use it to serve the Lord always.

Brittany

You are soft spoken and gentle in nature, and yet a strong person. You are very compassionate and love to help people. Your housekeeping skills and desire to keep things tidy reflects how you value order. How I treasure the times when you help me cook and bake special things. You have wisdom beyond your years and insight into situations that are remarkable and you will flourish as you build on the foundation of Christ.

Desirae

Your infectious quick-witted temperament can put a smile on my face on the gloomiest day and cheer me up. You are outspoken and your swift response to situations keeps your teachers on their toes. You love to help people and are always willing and capable of stepping in and lending a hand whether in the kitchen or with any project. When you come to our house in a baking mood, we can always look forward to Boiled Raisin Cake a few hours later. You have incredible potential to accomplish anything you put your heart and mind to; my prayer is that you will use it to be a world changer for Jesus.

Marita

Even as a wee one, your spunk and spark gave us many laughs and opportunities to see your strong will. You speak your mind well. Your tender heart, especially for animals was demonstrated numerous times as you nurtured several litters of kittens at once. You are doing a marvelous job of learning how to cook, bake, sew and paint - skills that will be very beneficial in your future. You have grown into a beautiful young woman of God and it is a great blessing to see your heart to follow Him.

Jamison

You are fast becoming a great young man – hard working, willing to take on the responsibilities given to you around the house or farmyard without complaint, and delightful to spend time with. Talented in doodling and drawing, your cartoons are most interesting! Music is a big part of your life and we were blessed one Sunday morning when we had the privilege of hearing you play drums during worship. You love to learn new things and you've done a great job learning to play your guitar … and now playing in a band! The talents God has given you along with your gentle nature is a remarkable dynamic He can use to further His kingdom.

Janaya

Your angelic smile and nature wins the hearts of everyone you meet. You love to play table games and I enjoy seeing the smile on your face when you beat me time and again. The quiet times we have spent doing jigsaw puzzles together are precious to me. You have painted some beautiful pictures and I am excited to see you develop this talent. You are a lovely reflection of Jesus and this is becoming more and more evident as you grow into womanhood.

Tribute To My Siblings

As you read this book, I'm sure you will also relive the many memories that came to my mind of our life together. The laughter and tears we experienced during the difficult pioneer years forged a bond that has remained, but those hard years were the best years we would ever know together. You have all been such an integral part of my story and I am grateful and blessed to have such a great family to share it with. I love you and thank God for each one of you.

John and Marge Neudorf
John married Marge Petkau on November 7, 1954. They raised nine children and have thirty-two grandchildren and eight great-grandchildren. They celebrated their 56th anniversary in 2010. They lost David on January 6, 2002.

Margaret and Fred Unrau
Margaret married Fred Unrau on January 11, 1959. They raised five children and have twenty-eight grandchildren and three great-grandchildren. They celebrated their 51st wedding anniversary in 2010.

Pete and Sarah Neudorf
Pete married Sarah Friesen on August 13, 1961. They raised six children and have nineteen grandchildren and four great-grandchildren. They were married for almost 47 years. Pete passed away on July 24, 2007.

Annie and Jake Wiebe
Annie married Jake Wiebe on August 25, 1957. They raised eight children and have twenty-eight grandchildren and thirteen great-grandchildren. They celebrated their 53rd wedding anniversary on August 25, 2010.

Jake and Mary Neudorf
Jake married Mary Wiebe on June 14, 1964. They raised seven children and have twenty-one grandchildren. They were married for forty years. Jake passed away on February 6, 2004.

Betty and Andrew Knelsen
Betty married Andrew Knelsen on July 29, 1967. They raised four children and have three grandchildren. They celebrated their 43rd wedding anniversary in 2010.

Helen and Jim Kincaid
Helen married Jim Kincaid on February 4, 1967 and they raised three daughters and have four grandchildren. They celebrated their 43rd wedding anniversary in 2010.

Mary and Jake Friesen

Mary married Jake Friesen on July 9, 1967. They raised six children and have fourteen grandchildren and four great-grandchildren. They lost Joel on February 26, 1984. They celebrated their 43rd wedding anniversary in 2010.

Bill and Sara Neudorf

Bill married Sara Bueckert on December 23, 1971. They raised four children, and have six grandchildren. They lost Bobbi on September 21, 2009. They celebrated their 39th wedding anniversary in 2010.

Babe and Johnny Knelsen

Babe married Johnny Knelsen on August 4, 1968. They raised five children and have eleven grandchildren. They were married for 41 years. Babe lost Johnny on December 8, 2009.

Martha and Bill Neufeld

Martha married Bill Neufeld on October 12, 1968. They raised five children and have four grandchildren. They celebrated their 41st wedding anniversary in 2010.

Leonard and Lena Neudorf
Leonard married Lena Knelsen on August 7, 1976. They raised four children and have six grandchildren. They celebrated their 34th wedding anniversary in 2010.

Esther and Brad Friesen
Esther married Brad Friesen on January 5, 1991. They raised two children and celebrated their 19th wedding anniversary in 2010.

Our family, siblings with spouses, taken June 19, 2003.
In the back row from left to right: Sarah, Tena, Carl, John, Fred, Jake, Andrew, Jake, Johnny, Bill and Mary.
In the middle row: Pete, Marge, Margaret, Annie, Betty, Mary, Babe, Martha and Jake.
In the front row: Jim, Helen, Bill, Sara, Lena, Leonard, Esther and Brad.

Acknowledgements

Memories are a family affair and first and foremost I want to acknowledge my gratitude to my parents (who have both passed on) for the memories they shared of their life growing up in Mennonite villages, sheltered from any influences by the world around them. As I was researching Mennonite life I began to understand more fully some of the things they had shared. Many times when I needed some information, I thought, "if only I could ask Mom and Dad." Sadly, all their history – which wasn't recorded to memory – is buried with them. Also, I'm thankful to Mom and Dad for setting my feet on the right path and giving me direction – for the example they set; the courage, determination, and a steadfast faith that influenced and molded me in my youth.

Thank you to my brothers and sisters for their patience and understanding when I called at all hours needing confirmation and clarification on dates, times, and incidents, or to ask for yet another photo. Often we began to reminisce and many incidents – almost forgotten – surfaced, and I reached for my pen and paper. I enjoyed reminiscing together, recalling our favorite memories of the fun we shared growing up, as well as the difficult times that shaped our lives and conditioned us for survival. As I was writing, many painful experiences opened the floodgates of my memory and rivers of tears began to flow. It was difficult to unlock those doors and relive the pain that I had carefully tucked away for so many years.

I was thankful for the three-year diary I kept from 1958 to 1961 which helped me pinpoint dates and events with accuracy.

I am also indebted to the following for their advice, assistance, support and encouragement.

I'm deeply grateful to Richard Friesen, New Westminster, BC for his invaluable help recording much of the Mennonite history – all the time he spent editing and critiquing my early draft and again later – and the time spent on the telephone.

A special thank you is extended to Bill Janzen, Calgary, Alberta for believing in me, his interest in my project and the valuable advice he gave me in the early stages of my writing – for placing research books in my hands which I didn't know existed, for the unlimited use of his large photo collection and the experiences he shared of his years working with the Mennonites in Mexico. Most of all I want to thank him for his encouragement which motivated me to keep writing when many times I felt like giving up.

Thanks also to Dick McLean, Grande Prairie, Alberta for his interest in my story and all the time he spent proof reading and editing my manuscript.

Thank you to John Janzen, Winnipeg, Manitoba who thought I had a story worth telling and led me to the correct sources of information I needed on the history of the Mennonite people, for reading my manuscript in the early stages, and making corrections.

To Becky Hefty, Lakeside, Montana who did most of the corrections and the meticulous editing that gave shape to the book.

Thank you to Kathy Janzen, La Crete, Alberta for going out of her way and forwarding the books from her library that I needed for research.

To Michelle Burton, Tumbler Ridge, BC, who selflessly gave of herself – making the time to photocopy my manuscript and coming to help with computer settings and e-mailing the manuscript when I was confined to the house.

Thank you to William Schroeder for the unlimited use of the *Mennonite Historical Atlas*. Many times a map explained more than I could have written in a thousand words.

My daughter LaDawn, Lakeside, Montana, deserves special thanks, first of all for sharing my passion to discover more about our Mennonite heritage. For all the weeks she set aside to help with editing, and I was finally able to get my manuscript to the printer. But most of all for her encouragement that helped me finish the project.

Thank you to my grandson, Jamael for making suggestions for a title. I had long finished writing the story and still couldn't come up with a title. While traveling to Montana we were sitting in the back seat of the car and I was relaying some of my life's story to him, when suddenly he said, "Pushing through, Grandma." Yes, I had pushed through!

Thank you to Tracy Krauss for doing the final edit on short notice.

I would like to relay a special thank you to Lorraine Funk for the many hours she contributed to this project; for her consulting services that opened my eyes to the huge amount of work that would be involved in getting the book into my hands.

Special thanks to Carl who was so patient and understanding and encouraged me to make yet another trip to Montana to work on my manuscript – when he knew he would be left to cook for himself. He didn't complain when my mind blanked or when I forgot about the world around me and was still sitting at the computer at midnight. He never even complained about the hot dog he prepared for himself for supper.

Thank you all for investing your time. Without your valuable contributions this book couldn't possibly have made it to print. I will acknowledge here, that I take responsibility for whatever mistakes or oversights are contained herein. Because of the particular nature of this book, I did rely a great deal on personal memory, and although I pride myself on recall, I know that others may remember events in other ways.

In an effort to respect the personal lives of individuals, I have purposefully omitted portions of my life that were intricately interwoven with theirs. The stories were not mine alone to tell.

The Illustrator

Abe Dyck was born in Swift Current, Saskatchewan and raised at La Crete, Alberta. Other than taking art courses from the International Correspondence School, Abe is a self-taught artist. He currently resides in Slave Lake, Alberta.

GLOSSARY OF LOW GERMAN WORDS

Bobbat: Steamed dumplings on top of fried chicken.

Borscht: Soup made with cabbage, dill and other vegetables.

Brohd'fat: Grease left in frying pan after frying ham or sausage.

Darp: A village.

Ditje'maltj: Thickened milk (unsweetened yoghurt) which turns into cottage cheese with heat; a popular Mennonite dish.

Fat'küake: Fruit fritters.

Fibel: An elementary reader.

Gang: A passageway.

Glomms: Cottage cheese.

Je'sang'büak: Songbook: German songbook without notes.

Jreewe'schmolt: Sediment from rendering lard.

Kompst'borscht: Cabbage soup usually made with chicken.

Kruzhel'mets: Fancy lace cap Mennonite ladies wear under their shawl.

Läwa'worscht: Liver sausage.

Miea'grope: Large cast iron cauldron used to render lard when butchering pigs.

Mooss: Cold fruit soup.

Pan'küake: Crepes or pancakes.

Plaut'dietsch: Low German language.

Plüme'moos: Fruit soup made with prunes and other dried fruit.

Rea'holt: Long wooden paddle, stir stick.

Rebb'späa: Spare-ribs tossed into lard while processing.

Roll'küake: Deep-fried dough served with watermelon.

Schlop'beintj: Trundle bed, seating accommodation during the day and a pull-out bed for the night.

Schnetje: Baking powder biscuits.

Schwiens'schwoat: Pig rind.

Sill'fleesch: Pickled pork.

Sill'tjees: Headcheese.

Socke: High slippers made with sheep's wool.

Somma'borscht: Soup made with potatoes and garden greens, sour cream or buttermilk.

Somma'krankheit: Twenty-four hour flu with diarrhea.

Somma'tjäatj: Small house separated from the main dwelling in which the cooking was done in the summer.

Süa'komst'borscht: Sauerkraut soup.

Süa'ramp: Sorrel.

Tjrinjel: Fancy flatbread, twisted buns.

Vaspa: Afternoon coffee break.

Ve'lafnis: Mennonite wedding celebration held one week before the wedding.

Worscht: Sausage.

Wrennetje: Perogies made with cottage cheese or other filling.

SOURCE

Thiessen, Jack. *The Mennonite Low German Dictionary.* Max Kade Institute for German–American Studies, Madison, Wisconsin, USA. 2003.

PHOTO CREDITS

Lois Hudson

Andrew Knelsen

Ben Peters

Isaac Dyck

Bill Janzen

Pauline Zeschuck

Annie Wiebe

Margaret Unrau

Marge Neudorf

Helen Kincaid

LaDawn Dyck

Randy Neufeld

Jake J. Wolfe

Sara (Lehn) Harder

ADDENDUM

MENNONITE TRADITIONS

MENNONITE MIGRATIONS TO:

To order additional copies, contact:

Tena Friesen
Box 1168
Tumbler Ridge, BC
Canada V0C 2W0

Phone: 250-242-3636
Cell: 250-242-8443
Email: tenafriesen@gmail.com

Clare

Dr Claire Craig

Expired